Consolidated-

Consolidated-Vultee
PB4Y-2 Privateer
The Operational History of the U.S. Navy's World War II Patrol/Bomber Aircraft

Alan C. Carey

Schiffer Military History
Atglen, PA

Dedication

In memory of my father

Robert Watson Carey Sr., ARM3c
(9 February 1926-3 January 2004)
Veteran of Navy Bombing Squadron 109 (1943-44)
Distinguished Flying Cross with Gold Star
Air Medal with two Silver Stars
Navy Commendation with "V" Device

Book Design by Ian Robertson.

Library of Congress Catalog Number: 2005920852

Printed in China.
ISBN: 0-7643-2166-8

We are interested in hearing from authors with book ideas on related topics.

Published by Schiffer Publishing Ltd.
4880 Lower Valley Road
Atglen, PA 19310
Phone: (610) 593-1777
FAX: (610) 593-2002
E-mail: Info@schifferbooks.com.
Visit our web site at: www.schifferbooks.com
Please write for a free catalog.
This book may be purchased from the publisher.
Please include $3.95 postage.
Try your bookstore first.

In Europe, Schiffer books are distributed by:
Bushwood Books
6 Marksbury Avenue
Kew Gardens
Surrey TW9 4JF
England
Phone: 44 (0) 20 8392-8585
FAX: 44 (0) 20 8392-9876
E-mail: Bushwd@aol.com.
Free postage in the UK. Europe: air mail at cost.
Try your bookstore first.

Contents

	Acknowledgments	6
	Introduction	7
Chapter 1	Development and Production	8
Chapter 2	Privateer Operations in World War II: Tinian (January-May 1945)	37
Chapter 3	Iwo Jima (June-August 1945)	50
Chapter 4	Okinawa (April-May 1945)	59
Chapter 5	Okinawa (June-August 1945)	71
Chapter 6	World War II Operations: Clark Field, Philippines (March-August 1945)	82
Chapter 7	World War II Operations: Palawan and Mindoro, Philippines	91
Chapter 8	Additional World War II Squadrons	100
Chapter 9	Cold War Service (1946-1956)	106
Chapter 10	Korean War Service	122
Chapter 11	French AÈronavale and RoCAF Privateer Operations	133
Chapter 12	Privateers Since 1961	139
	Color Gallery	145
Appendix A	World War II Aerial Kills by Individual PB4Y-2 Patrol Plane Commanders	154
Appendix B	World War II Squadron Combat Records	155
Appendix C	World War II PB4Y-2 Combat and Operational Losses (October 1944-August 1945)	155
Appendix D	World War II PB4Y-2 Privateer Nose Art	156
Appendix E	PB4Y-2 Privateer Operational and Combat Losses (1944-1956)	158
Appendix F	United States Coast Guard, Aéronavale, Civilian, and Latin American Privateer Data	161
Appendix G	United States Navy PB4Y-2 Units (1944-1953)	162
Appendix H	United States Navy Tail Codes (1946-1956)	163
Appendix I	World War II Personnel Killed or Missing in Action (1944-1945)	164
Appendix J	World War II-Era Operational Fatalities (1944-1945)	166
Appendix K	Post-World War II Operational Fatalities (1946-1953)	167
Appendix L	Enlisted U.S. Navy Aviation Ratings	169
Appendix M	French Aéronavale Fatalties (1951-1957)	170
	Notes	171
	Bibliography	173
	Index	174

Acknowledgments

I want to thank the following veterans, individuals, organizations, and those who wished to remain anonymous for providing information on the Privateer's history. I also offer my sincerest apologies for any omissions.

Veterans
Alex G. Alexander (VP-9)
Roy Balke (VPB-109)
David E. Bronson (VPB-116)
Bill Duckett (VPB-123)
Frank Durban (VP-871)
Orvis N. Fitts (VPB-117)
Eddie Harding (VPB-122)
Donald Hartvig (VPB-108)
Norman Houle (VPB-143)
A.C. Jeanguenat (VPB-108)
Richard Jeffreys Jr., (VPB-121)
Wilmer L. Kerns (VP-772)
Earl Mann (VPB-118)
Jim Page (VP-28)
Ray Parsons (VPW-1/2)
Thomas Pierce (VPB-124)
Ted Rowcliffe (VPB-124)
Maurice "Shep" Shapiro (VP-871/VP-19
Ted Shireman (VPW-2)
Frank Tutu (VP-772),
Bill Woodward (VPB-104)

Individuals
Jim Augustus
Allan Blue
Curt Brownlow
Robert Feuilloy
David Giorgini
Steve Hawley
Minoru Kamada
Chip Krokoski
Al Marks
Davis McAlister
Mahlon Miller
Joseph E. Racenet
James Sawruk
David Smith
Bill Thys
Stan Walker

Organizations
B-24 Liberator Club
Hawkins and Powers Aviation, Inc
National Archives and Records Administration at College Park, Maryland
Naval Historical Center, Washington, D.C.
Tailhook Association
U.S. Navy Patrol Squadrons at www.vpnavy
Wings of China Publications, Wai Yip, Editor

Introduction

The Consolidated-Vultee (Convair) PB4Y-2 Privateer was a development of the company's B-24 Liberator heavy bomber of World War II and, after 60 years, it continues to serve as a slurry bomber fighting wildfires throughout the western United States. *Consolidated-Vultee PB4Y-2 Privateer: The Operational History of the U.S. Navy's World War II Patrol/Bomber Aircraft*, covers the airplane's 60-plus year service history with the United States Navy and Coast Guard, the French Aéronavale, the Republic of China Air Force, various countries of Latin America, and finally as a slurry bomber for aerial fire fighting companies.

As a patrol bomber during World War II, the Privateer won the trust and confidence of combat aircrews due to its rugged construction, which allowed it to withstand a considerable amount of battle damage, and in its defensive armament that gave it the capability to go head-to-head with Japanese fighters. Expressing his confidence and love of the PB4Y-2, Orvis N. Fitts, as a patrol plane commander during the closing days of World War II with the *Blue Raiders* of VPB-117, said:

"The Privateer was the best long-range patrol bomber of World War II. It was more responsive on the controls than the Liberator, and I just plain liked to fly the Privateer. It was a great aircraft to fly."[1]

1

Development and Production

Development and Production

In mid-1942 the United States Navy acquired several hundred Consolidated B-24 Liberators from the Army Air Force for long-range reconnaissance and anti-submarine warfare (ASW). However, the Navy questioned the time and cost of modifying ex-Army B-24s, as its needs were considerably different. What the Navy wanted was a long-range reconnaissance platform capable of staying on patrol over an extended period, with the capacity to locate specific enemy targets via state-of-the-art electronics gear, while retaining the capability to defend itself from enemy fighters. Therefore, a considerable amount of effort was exerted to develop a modified version of the Liberator that would fulfill the Navy's requirements. Convair's attempt to make a few design changes to an existing model eventually evolved to the development of a 70,000-pound aircraft bristling with 12 .50-caliber machine guns that could carry and deliver ordnance ranging from bombs, depth charges, and napalm to guided missiles.

Structural Modifications

The Privateer was very similar to the Liberator, but two distinguishing modifications set it apart. In terms of similarities, the B-24's Davis wing was retained on the PB4Y-2, but the Pratt & Whitney R-1830-65 engines, which powered the Liberator, were exchanged for the R-1830-94. This modification required the engine nacelles on the PB4Y-2 to be reconfigured by rotating them 90 degrees, resulting in the carburetor air intakes and oil cooling systems being

The PB4Y-1 Liberator was the predecessor of the PB4Y-2 Privateer and had a distinguished career during the Second World War, serving with the U.S. Navy and Marine Corps throughout the Pacific, European, and Mediterranean Theaters. Early Navy Liberators in the Pacific Theater sported an olive drab camouflage. Pictured here is *Sugar* (Bureau Number 32098), which saw action in the Central Pacific between November 1943 and July 1944, and was the personal aircraft of VB-108's skipper Commander E.C. Renfro. (Author's Collection)

Photographed in flight is XPB4Y-2 (Bureau Number 32086). According to Allan Blue, an aviation historian, this aircraft's identity was determined by looking at the engine nacelles, which are the vertical type. The other two X jobs retained the original B-24 engine configuration. The purpose of the mast-like piece of equipment that appears to extend forward of the cockpit has yet to be determined. (Author's Collection)

located on the top and bottom of the engines. The superchargers needed for high altitude operations were deleted to save weight, since the Privateer was to operate at low altitudes. The fuselage of both models also looked similar in appearance, but the Privateer's length was extended approximately seven feet with the addition of a flight engineer station. According to Reuben Fleet, the founder of Consolidated Aircraft Company:

"The Navy was anxious to get a third man—a flight engineer—in the cockpit, so we extended the fuselage forward of the wing."

The extension also allowed room for the installation of Electronic Countermeasure Gear (ECM).[2]

Two distinguishing modifications featured on the Privateer—the tail assembly and defensive armament—differed from that of the B-24 Liberator. The empennage of the Privateer was changed from the twin-tail assembly configuration featured on the B-24 to a conventional vertical and horizontal stabilizer. Three aircraft with the Navy Bureau of Aeronautics (serial numbers (BuNo) 32086, 32095, and 32096) were modified and designated as XPB4Y-2s (Convair Model 40, later designated as the Model 100). Initially, the three X ships were originally flown with the twin tail assembly; however, based on data collected from wind tunnel tests at the University of Washington, Convair engineers reasoned that the aircraft would be more stable with a single fin configuration, rather than the standard twin tail assembly. Two of the X-models were fitted

A side profile of XPB4Y-2 (Bureau Number 32086) sporting the standard olive-drab coloration. World War II-era Privateers were usually painted a tri-colored scheme and later an overall glossy sea blue. (Author's Collection)

An aft view shot of an XPB4Y-2 may be that of Bureau Number 32086, circa 1944. She was stricken from the Navy's inventory on 30 June 1947 at Norfolk, Virginia. (Author's Collection)

with a Douglas C-54 Skymaster-style single vertical fin, but flight tests conducted at the Naval Air Test Center Patuxent, Maryland, during early 1944 showed the need for a taller vertical fin, and such was installed on all existing and future production aircraft.

The PB4Y-2 did have some initial teething problems involving the new engines, as retired Master Chief Petty Officer and VPB-118 veteran Earl R. Mann recalls:

"We experienced some 'loss of engine' problems. The Pratt & Whitney 1830-94 engine had been changed from utilizing a turbo supercharger with an exhaust waste gate, to a two-stage blower system. The new engines were burning holes in the top of the pistons. We worked with Consolidated Aircraft and Pratt & Whitney, and they ascertained that the problem was 'too hot a sparkplug.' They changed the sparkplug specifications to a 'cooler' sparkplug, and we never experienced any further problems, even with 'Full Military Power' application, and sometimes 'Redlining,' or exceeding specifications in combat situations."

Defensive Modifications

The military version of the Privateer was a heavily armed gun platform with 12 .50-caliber machine guns housed in hydraulically or electric driven turrets, compared to the B-24 Liberator's eight turreted and two hand-held waist .50-caliber machine guns. The airplane's distinguishing armament consisted of the ERCO 250SH-3 Bow Turret, a pair of ERCO 250-TH Waist Blisters, and two Martin 250CE-16 and 250CE-17 Upper Deck Turrets, but it retained the standard A-6 Tail Turret found on the B-24/PB4Y-1 Liberator. For protection against enemy fire, each turret had armor plating and bulletproof glass installed in front of the gunner.

XPB4Y-2 (Bureau Number 32096) at NAS Patuxent River, Maryland, on 6 June 1944. This photograph shows some of the blisters underneath the fuselage, which housed various air-to-surface radar and radar countermeasures antennae. The blister directly behind the bombardier's window housed the AN/APA-17 high-frequency direction finder; the blister above the nose wheel is the AS-124/APR; the blister behind the nose wheel is the AS-67/APQ-2B set used with the AN/APQ-2 transmitter. The Navy struck Bureau Number 32096 from its inventory on 30 June 1945 at Patuxent. (Author's Collection)

A full frontal view of an early model Privateer with the MPC 250-CE1 nose turret possibly photographed at the Convair plant in San Diego, California. This view also shows the paired arrangement for radar antennas, which provided coverage for each side of the aircraft. Behind the Privateer are PB4Y-1 Liberators that appear to be undergoing modifications since they lack nose or tail turrets. (Author's Collection)

This late-model PB4Y-2 photographed over California (Bureau Number 59533) with the ERCO bow turret has the tri-color paint scheme, which was standard on U.S. Naval aircraft after September 1943. This aircraft served with VPB-109 on Okinawa and was stricken from the squadron's inventory on 24 May 1945. (Author's Collection)

PB4Y-2 Privateers under assembly at the Convair plant in San Diego, California, on 18 March 1944. (Courtesy of Convair via Allan Blue)

Below: The seven compartments of the PB4Y-2 illustrated in the Pilot's Handbook of Flight Operating Instructions, Naval Aeronautics Publication AN 01-5EN-1, dated 15 April 1945. Hereafter referred to as Pilot's Handbook. (Author's Collection)

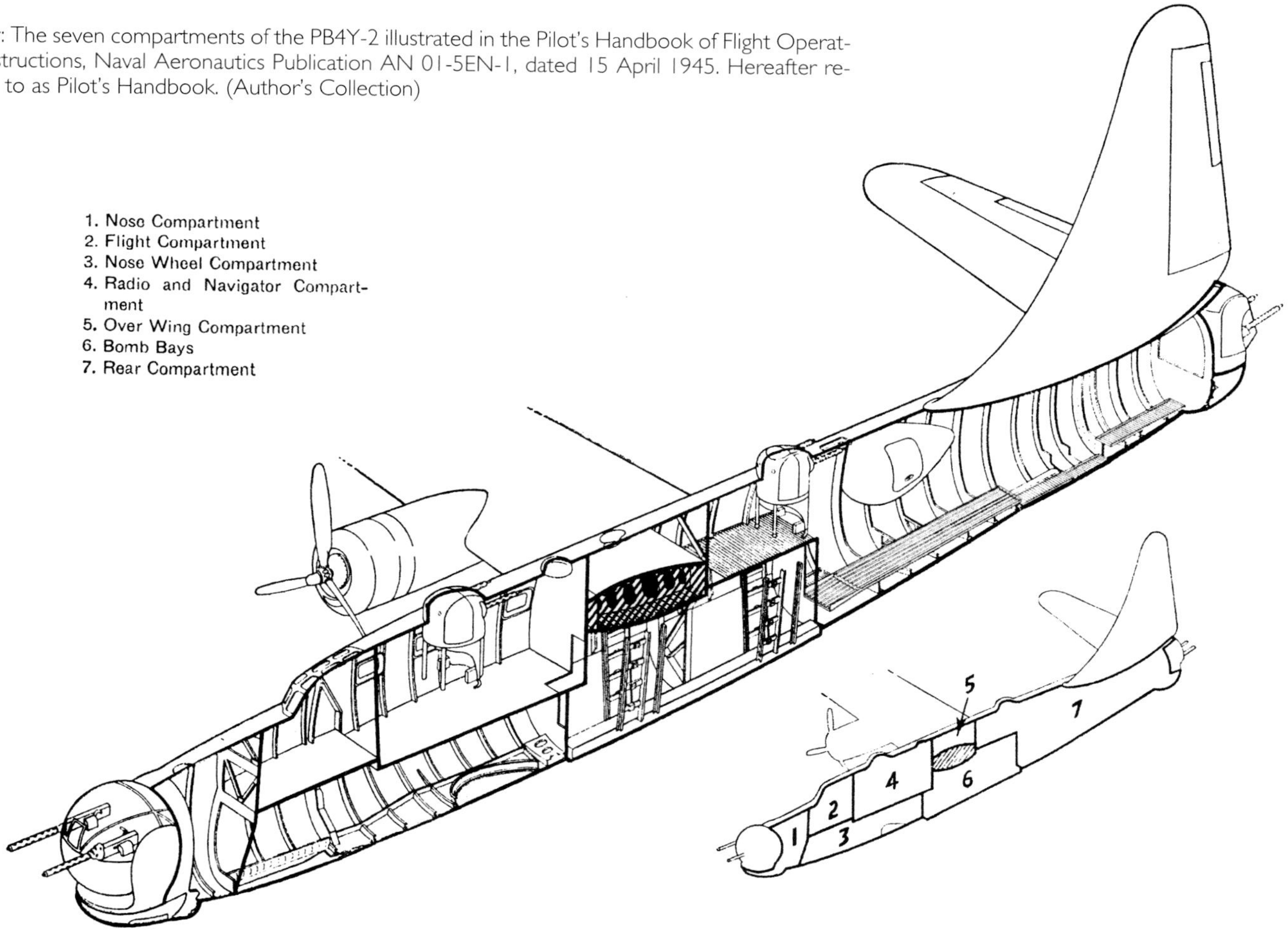

1. Nose Compartment
2. Flight Compartment
3. Nose Wheel Compartment
4. Radio and Navigator Compartment
5. Over Wing Compartment
6. Bomb Bays
7. Rear Compartment

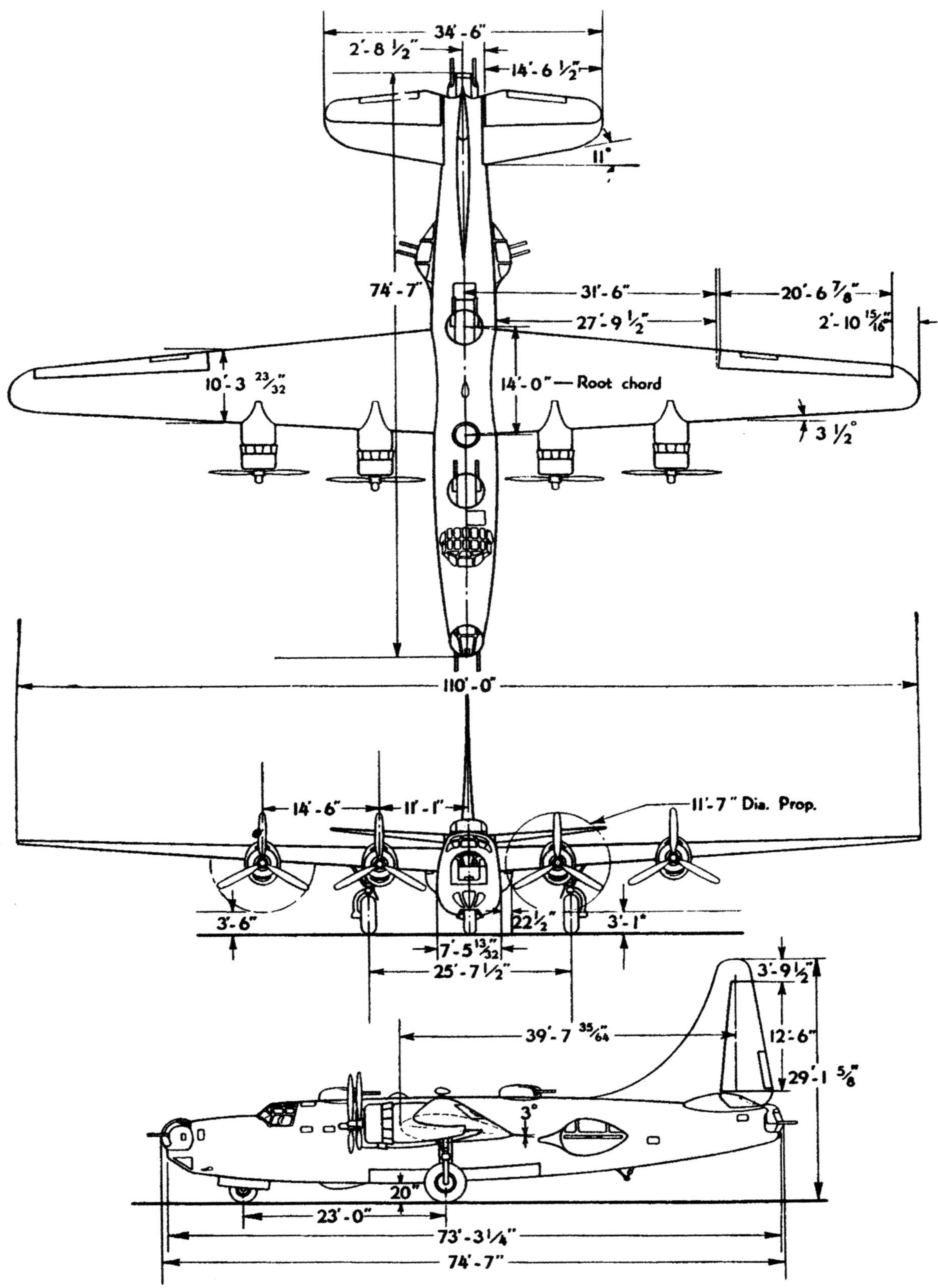

This schematic diagram shows the overall dimensions of the PB4Y-2 Privateer. (Author's Collection)

ERCO 250SH-3 Bow Turret

The ERCO bow turret was a hydraulic powered, circular gun platform consisting of two .50-caliber machine guns, which had become standard on most PB4Y-1 Liberators. The guns of the 250SH-3 bow turret, supplied with four magazines holding 800 rounds of ammunition, could rotate 85 degrees either side of the longitudinal centerline of the plane, elevated 82 degrees above neutral, and depressed 83 degrees.

ERCO 250-TH Waist Blisters

The open waist positions of the B-24 Liberator, with their single hand-held .50-caliber M2 machine guns, were replaced by the hydraulically powered teardrop 250-TH waist blisters. The twin .50-caliber machine guns housed in the turret could swing 79 degrees aft, 50 degrees forward, 60 degrees up, and 95 degrees down. Four canisters, each containing 400 rounds of ammunition, were stored aft of the turrets, and flexible feed chutes, which could hold up to 100 rounds of ammunition, provided a total supply of 500 rounds of ammunition per gun. Fire interrupters were installed to prevent the guns from firing while they were pointed at the horizontal stabilizer or wings.

Martin 250CE-16 and 250CE-17 Upper Deck Turret

The electric powered Martin 250CE-16 (forward) and 250CE-17 rear (aft) upper turrets, supplied with 800 rounds of ammunition, were capable of rotating 360 degrees, and could be elevated from 6.5 to 85 degrees. Profile fire interrupters were installed to prevent the guns from firing towards the tail structure.

MPC 250-CH-6 Tail Turret

The hydraulically powered MPC 250-CH-6 tail turret could rotate 71.5 degrees either side of the longitudinal angles of the plane, and

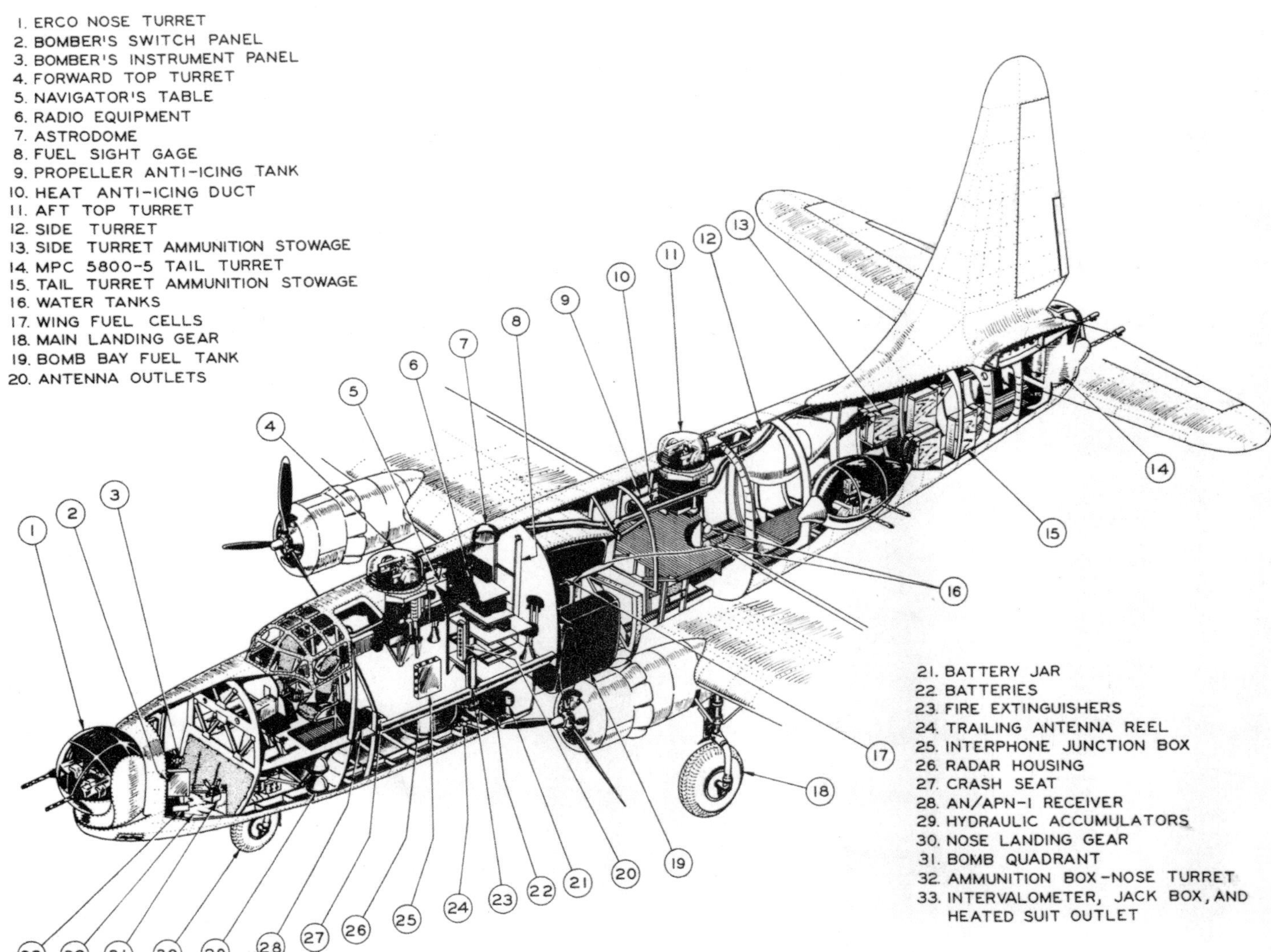

A detailed cutaway of the fuselage in the Pilot's Handbook showing standard equipment found on a World War II-era PB4Y-2. (Author's Collection)

the guns could be elevated 70 degrees and depressed 34 degrees from a horizontal position. Each gun was supplied with 1,000 rounds of ammunition stored in containers in the aft compartment of the plane.

Offensive Armament

The Privateer was capable of carrying a standard bomb load of 8,000 pounds or two SWOD Mk-9 *Bat* guided missiles—later designated as the ASM-N-2—as well as aerial mines, depth charges, napalm, or acoustical torpedoes. The main bombardier instruments, located on the left side of the plane, consisted of the quadrant, instrument panel, control panel, intervalometer, and firing key. All bombing control units, except for the pilot's emergency release handle, were located in the nose section of the aircraft, and were typically operated by an enlisted bombardier, usually with the rating of Aviation Ordnance Mate Aerial Bombardier, abbreviated as AOM (AB).

SWOD Mk-9 *Bat*

During World War II Navy Patrol and Bombing Squadrons (VPB) 109, 123, and 124 were equipped with the radar-controlled missile, SWOD Mk-9 (Special Weapons Ordnance Device), nicknamed the *Bat*, which described its radar homing mechanism. A late development of the discarded *Pelican* missile program, which was terminated in the fall of 1944, the plywood constructed device enclosed

1. Climb Indicator
2. Pilot's Power Panel
3. Brake Hydraulic Pressure Gages
4. Main Hydraulic System Pressure Gage
5. Air Speed Indicator
6. Gyro Horizon
7. Pilot Director Indicator
8. Directional Gyro
9. Bomb Door and Bomb Release Indicator Lights
10. Pilot's Direct Vision Panel
11. Removable Double Windshield Pane
12. Windshield Defroster Hot Air Duct
13. Propeller Feathering Switches
14. Gyro Flux Gate Compass Repeater
15. Clock
16. Radio Compass Bearing Indicator
17. Radio Altimeter Limit Lights
18. Radio Altimeter Limit Switch
19. Radio Altimeter
20. Mark 3 Automatic Pilot Control Panel
21. Mark 3 Automatic Pilot Servo Speed Controls
22. Altimeter
23. Flap Position Indicator
24. Turn-and-Bank Indicator
25. Pilot's Elevator-aileron Control Wheel

Figure 4 — Main Instrument Panel, Pilot's Side

(From the Pilot's Handbook in the Author's Collection)

1. Flight Report and Check List Holder
2. Pilot's Interphone Control Box
3. Interphone Jack Box
4. Controls for IFF Signal Equipment
5. Instruction Plate for SCR-269G Radio Compass
6. Cabin Heat Thermostat
7. Latch for Side Window Panel
8. Ash Tray
9. Pilot-Bombardier's Speaking Tube
10. Map Reading Light
11. Fluorescent Light
12. Pilot's Power (Circuit Breaker) Panel
13. Static Pressure Selector Valve
14. Pilot's Oxygen Tank and Regulator
15. Pilot's Seat

Figure 10 — Pilot's Power Panel and Interphone Box

(From the Pilot's Handbook in the Author's Collection)

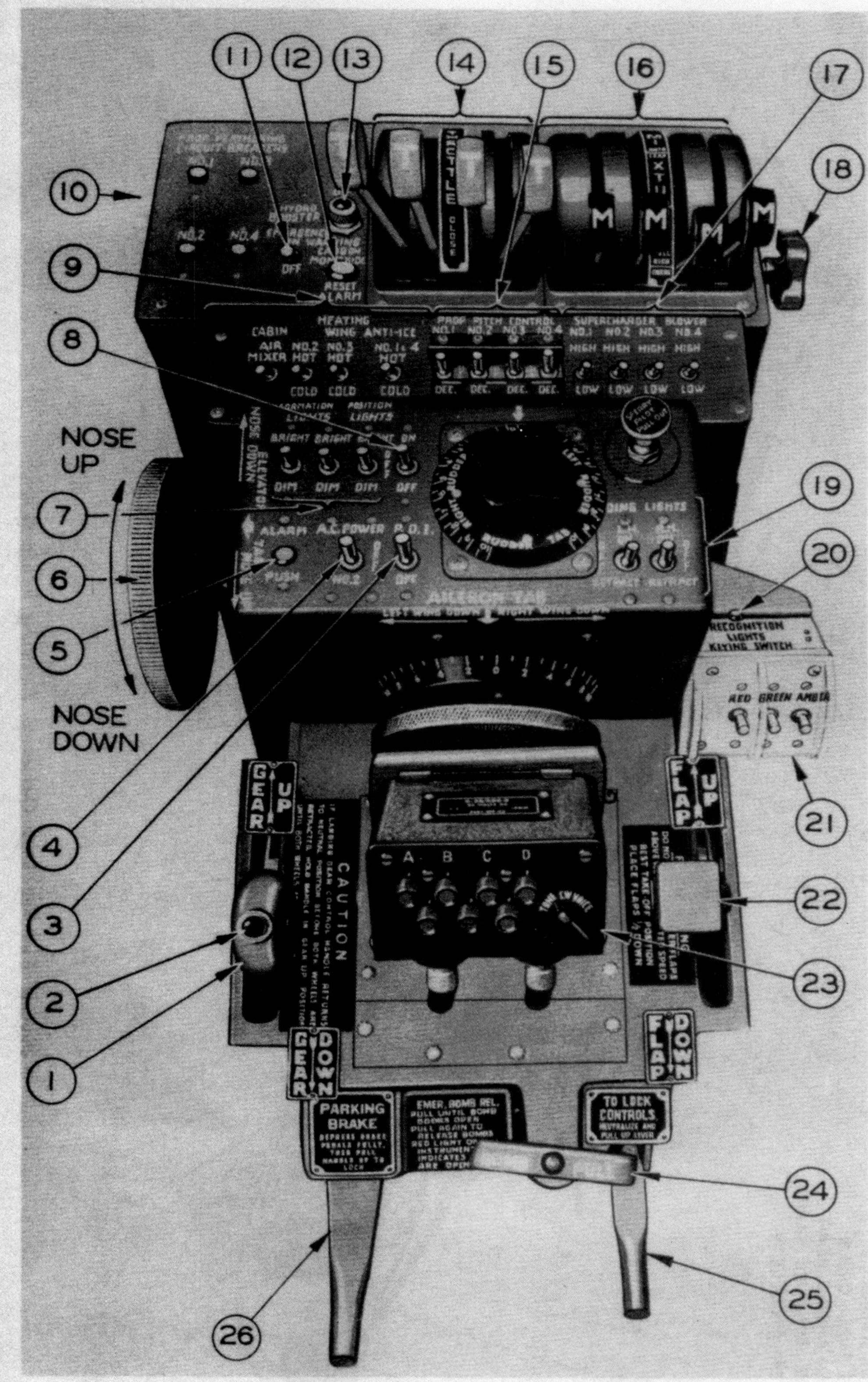

1. Landing Gear Control Lever
2. Landing Gear Safety Switch Push Button
3. PDI Switch
4. A-C Power Inverter Switch
5. Bail-out Alarm Button
6. Elevator Tab Control Wheel
7. Formation and Position Light Switches
8. Bomb Release Safety Switch
9. Cabin Heat Switches
10. Propeller Feathering Pump Circuit Breakers
11. Electric Hydraulic Pump Switch
12. Carbon Monoxide Indicator Reset Button
13. Carbon Monoxide Warning Light
14. Throttle Quadrant
15. Propeller Governor Control Switches
16. Mixture Control Quadrant
17. Supercharger Shift Control Switches
18. Control Quadrant Friction Adjuster
19. Landing Light Switches
20. Recognition Light Key
21. Recognition Light Selector Switches
22. Flap Control Lever
23. AN/ARC VHF Control Box
24. Pilots' Emergency Bomb Release
25. Surface Controls Lock Handle
26. Parking Brake Handle

Figure 3 — Pilots' Pedestal

(From the Pilot's Handbook in the Author's Collection)

1. Pilot Director Indicator
2. Mark 3 Automatic Pilot On-off Control
3. Throttle and Mixture Quadrants
4. Landing Gear and ASG Indicator Lights
5. Fuel Flowmeters
6. Mark 3 Automatic Pilot Control Panel
7. Manifold Pressure Gages
8. Radio Compass Bearing Indicator
9. Compass Light Dimmer Switch
10. Tachometers
11. Magnetic Compass
12. Outside Air Temperature Gage
13. Propeller Feathering Switches
14. Windshield Defroster Hot Air Duct
15. Removable Double Windshield Pane
16. Copilot's Direct Vision Panel
17. Propeller Governor Indicator Lights
18. Cylinder Temperature Gages
19. Fuel Pressure Gages
20. Oil Pressure Gages
21. Oil Dilution Switches
22. Carburetor Alternate Air and Air Filter Control
23. Fuel Booster Pump Switches
24. Cowl Flap Switches
25. Copilot's Power Panel
26. Propeller Anti-icer Pump Rheostat
27. Primer Switches
28. Copilot's Microphone Switch
29. Starter and Meshing Switches
30. Copilot's Elevator-aileron Control Wheel
31. Oil Temperature Gages

Figure 5 — Main Instrument Panel, Copilot's Side

(From the Pilot's Handbook in the Author's Collection)

1. Copilot's Microphone Switch
2. Instrument Panel
3. Copilot's Wheel
4. Engine Controls Switch Panel
5. Copilot's Map Reading Light
6. Copilot's Fluorescent Light
7. Copilot's Power Panel
8. Fluorescent Light Rheostat

Figure 11 — Copilot's Power Panel

(From the Pilot's Handbook in the Author's Collection)

1. Interval Control
2. Bomb Control Quadrant and Levers
3. Pilot-Bombardier's Speaking Tube
4. Projector Light
5. Bomb Computing Chart
6. Outside Air Temperature Gage
7. Altimeter and Air-speed Indicator
8. Bombardier's Control Panel
9. Bomb Release Firing Switch
10. Interphone Station Box

Figure 50 — Bombardier's Instruments and Controls

The Bombardier's instruments and controls was located forward of the cockpit and aft of the bow turret as shown in the Pilot's Handbook. (Author's Collection)

a one thousand pound general-purpose bomb. On a Privateer, a missile was suspended under each wing, outboard of the engines, and both units were centrally controlled within the plane until aircraft's onboard radar locked on given targets for directional homing. Approximately 3,000 were built, and operational use of the ASM-N-2 *Bat* continued after the war with squadrons VP-104 and 115. By the early 1950s the device had become obsolete.

Technical Data

1945 Designation	1947 Designation	1948-1950 Designation
SWOD Mk-9 Model 0	ASM-2	ASM-N-2
SWOD Mk-9 Model 1	ASM-2A	ASM-N-2A
Length	11 feet 11 inches	
Wingspan	10 feet	
Weight	1,800 pounds (approximate)	
Range	20 miles	
Warhead	1,000-pound general-purpose bomb	

Electronics Gear

When the Privateer entered service, it carried state-of-the-art electronic counter-measures (ECM) gear for detecting, interfering with, or exploiting for intelligence purposes, any electromagnetic energy that an enemy might transmit for military purposes. After World War II, from approximately 1948 to 1953, and especially during the Korean conflict, the aircraft was utilized as a platform for electronics intelligence gathering (ELINT) against North Korea, China, and the Soviet Union. Throughout the aircraft's military service, the Privateer carried an array of electronics gear consisting of, but not limited to, the following equipment:

Airborne Search, Bombing, and Detection Radar

AN/APS-2 S-Band Search Radar & Beacon: 3,000 MHz search radar that could detect ships up to 60 miles and used with the low level radar bombsite AN/APQ-5.

AN/APS-15 X-Band Bombing & Navigation Radar (named *Mickey*): 10,000 MHz bombing and navigation aid designed for

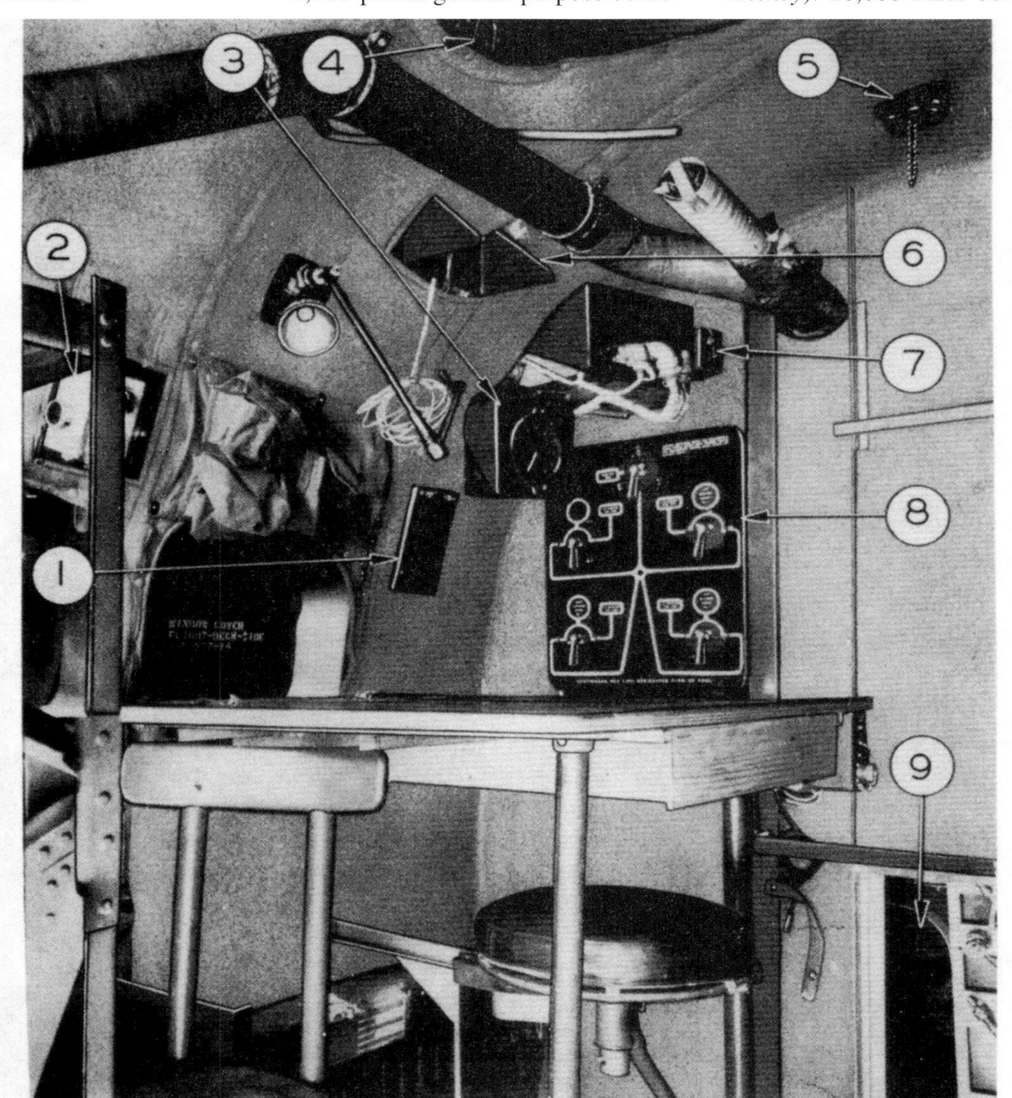

1. Gyro Flux Gate Caging Circuit Breaker
2. Interphone Station Box
3. Gyro Flux Gate Compass Master Indicator
4. Astrodome
5. Signal Piston Adapter
6. Astrograph Bracket (early airplanes only)
7. Gyro Flux Gate Caging Control and Amplifier Box
8. Main Fuel Selector Panel
9. Door to Bomb Bays

Figure 48 — Navigator's Station

The navigator's station was located on the right side of the aircraft and aft of the forward top turret as shown in the Pilot's Handbook. (Author's Collection)

bombing through overcast that gave a true representation of the surface.
AN/APS-44 Search Radar

Airborne Navigation Radar
AN/APN-1 Radio Altimeter
AN/APN-4 LORAN

Airborne Fire Control Radar
The following was a radar gun site apparently used in the tail turret of the B-29 and PB4Y-2.
AN/APG-15 S-Band Tail Gun Radar

Airborne Identification Radar
AN/APX-2 IFF Transponder Set
AN/APX-8 IFF Set

Airborne Radar Intercept Receivers
The following systems were designed to collect radar intelligence.
AN/APR-1
AN/APR-2
AN/APR-5

1. Heating System Duct Register
2. Special Equipment Rack
3. Defroster Duct
4. Navigator's Chart Case
5. Projector Lights
6. Junction Box
7. Interphone Station Box
8. Heated Flying Suit Receptacle and Switch
9. Ash Trays
10. A-C Power Receptacles
11. Navigator's Table
12. Writing Arm
13. Special Operator's Seat and Safety Belt
14. Oxygen Equipment
15. Stowage Bracket for Oxygen Equipment

Figure 44 — Special Operator's Station

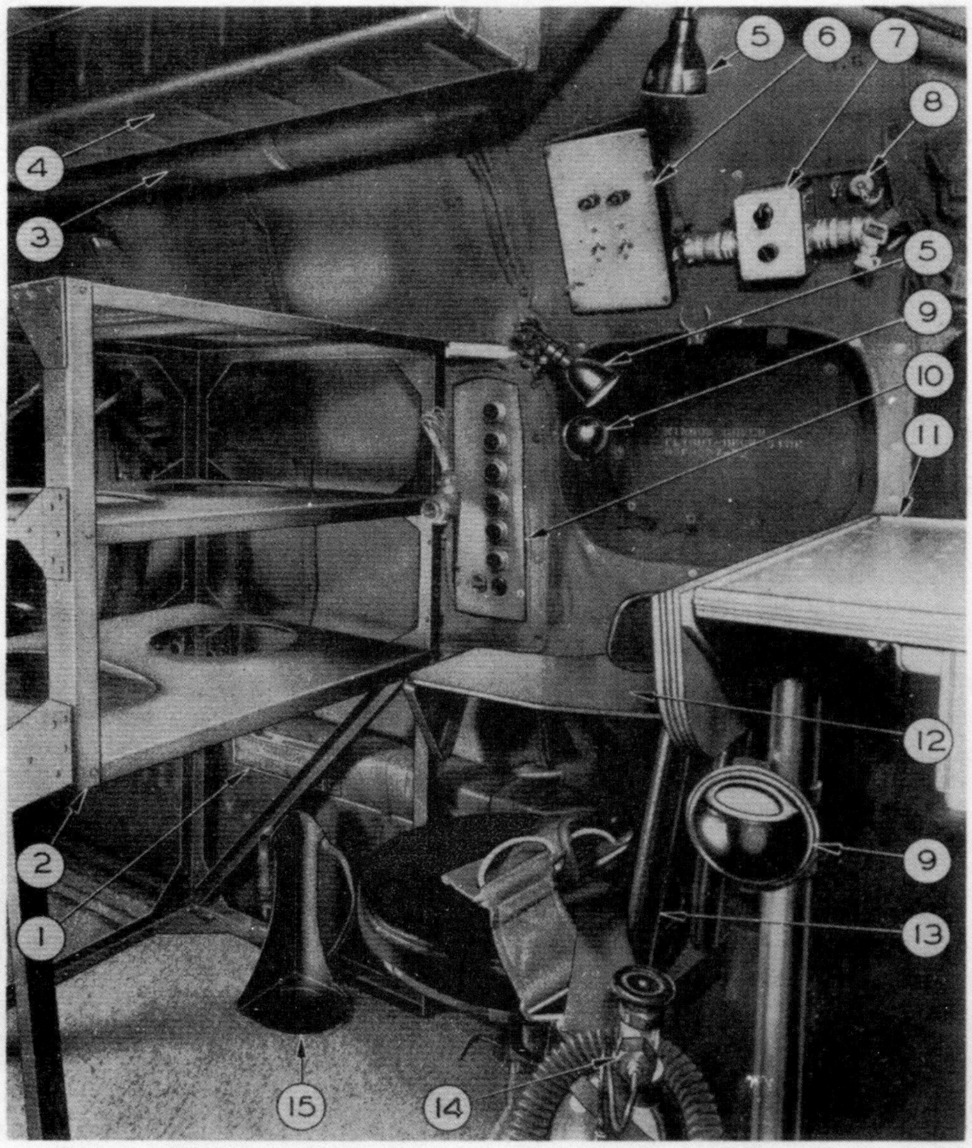

The special operator's station was located forward of the Navigator's Station are housed Electronic Countermeasures gear (ECM) as shown in the Pilot's Handbook. (Author's Collection)

Airborne Radar Transmitters

The following were radar-jamming systems.

AN/APT-1 (named *Dina*)
AN/APT-5 (named *Carpet*)
AN/APQ-2 450-750 MHz High Power Barrage Jamming Transmitter (named *Rug*)

Airborne Radar Auxiliary Assemblies

AN/APA-17 250-1000 MHz Broadband Direction Finding Radar

Airborne Radio Navigation Equipment

AN/ARN-8 Marker Beacon Receiver

Airborne Radio Communication

AN/ARC-1 VHF Transceiver

Airborne Radio Intercept Receivers

The following are airborne search receivers designed to locate frequency channels of radar and radio systems.

ANN/ARR-5
AN/ARR-7

Antenna Systems

AS-124/APR
AS-125/APR used with the AN/APR-5
AS-67/APQ-2B used with AN/APQ-2 transmitter

1. Flying Suit Heater Receptacle
2. Antenna Transfer Switch
3. Antenna Reel Control Box
4. Radio Operator's Interphone Jack Box
5. Radio Operator's Interphone Control Box
6. Fostoria Light
7. Radio Operator's Radio Junction Box
8. Radio Operator's ARC-5 Control Box
9. Ceiling Light
10. Antenna Panels
11. LM-14 Frequency Meter
12. Interphone Amplifier
13. ATC Transmitter
14. RAX Receivers
15. Radio Table
16. Key
17. Antenna Loading Coil

Figure 42 — Radio Operator's Station

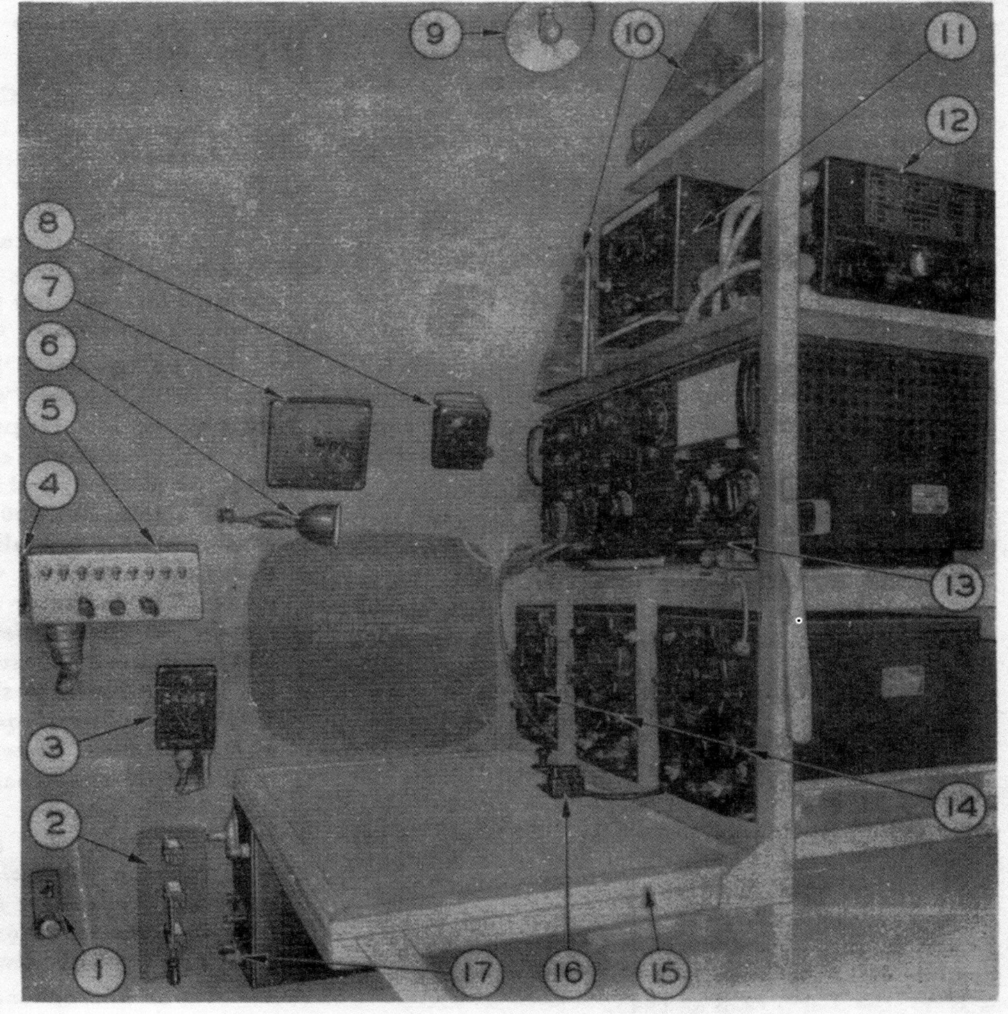

The radio operator's station was located on the left side of the aircraft and aft of the forward top turret as shown in the Pilot's Handbook. (Author's Collection)

Production

At first the aircraft was named the *Sea Liberator*; however, since approximately 50 percent of the bomber's internal components were changed and the belly turret deleted it was essentially a new model, and was finally given the name *Privateer*. In historical terms, a privateer was a ship commissioned by a government to capture or destroy enemy ships. It was aptly named, since Privateers encountered and destroyed or damaged hundreds of Japanese merchant ships between January and August 1945.[3]

The first prototype made its first flight on 20 September 1943, with production beginning in March 1944 at the Convair plant in San Diego, California. The original contract of 15 October 1943 called for 660 aircraft, but the Navy requested 710 more the following year. The end of the war resulted in most of the second order being canceled, and total production topped out at 736 PB4Y-2 Privateers, with the last plane coming off the assembly line in October 1945 (Bureau of Aeronautic Numbers 59350 to 60009 and 66245 to 66324).[4]

During the course of its service life with the United States Navy and Coast Guard, a number of PB4Y-2s were modified to fulfill specialized missions. The first 100 Privateers built were the C Model, which retained the standard Consolidated B-24 Motor Products nose turret. In April 1945 some Privateers were modified to carry the SWOD Mk-9 by fitting underwing release points for the device and were designated as the PB4Y-2B.

During the post war years, additional aircraft were converted for other specific reasons. The PB4Y-2M was a meteorological research version obtained by removing the turrets and adding a B-24D-type nose transparency; the PB4Y-2S carried special antisubmarine radar, while the PB4Y-2K was a target drone operated by the Naval Air Development Center. In 1951 the bomber designation was dropped, and the various versions were redesignated as

1. Oxygen Equipment
2. Radar Equipment Rack and Cables
3. Special Equipment Control Head
4. Junction Box and Circuit Breakers
5. Radar Nacelle Instruction Card
6. Inclinometer
7. Ash Tray
8. Writing Arm
9. Interphone Station Box
10. Radar Operator's Seat and Safety Belt

Figure 45 — Radar Operator's Station

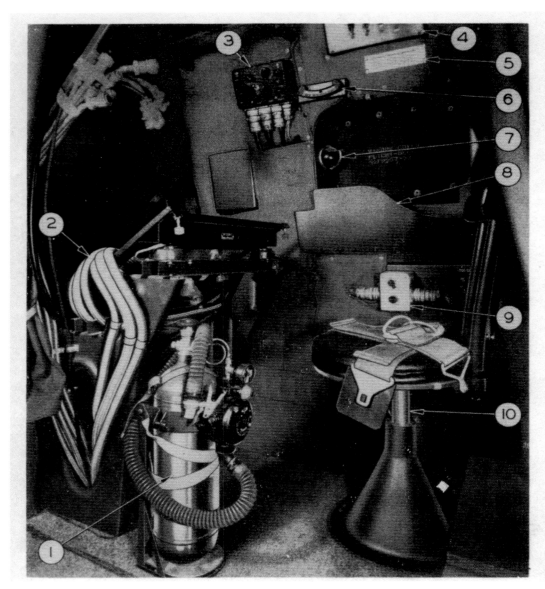

The radar operator's station was located forward of the Radio Operator's Station as shown in the Pilot's Handbook. (Author's Collection)

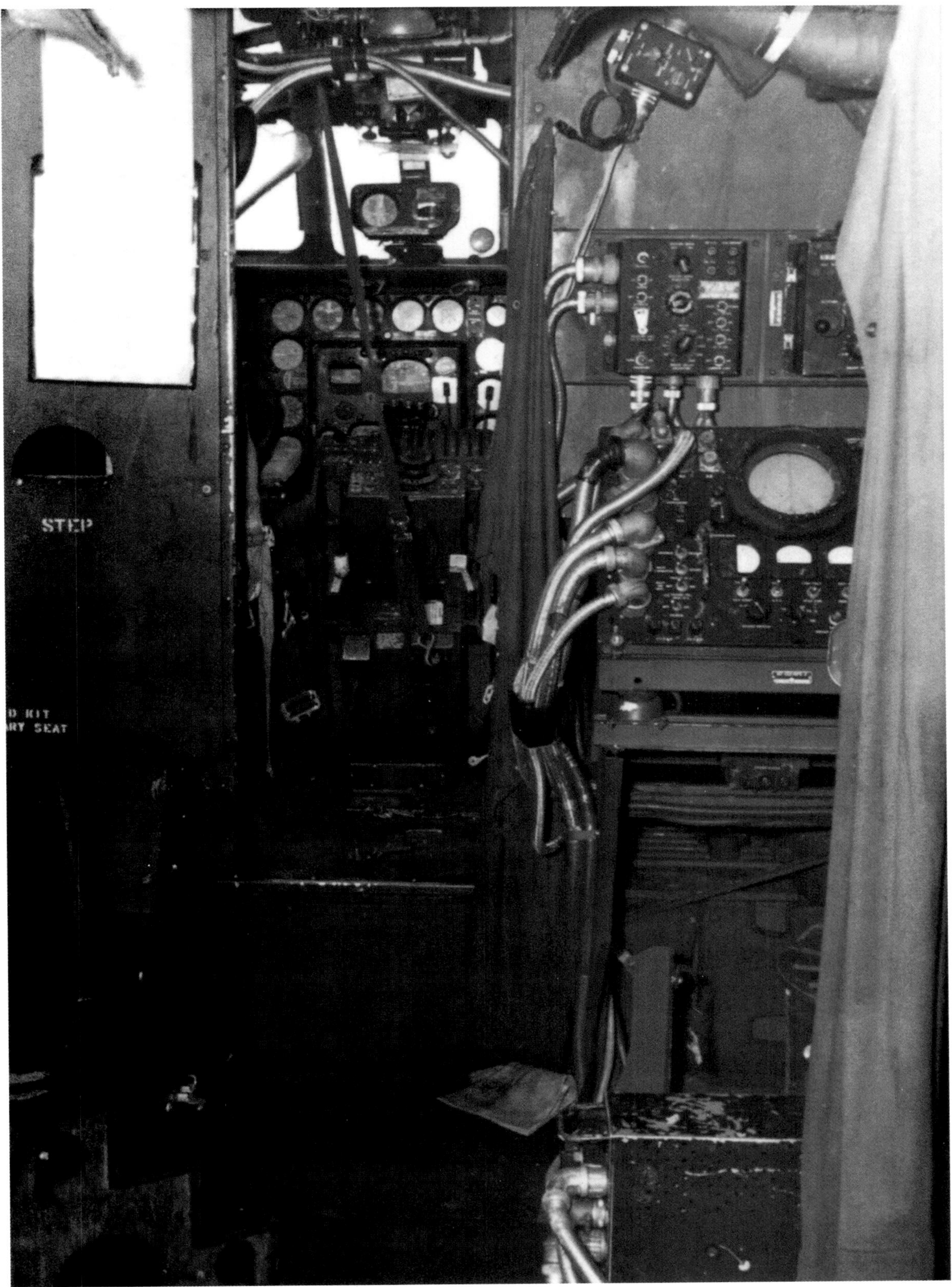

This interior view of a post-World War II Privateer belonging to VP-881 shows the AN/APS-15 radar system to the right. The main unit is the indicator/receiver while the left control box is for scan control and the box on the right is the bombing computer control. John Szewczyk via Allan Blue provided the information on the radar system. (Photograph: Marion C. Giorgini via David Giorgini)

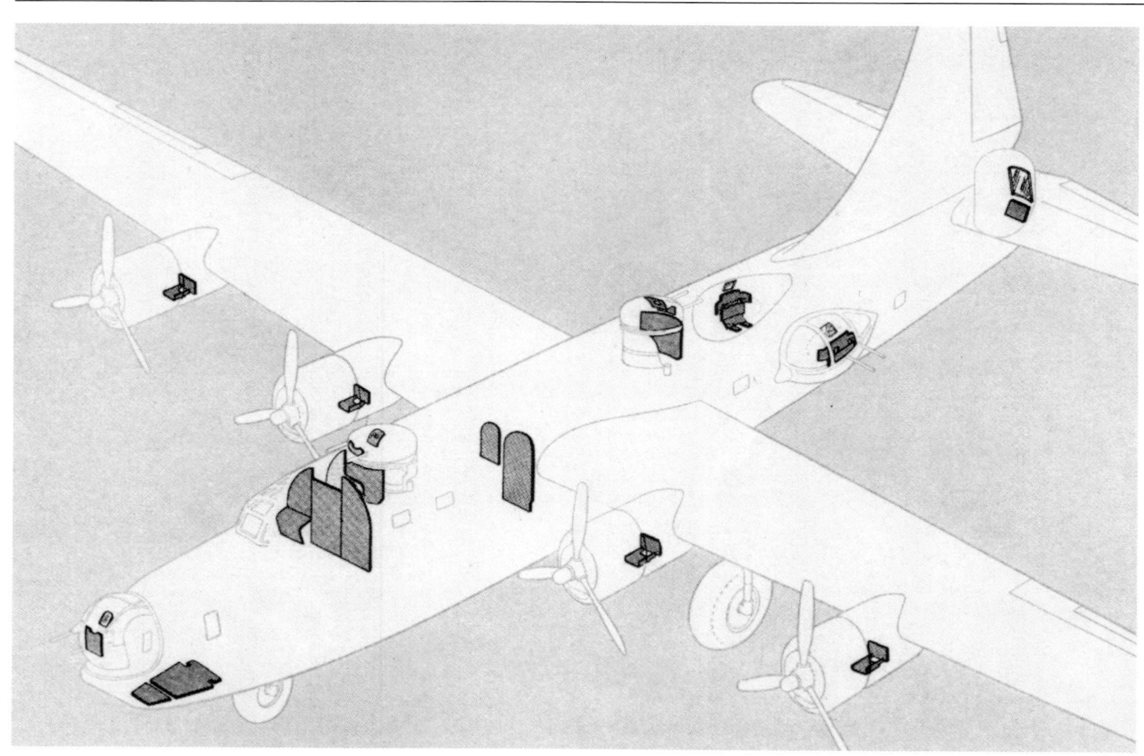

A diagram showing the location of armor plating as presented in the PB4Y-2 General and Armament Manual published by Consolidated Vultee Aircraft Corporation dated 1944. Hereafter referred to as the Armament Manual. (Author's Collection)

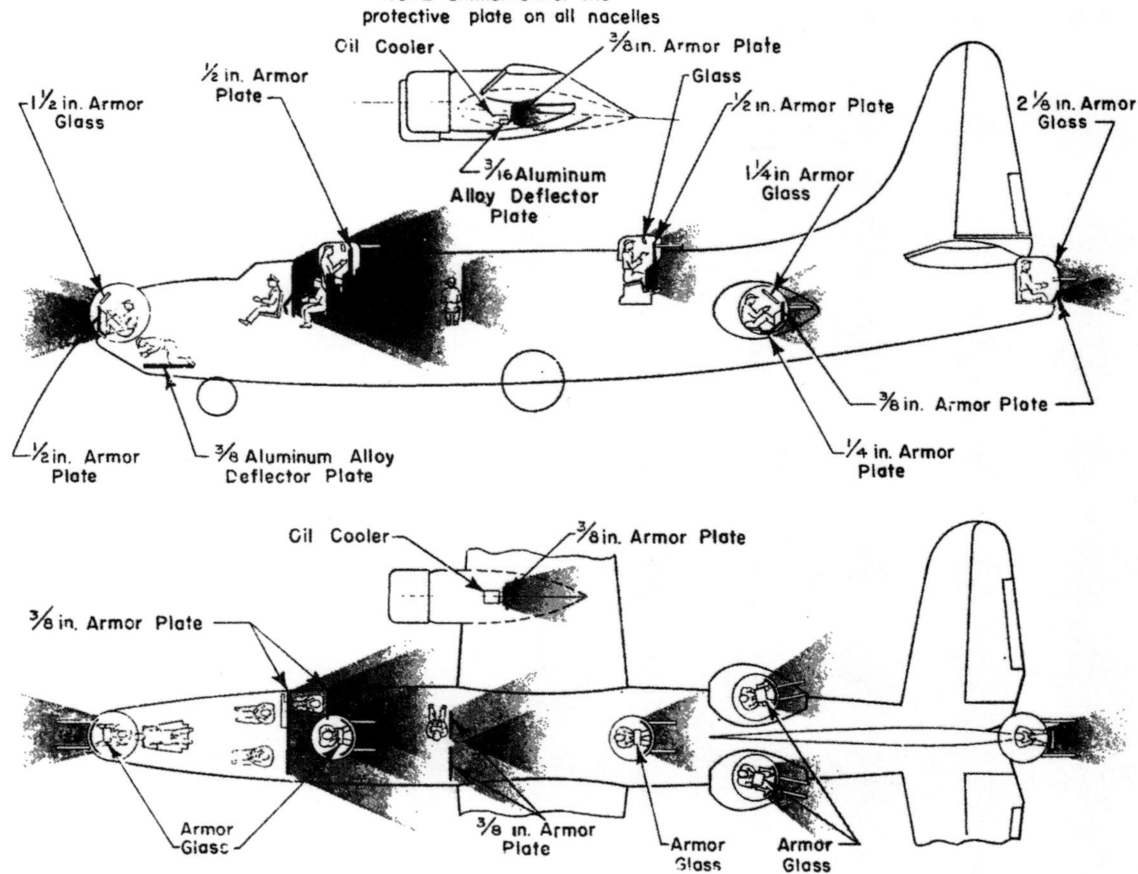

An illustration showing the type, thickness, and zones of armored protection as presented in the Armament Manual. (Author's Collection)

the P4Y-2, P4Y-2B, P4Y-2S, or the P4Y-2K, while the United States Coast Guard version (P4Y-2G) was introduced. In September 1962 the last remaining PB4Y-2s in the U.S. Navy's inventory were redesignated P-4B. However, the original model designation is typically used when referring to the aircraft.

Specifications	**PB4Y-2 Privateer**	**PB4Y-1D Liberator**
Power Plant	R-1830-94-Single Stage,	R-1830-65 Turbo Supercharged Two-Speed Integral Blower
Length	74 ft 7 in	67 ft 3 in
Wingspan	110 ft	Same
Height	29 ft 2 in	17 ft 11 in
Wing Area	1,048 square feet	Same
Empty Weight	37,765 pounds	36, 950
Gross Weight	65,000 pounds	56,000 pounds
Max Gross Weight	70,231	60,000 pounds
Armament	1 Nose Turret with 2 .50-cal guns	Same
	2 Top Turrets with 2 .50-cal guns	1 Top Turret with 2 .50-cal guns
	2 Side Turrets with 2 .50-cal guns	2 Hand-held .50-cal guns
	1 Tail Turret with 2 .50-cal guns	Same
		1 Belly Turret with 2 .50-cal guns Some later versions carried the APS-15 instead of this turret
Bomb Load	8,000 pounds	8,800 pounds
Maximum Speed	250 mph	279 mph
Cruising Speed	200 mph	200 mph
Service Ceiling	21,200 ft	31,800 ft
Range	2,630 miles with full payload	2,960 miles
Crew	11-13	10-11

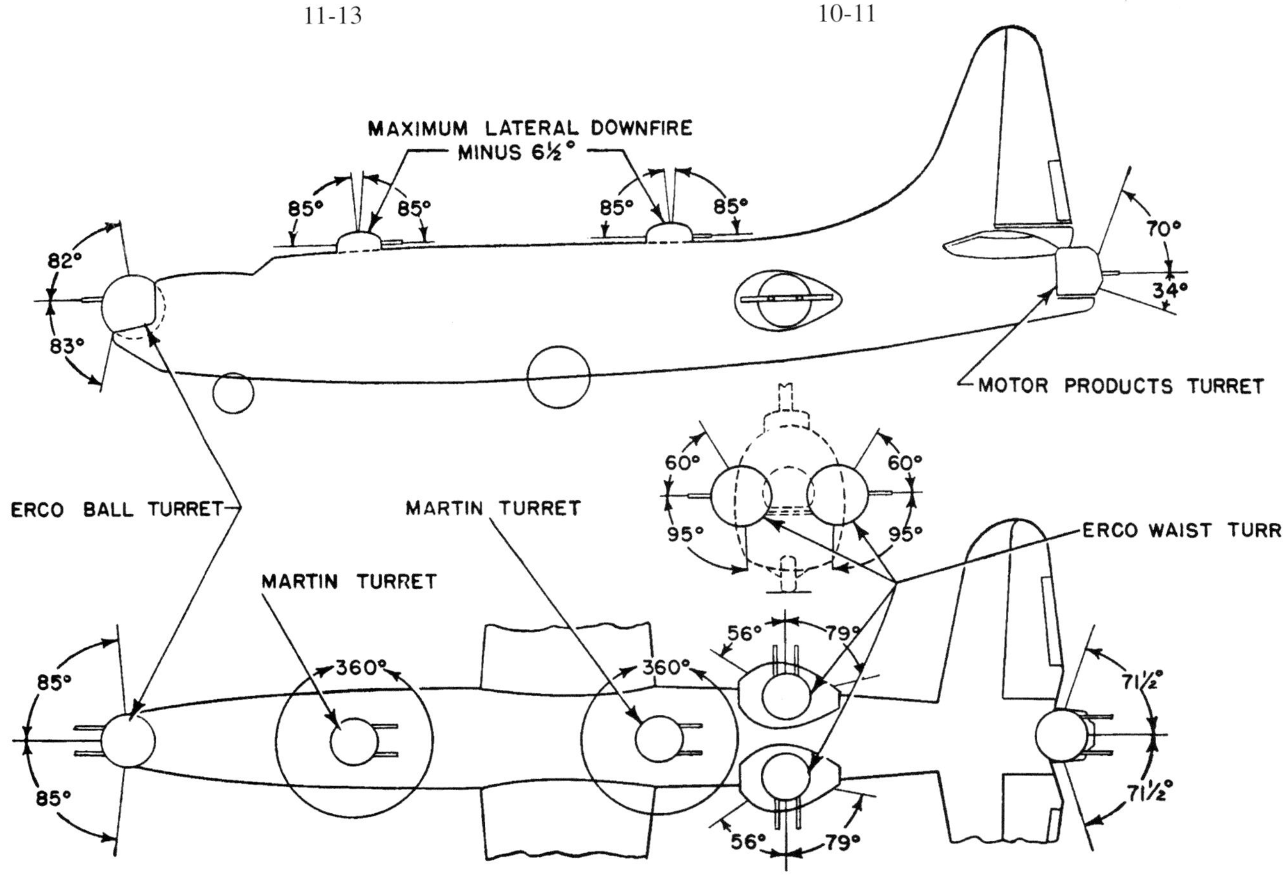

An illustration showing angles of fire for each turret position of the PB4Y-2 as shown in the Armament Manual. (Author's Collection)

Figure 30—Erco Nose Turret

1. Ventilator
2. Armor Glass
3. Armor Plate
4. Sighting Window (Metal Guard Inserted)
5. Gun Camera Mounting Pad
6. Ejected Link Receiver Chute
7. Ejected Link Receiver Chute
8. Gunner's Shoulder Strap
9. Control Valve
10. Door Hinge
11. Door Handle
12. Elevation Declutch Handle
13. Front Ammunition Can
14. Emergency Tilting Handle Receptacle
15. Emergency Tilting Handle Receptacle
16. Switch Panel
17. Control Handle
18. Hydraulic Pump Handle
19. Door Latch Handle

A frontal and rear view of the Engineering and Research Corporation's (ERCO) 250SH-3 Bow Turret as shown in the Armament Manual. (Author's Collection)

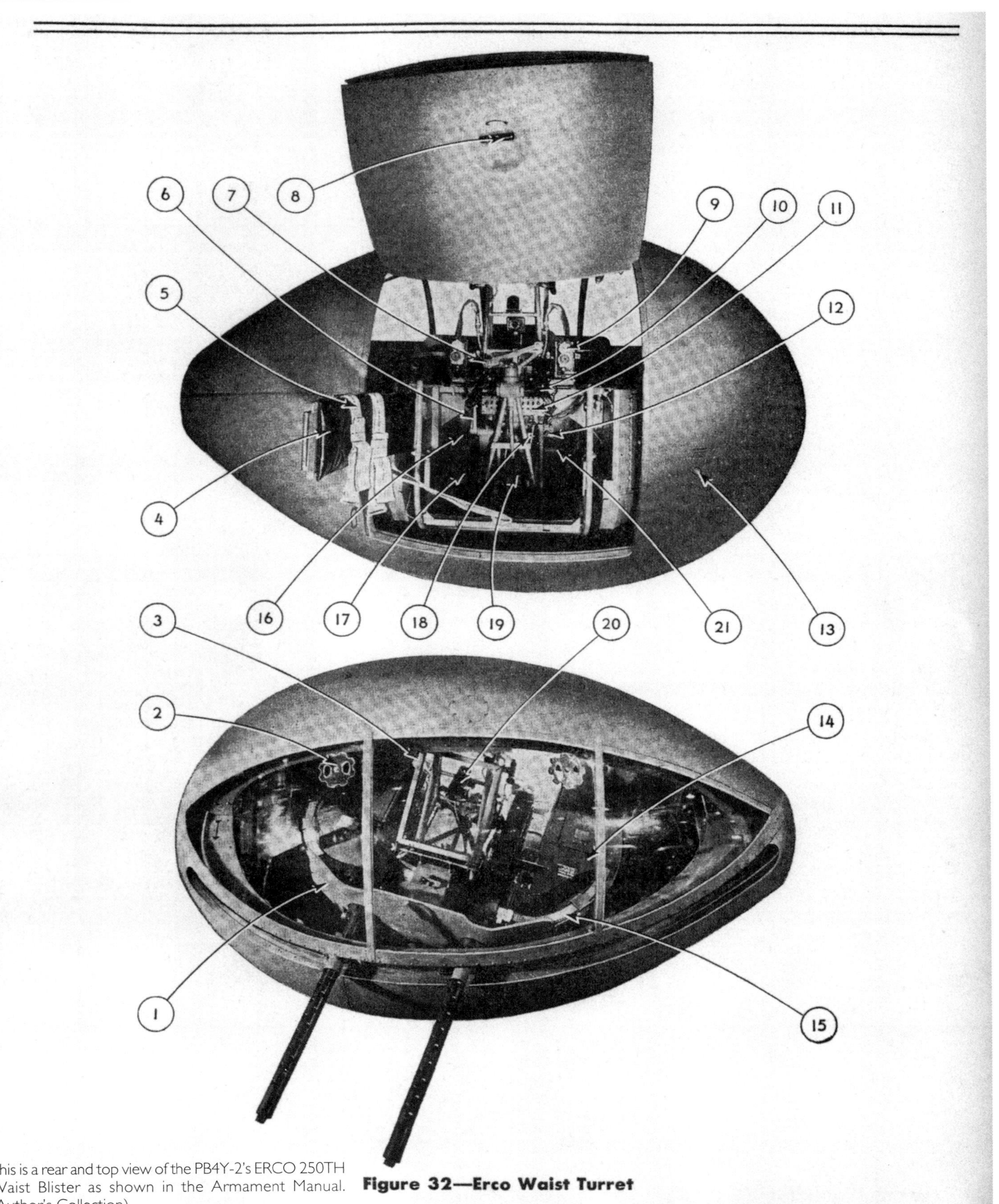

This is a rear and top view of the PB4Y-2's ERCO 250TH Waist Blister as shown in the Armament Manual. (Author's Collection)

Figure 32—Erco Waist Turret

RY-3 Privateer Express

The Model 101 RY-3 Privateer Express was an unarmed transport version of the PB4Y-2, with a fuselage having a series of windows, a single loading hatch, and capable of carrying a maximum of 28 passengers, or up to 16,641 pounds of cargo. Manufactured at the Convair plant in San Diego, the total production run of the RY-3 was 34 aircraft, and they carried the Bureau of Aeronautics serial numbers 90020 to 90050 and 90057 to 90059. Between 1945 and 1946, RY-3s served with No. 231 and 232 Squadrons of Royal Air Force (RAF) Transport Command as the Liberator C.IX with the serial numbers JT-973 through JT-999 and JV-936. In 1946 RY-3s in the RAF inventory were either sent back to the United States or scrapped. The United States Marine Corps operated a few of the transport versions, while the Royal Canadian Air Force (RCAF) operated one with the name *Rockcliffe Icewagon*, serial number JT-973 (Bureau Number 90021), on ice-research missions before it was scrapped in 1948.

RY-3 Specifications

Length	75 ft 5.25 in
Wingspan	110 ft
Height	29 ft 2 in
Wing Area	1,048 square feet
Empty Weight	31,000 pounds
Gross weight	60,000 pounds
Power Plant	R-1830-94
Maximum speed	248 mph
Cruising Speed	158 mph
Service ceiling	18,300 ft

Figure 33—Erco Waist Turret

1. Upper Armor Plate
2. Ventilator
3. Armor Glass
4. Gunner's Back Rest
5. Gunner's Shoulder Straps
6. Azimuth Manual Crank
7. Control Valve Cable and Pulleys
8. Door Handle
9. Firing Solenoid
10. Control Handle
11. Switch Panel
12. Foot Firing Lock
13. Emergency Elevation Release
14. Ejected Link Container
15. Ejected Link Chute
16. Intermediate Armor Plate
17. Diagonal Armor Plate
18. Azimuth Declutch Handle
19. Shell Feed Chute
20. Gun Sight
21. Foot Firing Pedal
22. Gun Camera Mount
23. Manual Elevation Crank
24. Trouble Lights
25. Gun Band Enclosure

A frontal view of the waist blister as shown in the Armament Manual. (Author's Collection)

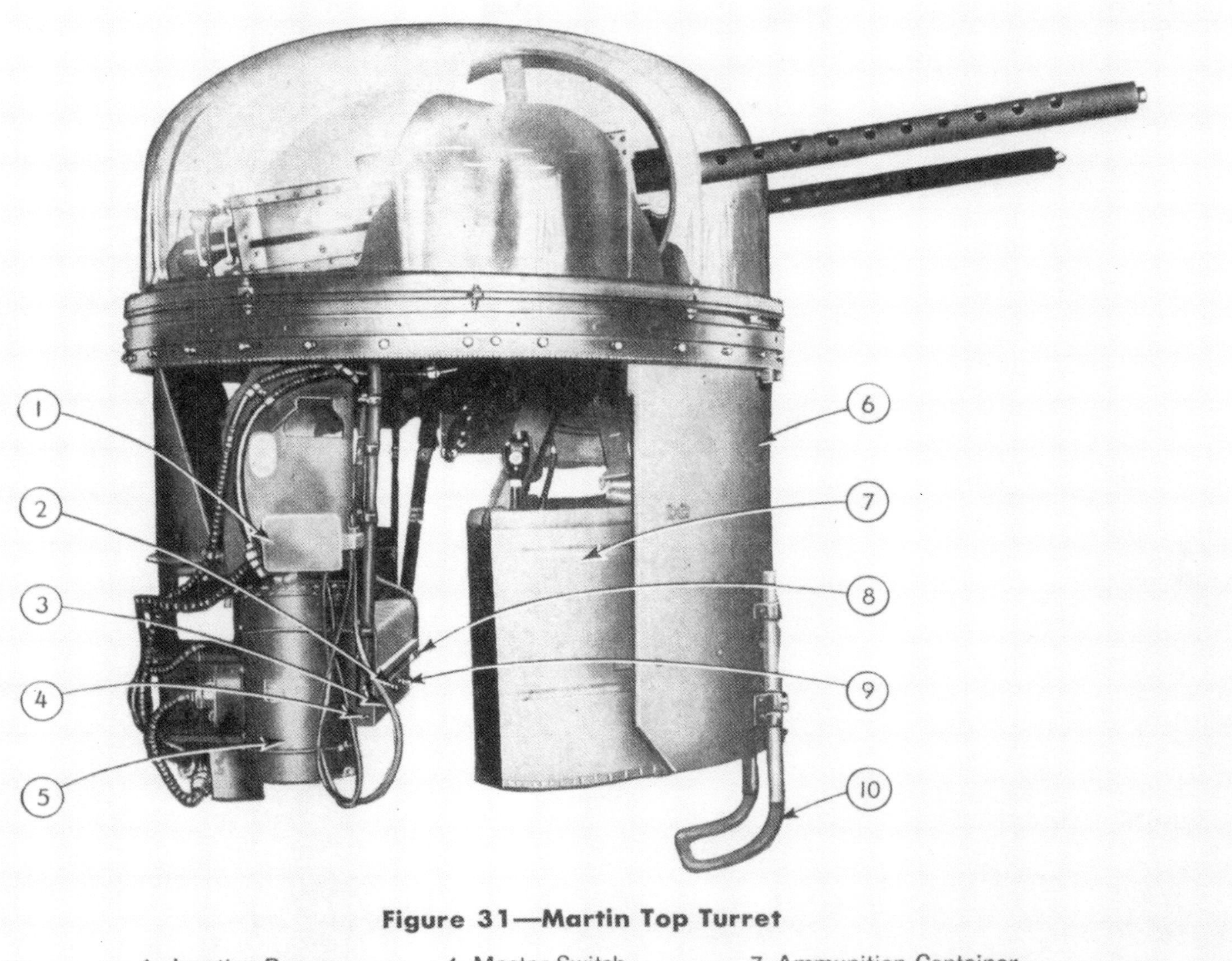

A side profile of the PB4Y-2's Martin 250CE-16/17 Upper (Deck) Turret as shown in the Armament Manual. (Author's Collection)

World War II PB4Y-2 Camouflage and Markings

Early World War II-era Privateers were painted the standard tri-color scheme adopted by the United States Navy, consisting of sea blue top surfaces, intermediate blue side surfaces, and insignia white lower surfaces. By mid-1945 Privateers began appearing with either an overall flat sea blue or glossy sea blue color scheme. Letters and markings were painted insignia white, with the model designation and the bureau number being applied to both sides of the vertical stabilizer.

During World War II, it appears the United States Navy established and applied an unusual aircraft and squadron identifier or call sign system on PB4Y-2s. Most aircraft were marked on both sides of the forward fuselage and consisted of a letter, for example an "X," followed by the last three digits of the aircraft's bureau number. However, this writer has yet to find concrete evidence that either proves or disproves the validity that it was a true identification or call sign system, since several different squadrons were supplied with Privateers that bore the same letter code. Other aircraft were identified by having the last three digits or the entire five-digit bureau number stenciled on the forward fuselage, while some lacked any type of identification code, except for the model type and bureau number displayed on the upper portion of the vertical stabilizer. All codes on the forward fuselage were painted black or insignia white, although some nose artists incorporated various colors into the code to match the artwork. The following table lists possible squadron identification symbols that appear in World War II-era photographs:

Figure 34—Motor Products Tail Turret—Front View

1. Hand Grip
2. Entrance Door Window
3. Azimuth Manual Crank Shaft
4. Azimuth Manual Control Hand Crank
5. Tie Rod
6. Hoisting Lug
7. Foot Firing Cable
8. Shell Chute
9. Entrance Door
10. Hand Rest

This is a frontal view of the PB4Y-2's MPC 250-CH-6 Tail Turret as shown in the Armament Manual. (Author's Collection)

Squadron	Code
VPB-106	X and or three digits
VPB-108	Z and three digits
VPB-109	V and three digits
VPB-116	R and three digits
VPB-117	R and three digits on the PB4Y-2
VPB-118	Three digits
VPB-119	R and three digits
VPB-120	Unknown (possibly entire bureau number)
VPB-121	Y and three digits
VPB-122	Three digits
VPB-123	X and three digits
VPB-124	X and three digits

Post-War PB4Y-2 Camouflage and Markings

In late 1945 naval aircraft, including the Privateer, were repainted an overall glossy sea blue; the anti-glare panel forward of the cockpit was painted a non-specular sea blue, while the model type, number, and squadron identifier codes were painted insignia white. During the late 1950s and early 1960s, Privateers used as P4Y-2K drones were painted fluorescent red-orange. In 1947 an international orange band was applied to United States Naval Reserve Privateers, forward of the empennage. In February 1949 propeller-warning stripes, with insignia white lettering, were added within an insignia red stripe on the fuselage. In addition, the words

Danger Danger were added perpendicular to the word *propeller* with an arrow pointing towards the stripe. In 1948 squadron tail

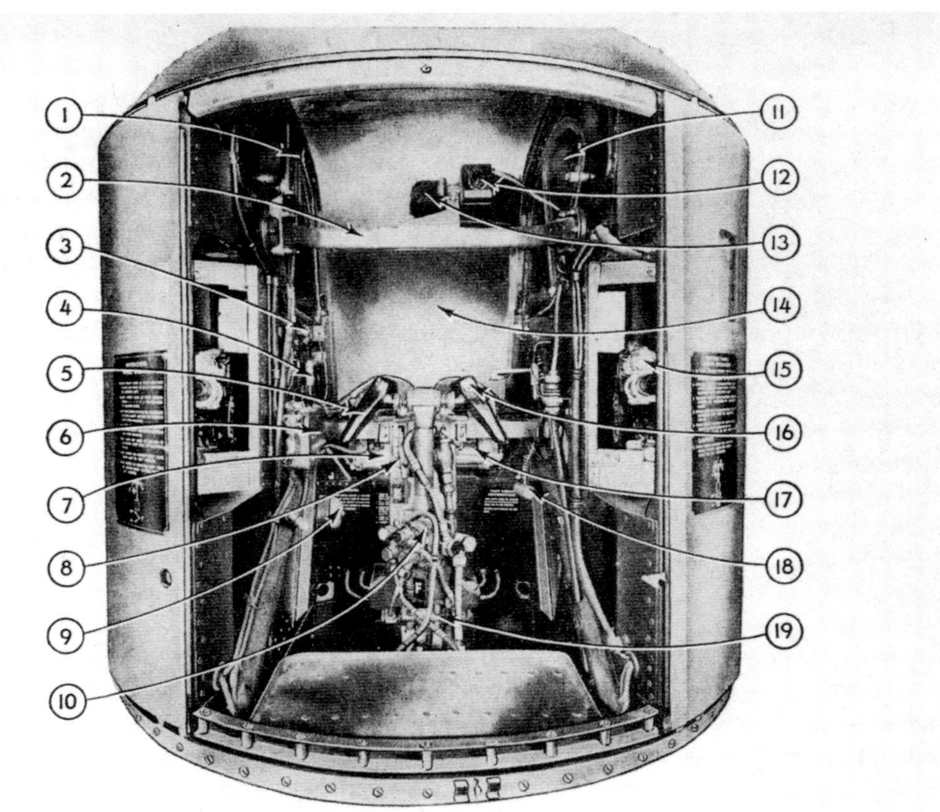

Figure 35—Motor Products Tail Turret—Rear View

1. Gun Camera Mount
2. Gun Sight Yoke
3. Elevation Manual Crank Shaft
4. Elevation Manual Control Hand Crank
5. Turret Control Handle
6. Switch Panel
7. Booster Motor
8. Shutoff Valve
9. Alarm Bell
10. Turret Control Valve
11. Ventilator
12. Gun Sight Rheostat
13. Gun Sight
14. Armor Glass
15. Gun Firing Solenoid
16. Microphone Button
17. Booster Motor
18. Gun Charger Handle
19. Dump Valve

This shows the rear view of the PB4Y-2's tail turret as shown in the Armament Manual. (Author's Collection)

A close-up view of the SWOD Mark-9 air-to-ground guided missile, called the *Bat*, installed under the right wing of a PB4Y-2. Note the aircraft appears to have a natural aluminum finish. (Courtesy: National Archives and Records Administration. Hereafter referred to as NARA)

This photograph shows a pair of SWOD Mark-9 *Bats* suspended under each wing of a PB4Y-2. During the Second World War VPB-109, 123, and 124 were equipped with the weapon, which produced mixed results when deployed against enemy shipping. This aircraft also displays the mast-like device shown on XPB4Y-2 Bureau Number 32086 pictured earlier in this chapter, giving credibility to one theory that the device was related to testing of the *Bat*. (Courtesy: NARA)

letters were applied to both sides of the vertical stabilizer on both active duty and reserve aircraft. In 1950 the word

Navy was applied to both sides of the aft fuselage, and it also appears that some reserve squadrons applied squadron letters to the upper and lower wing surfaces.

United States Coast Guard Coloring and Markings

The fuselages and wings of Coast Guard Privateers were usually painted an overall aluminum varnish, with yellow wing tips outlined in black, and an orange Yellow band outlined in Black was painted forward of the empennage. However, there is photographic evidence that shows a P4Y-2G with the glossy sea blue coloring. The words

U.S. Coast Guard were applied above the waist positions, and the abbreviation *USCG* was applied to the upper and lower wing surfaces. The last four digits of the bureau number were applied on both sides of the aft fuselage, with the aircraft designation P4Y-2G and the bureau number applied to both sides of the vertical stabilizer. Station lettering, such as those applied to Naval Privateers, does not seem to have been adopted by the Coast Guard.

Training Squadrons

Bombing and Operational Training Unit Four (VB-4 OTU), based at Whiting Field, Florida, and Hutchinson, Kansas, conducted initial training for PB4Y-2 crews, while advanced combat training was furnished by VPB-197 and VPB-200. VPB-197, based at Naval Auxiliary Air Station (NAAS) Camp Kearney, California, trained crews on the PB4Y-1 Liberator and PB4Y-2 Privateer before being disestablished on 1 April 1946. VPB-200 provided the final phases of combat training for replacement crews on the PB4Y-1 Liberator, PB4Y-2 Privateer, PV-1 Ventura, and PV-2 Harpoon from their base at NAS Kaneohe, Hawaii, beginning in August 1944. In October 1945 VPB-200 was absorbed into VPB-100, and the squadron was disestablished two months later in December.

A Jet Assisted Take-off (JATO) being performed by Bureau Number 59640 somewhere in the United States. The Navy conducted a number of JATO tests with the PB4Y-2 but JATO-assisted Privateers never went into combat. VPB-124 operated this particular aircraft from Okinawa in the summer of 1945 without JATO. (Courtesy: Roy Balke)

A U.S. Marine Corps RY-3 Privateer Express photographed in California. A transport version of the PB4Y-2, the RY-3 served primarily with the Marine Corps and the Royal Air Force between 1945 and 1946. This aircraft retained its natural aluminum appearance. (Courtesy: B-24 Liberator Club)

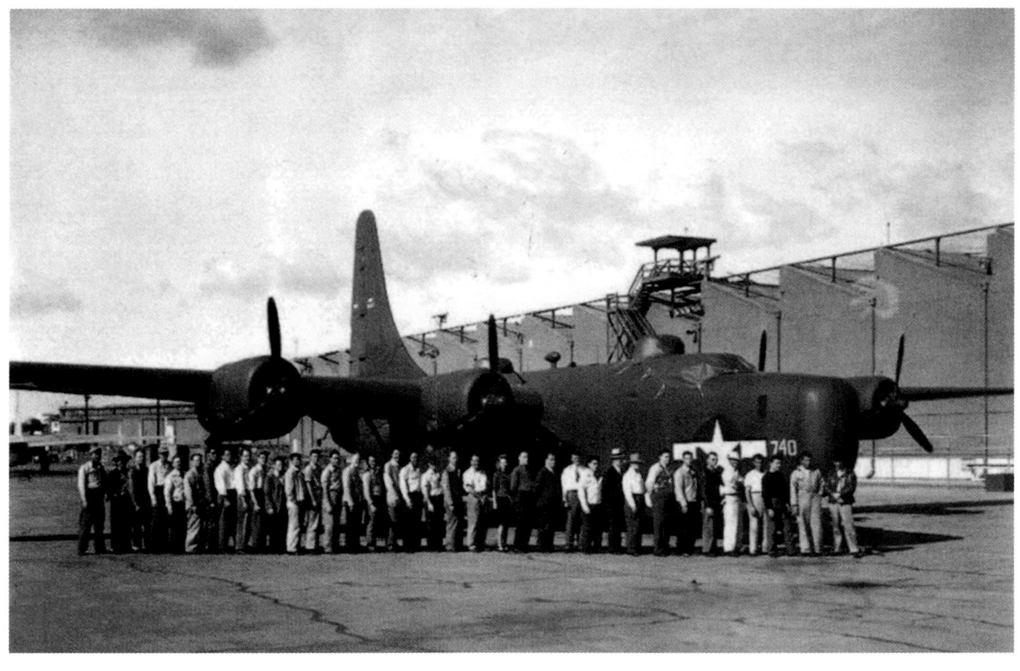

Convair workers stand next to the last production PB4Y-2 Privateer Bureau Number 66324 at the San Diego, California plant. (Courtesy Convair via Allan Blue)

2

Privateer Operations in World War II: Tinian (January-May 1945)

The first function of naval patrol aviation during World War II was to discover and report the location, nature, and movements of enemy forces. As the war in the Pacific progressed, patrol aviation was pressed into conducting air-sea rescue, mine-laying, defensive patrols around surface forces, and diversionary, harassing attacks against enemy bases, islands, and shipping. Since Navy Liberators, and later Privateers, could operate at a considerable range and carried 10 to 12 machine guns and a heavy bomb load, such aircraft conducted successful attacks on merchant shipping that contributed to the effort that ultimately strangled Japan's war-making capability.[5]

Setting the Stage

During the last eight months of the Pacific War, 16 United States Navy patrol squadrons equipped with the Liberator or Privateer, and sometimes both models, conducted missions against the Japanese from bases in the Central Pacific and the Philippine Islands. Ten combat squadrons (VPB-106, 108, 109, 118, 119, 120, 121, 122, 123, and 124) were the units initially assigned the aircraft. However, PB4Y-1 Liberator squadrons (VPB-102, 104, 111, 116, and 117), then serving in the Pacific Theater, started receiving the aircraft as replacements beginning in May 1945.

In the Central Pacific VPB-106, 108, 109, 118, 121, 123, and 124 operated under Fleet Air Wing Eighteen (FAW-18) and Landplane Detachment, Fleet Air Wing One (FAW-1), of the United States Third and Fifth Fleets. Between the capture of the Marianna Islands by American forces in August 1944 and the invasion of Iwo Jima in February 1945, United States airpower in the Central Pacific was utilized in the harassment and reconnaissance of by-passed Japanese-held islands in the Caroline and Marshall Islands. Part of this effort included PB4Y-1 squadrons VPB-102, 116, and briefly, VPB-117, before the latter squadron deployed to the Philippines. In addition, PB4Y-1 photographic squadrons VD-3, 4, and 5 conducted invaluable surveillance work over the Bonin Islands, Iwo Jima, Truk Atoll, and Okinawa. Navy PB4Y operations during this period were conducted from Eniwetok, in the Marshall Islands, and Saipan, Guam, and Tinian in the Marianna Islands.

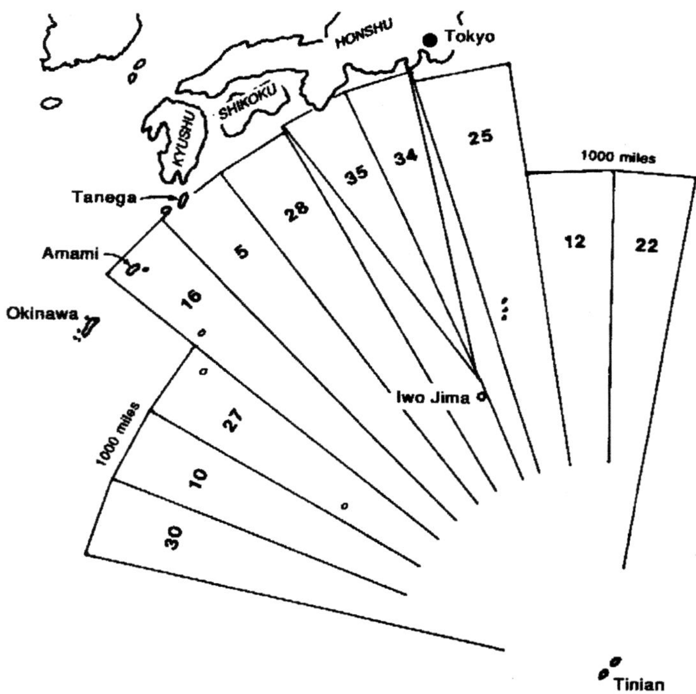

PB4Y search sectors in the Central Pacific extended outward from Tinian and Iwo Jima towards Japan. When Okinawa became a base of operations for PB4Y squadrons, the Korean Peninsula was included.

Navy's Torchy Tess (Bureau Number 59383), shown here at Yontan Field, Okinawa, operated with the *Old Crows* of VPB-118 and was an early model Privateer with the Consolidated nose turret. According to VPB-118 veteran Earl Mann and others, *Torchy Tess* was flown back to the United States in September 1945. (Courtesy: Davis McAlister)

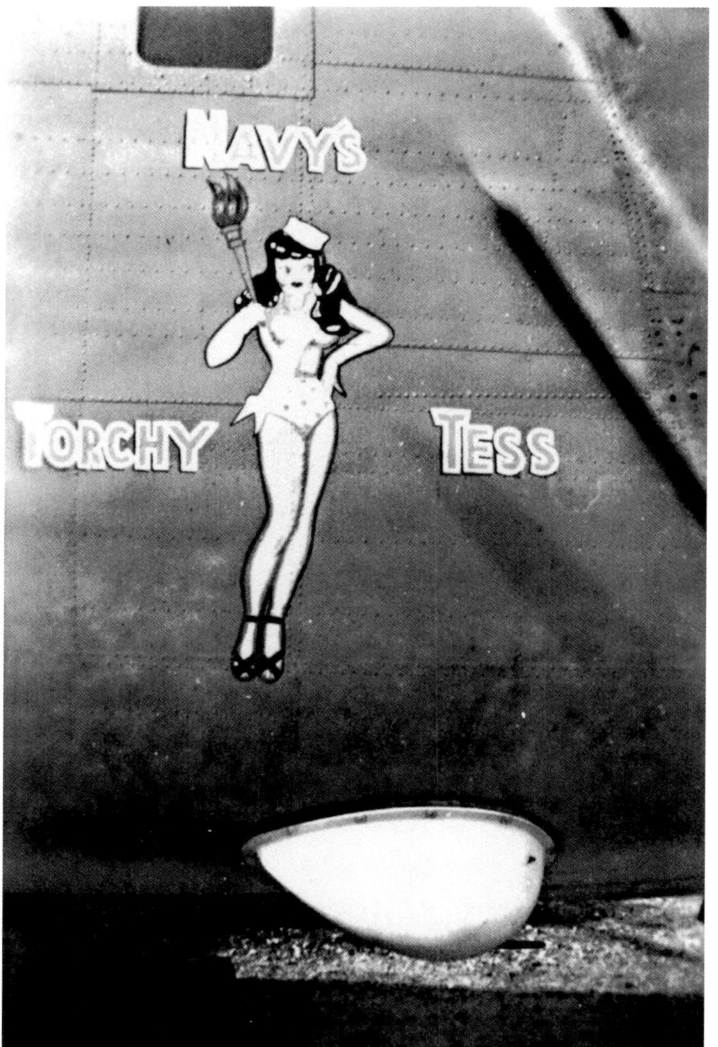

Close-up look at the nose art on *Navy's Torchy Tess* as it appeared on Okinawa between late April and early May 1945. (Courtesy: Davis McAlister)

A second phase of operations began in late March and early April 1945, when detachments of PB4Ys were sent to Iwo Jima for offensive operations against military and industrial targets in and around the Japanese home islands. A month later, within days of the initial American invasion of Okinawa in April 1945, Privateers were flying from Yontan Field for strikes against targets around Korea, Japan, and China. By July 1945 land-based squadrons operating from Okinawa and Iwo Jima stepped up attacks on enemy shipping in the Yellow, East China, and Japan Seas, along the coast of Japan, into the Inland Sea and Korea. The Chinese ports of Shanghai and Hangchow were in the process of being neutralized, as were Hong Kong and Formosa ports in the south. Additionally, the Korea-Japan shipping lanes across the Tsushima Straits were obliged to move in smaller convoys at night and rely on heavier escort. However, patrolling the coasts of China and Japan resulted in a high number of operational and combat related losses among several Privateer Squadrons between July and August 1945. During this period regular flight operations were canceled for nearly a week, as a typhoon moved towards the Japanese coast, and patrol squadrons were ordered to conduct special weather flights to track the storm. However, favorable weather the following week had planes from Okinawa going up in strength against shipping around Kyushu, Southern Honshu, and Korea, as well as over the Inland Sea, Sea of Japan, and the Yellow and East China Seas.

Tinian, Mariana Islands

Tinian is one of 15 islands that comprise the Marianas archipelago, and is located some 3,000 miles west of Hawaii. Beginning in June 1944, American forces invaded the four southern-most islands of the chain—Saipan, Tinian, Rota, and Guam—with Tinian being secured on 1 August 1944. Commander Kelly Harper's VPB-118, nicknamed the *Old Crows*, became the first PB4Y-2 Privateer squadron to conduct operations from an airbase on Tinian (named West Field) upon arriving between 10 and 14 January 1945.

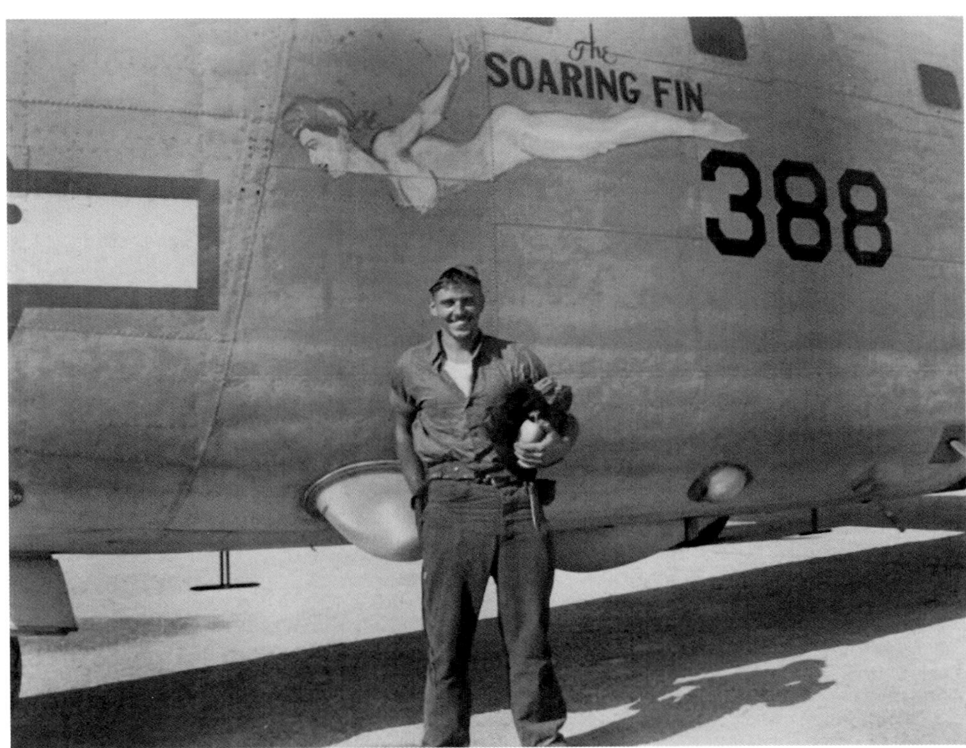

An unidentified member of VPB-118 stands next to *The Soaring Fin* (Bureau Number 59388). The squadron's Executive Officer, Lieutenant Commander Arthur F. Farwell, was forced to ditch this particular Privateer on 7 May 1945 when the aircraft sustained extensive damage from a Japanese merchant ship's anti-aircraft fire. (Courtesy: Earl Mann)

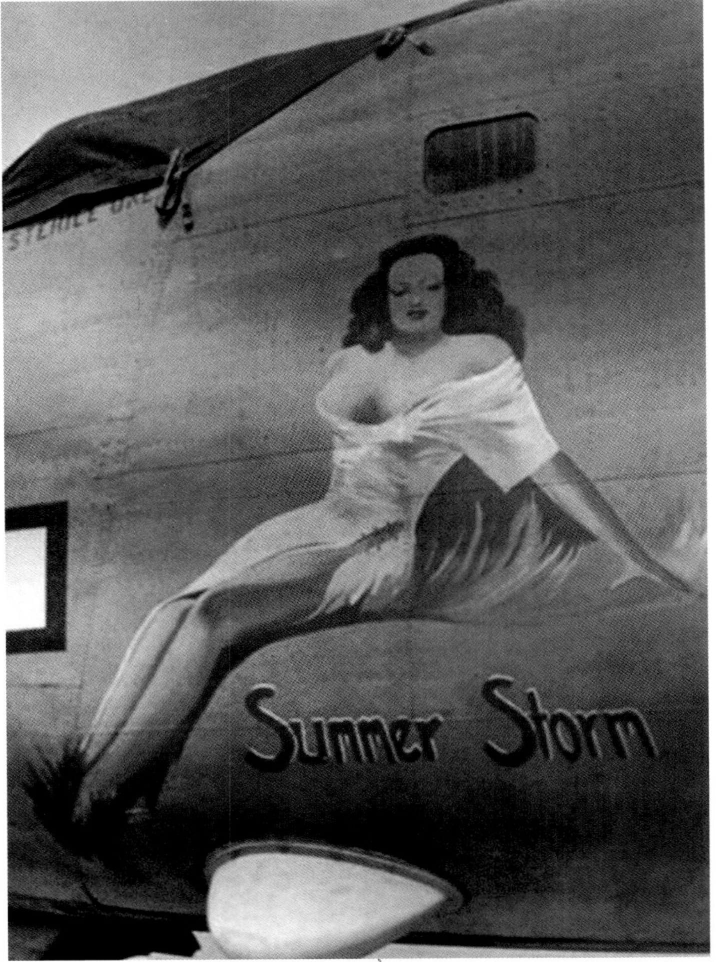

The squadron's first successful attack against Japanese merchant shipping occurred on 23 January when Lieutenant Edward G. Binning's Crew 13 damaged a 300-ton cargo ship near the Bonin Islands. The following month the *Old Crows* ran reconnaissance missions to Truk and Marcus Island to check for signs of Japanese movement during the American invasion of Iwo Jima. During the next several months, a majority of missions consisted of providing coverage for the United States Fifth Fleet, but on one occasion, a 1,200-ton freighter transport was found off Iwo Jima and damaged by Crew 6, commanded by Lieutenant Robert M. Finley.

Privateer operations doubled in size on Tinian upon the arrival of Commander William S. Sampson's *Wolverators* of VPB-106 between 13 and 16 February 1945. Before its arrival in the Central Pacific, one of 106's crews commanded by Lieutenant Francis H. Leik conducted the first ditching of a PB4Y-2. After running low on fuel during a navigation training flight, Leik ditched Privateer Bureau Number 59394 in the Gulf of California on 24 October 1944; the crew were rescued by a Mexican ship and returned to San Diego five days later. On Tinian, VPB-106's first contact with the enemy occurred on 20 February 1945 when a pair of planes commanded by Lieutenants James B. Schultz and Edward W. Ashley strafed a small wooden vessel and military barracks at Truk.[6]

During March 1945 a new phase of operations for Tinian-based patrol aviation began with reconnaissance flights to the Japanese

Summer Storm (Bureau Number 59380) assigned to Crew 8 of VPB-118 and commanded by Lieutenant Julian D. Serrill. On 22 April 1945, this aircraft was parked on Tinian when it was hit by a B-29 Superfortress. Three crewmembers of Crew 16 assigned to ferry the plane to Okinawa were aboard *Summer Storm* at the time of the crash. Don Berger, Richard Burns and Earl Mann managed to escape with minor injuries. (Courtesy: Earl Mann)

This Privateer of VPB-106 (Bureau Number 59386) hit a coral boulder upon landing at Tinian in February 1945 and was a total loss. (Author's Collection)

Personnel on Tinian in the process of salvaging useable parts from VPB-106's Privateer (Bureau Number 59386) that crashed on Tinian in the Mariana Islands. (Author's Collection)

home islands, providing fleet coverage, and neutralizing enemy picket boats. Specifically, patrol aviation was assigned screening duty for the United States Navy's Task Force 58 (TF-58) as it moved into position for carrier strikes on the Japanese mainland. The primary role of Navy Privateer and Liberator crews was to spot and engage enemy picket boats—ships in the 100 to 700-ton range being utilized as a form of early warning system to alert the mainland of approaching American planes. Four Privateers from VPB-118 patrolling on the 15th found such vessels off the Bonin Islands and inflicted severe damage to several of them during a combination of strafing and bombing attacks. Ten days later VPB-106 joined in the attacks, with Lieutenant Ashley inflicting serious damage to a pair of similar vessels located between Iwo Jima and Japan.

Fleet coverage required that search sectors be extended 1,000 to 1,200 miles from Tinian, which required planes flying the longest sectors to make a refueling stop at Iwo Jima. On one such flight, while returning from a patrol to Japan, Lieutenant Harry V. Duba, flying *Modest' O-Miss* (Bureau Number 59402), needed to land at Motoyama Field Number One on Iwo Jima to refuel before going on to Tinian. While making a steep-in approach to keep his plane from becoming a target of enemy soldiers firing from the end of the field, the Privateer hit a soft spot in the runway, which tore off the plane's right main landing gear and horizontal stabilizer. Lieutenant Duba and the rest of Crew 15 exited the aircraft unharmed, but *Modest' O-Miss* was a total loss.[7]

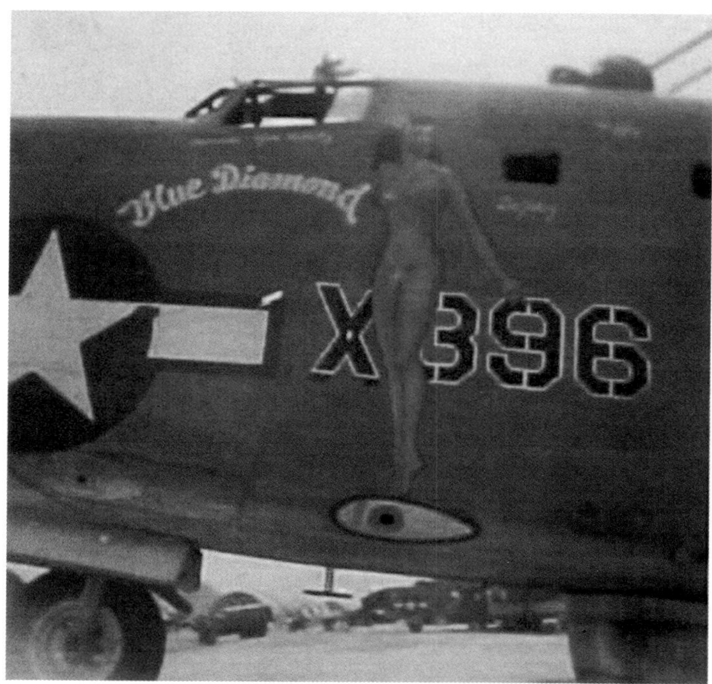

Blue Diamond (Bureau Number 59396) served in the Central Pacific and in the Philippines with *The Wolverators* of VPB-106. (Author's Collection)

Here is VPB-118's *Modest O' Miss* (Bureau Number 59402) after making a crash landing on Iwo Jima on 6 March 1945. The aircraft suffered extensive damage and was sent to the boneyard. (Courtesy: Steve Hawley)

A side view of *Modest O' Miss* on Iwo Jima. (Courtesy: Earl Mann)

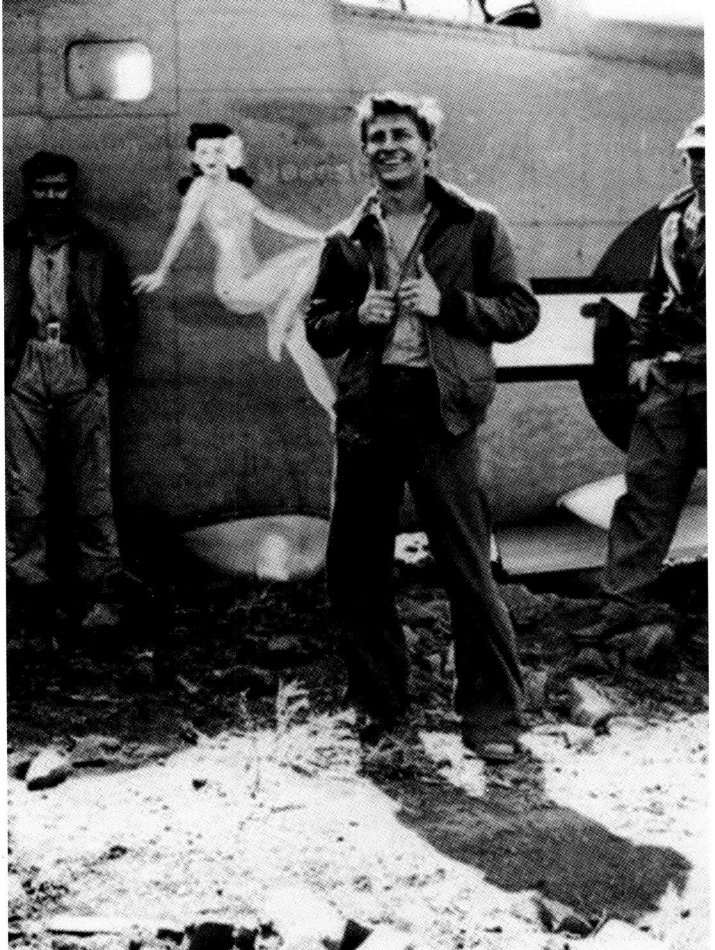

Unidentified crewmembers stand next to *Modest O' Miss* after crash landing at Iwo Jima on 6 March 1945. (Courtesy: Earl Mann)

PB4Y crews often went on 10 to 12-hour patrols without ever encountering the enemy, so their primary enemy was often boredom; yet, contact with Japanese forces, when it did occur, could often result in brief but intense combat. Of over 100 patrols conducted by VPB-106 during March 1945, only 11 resulted in enemy contacts. Picket boats were engaged on 6, 9, 10, 14, 17, and 24 March, with one encounter resulting in the loss of an entire crew, and during another attack a crewmember was seriously wounded. On the ninth, picket boats shot down Privateer Bureau Number 59497, commanded by Lieutenant Edward Ashley and carrying a crew of 12, plus three passengers who were along for the ride. Two survivors of the ill-fated Privateer, Seaman First Class Raymond W. Gray and Seaman First Class Charles W. Reddon, manged to survive the crash, only to be picked up by the Japanese. Apparently, both Gray and Reddon survived their captivity, and were repatriated back to the U.S. after Japan's surrender.

On the 14th a pair of 106 Privateers piloted by Lieutenants Joseph F. Huber and John F. Ripplinger teamed up with a pair of PV-1 Ventura bombers belonging to VPB-151 to destroy two enemy picket boats. During the ensuing battle, Huber's plane sustained serious damage to the control cables and his forward top turret gunner was seriously wounded in the legs by fragments from an exploding cannon shell.[8]

Attacks on picket boats continued throughout April, with VPB-118's Commander Harper' s Crew 1 teaming up with PV-1s of VPB-133 on the third. In the ensuing encounter with two enemy ships, Harper's plane *Pirate Queen* (Bureau Number 59404) was damaged, but made it safely back to Iwo Jima, where it was repaired and later flown back to Tinian. A day later, it was VPB-106's turn to reduce Japan's picket boat fleet, with Lieutenant Walter B. Hoblin sinking a 200-foot vessel 900 miles north of Tinian after the Privateer's radar operator picked up the vessel from a distance of

VPB-118's *Modest O' Miss II* (Bureau Number 59448) sported duplicate nose art as her predecessor (Bureau Number 59402) *Modest O' Miss I*. It appears that duplicate artwork was applied to both sides of the forward fuselage. (Courtesy: Author's Collection)

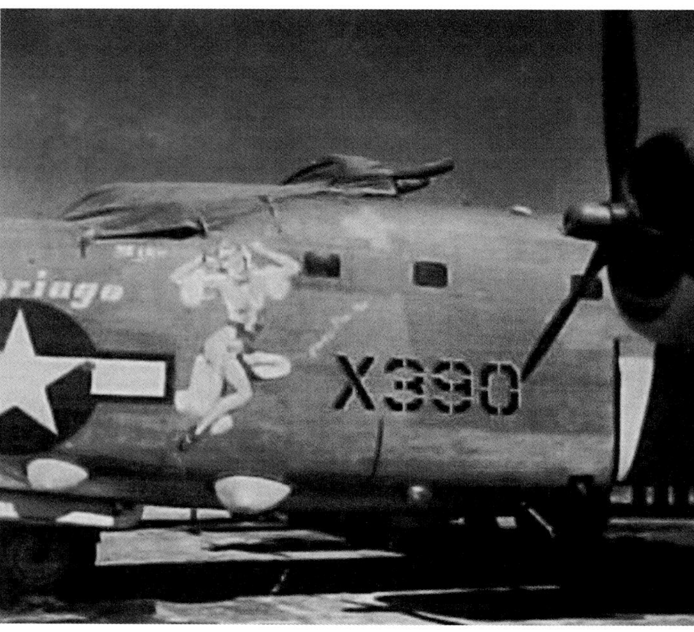

VPB-106's *Umbriago* (Bureau Number 59390) shown on Tinian between February and May 1945 (Author's Collection)

36 miles. Hoblin took the Privateer down, descending through a heavy overcast, before breaking out of it at 200 feet. The picket boat appeared, and Hoblin's bombardier dropped three 325-pound depth charges, with one scoring a direct hit on the vessel's fantail, which caused the picket to roll over and sink.

Chasing an Emily

After the fall of Iwo Jima, encounters with enemy aircraft became almost nonexistent until land-based air began approaching the Japanese homeland. Patrolling near Japan's home islands in search of picket boats provided PB4Y-2 crews with opportunities to test the aircraft's defensive capabilities against enemy aircraft. It began with VPB-118's Crew 12 conducting the first PB4Y-2 aerial kill of a Japanese aircraft in the Central Pacific area of operations.

Lieutenant Michael Keiser, patrol plane commander of *Flying Tail?* (Bureau Number 59379); an aptly named Privateer adorned with a large painting of a rather heavy-set nude woman, scored the squadron's first aerial kill on 12 March 1945 when a Kawanishi H8K (Emily) flying boat was intercepted and shot down off Amami Shima, an island between Okinawa and Kyushu. Initial contact was

A PB4Y-1 Liberator (upper center) photographed by a VPB-108 Privateer over Iwo Jima sometime between April and August 1945. (The contributor of this photograph wished to remain anonymous)

Aerial view of Iwo Jima as a VPB-108 Privateer makes a landing approach to Central Field. (The contributor of this photograph wished to remain anonymous)

A considerable number of Privateers during the Second World War sported risqué artwork of women. VPB-108's *Els Nocho* (Bureau Number 59460) seen here on Tinian Island was no exception. Barely visible in the far left background is another VPB-108 Privateer Bureau Number 59459 with the name *Lady Luck III*. (Author's Collection)

established when two Emily flying boats were spotted 7,000 feet above the Privateer, being escorted by seven Kawasaki Ki-45 (Nick) twin-engine fighters, but they were too far away, so Keiser did not pursue. Four minutes later three more Nicks were spotted as they approached, but none of them approached the American bomber.

Another four minutes elapsed before a single Emily was sighted 3,000 feet above the Privateer. Seeing his chance, Lieutenant Keiser pushed the PB4Y-2's throttles forward and headed for the enemy. The Japanese plane was taken completely by surprise as the Privateer's bow guns opened fire at maximum range, the first rounds chewing off pieces of the plane's tail. Seeing he was being pursued, the Emily's pilot nosed his plane down, turning to the right while its port waist position returned fire at the rapidly approaching American patrol bomber. However, the combined firepower of the Privateer's bow, top, and starboard waist turrets sent back a steady stream of machine gun fire, which quickly knocked out the Emily's sole means of defending itself. The flying boat then went into a steep glide from which it never recovered and hit the water, exploding on impact. A thick column of black smoke billowing some 5,000 feet into the sky marked the final resting place of the Japanese aircraft, her crew, and the first of nine aerial victories for VPB-118 [9]

An aerial shot of a PB4Y-2 Privateer from VPB-108 with Iwo Jima in the background. Note that the aircraft's upper tail section appears to be painted white, which was an unusual color variation for a PB4Y-2. (The contributor of this photograph wished to remain anonymous)

Arrival of VPB-108

VPB-108, led by Lieutenant Commander John E. Muldrow, became the third Privateer squadron to operate from Tinian, arriving between 4 and 7 April after operating from Peleliu in the Palau Islands for three weeks, 16 March-4 April 1945. Operations by VPB-108 from Tinian lasted only two weeks before most of the squadron's aircraft and crews departed for Central Field on Iwo Jima, leaving behind only a few flight personnel and the administrative offices on Tinian. During its brief tour of duty on Tinian, VPB-108 had the distinction of having the first recorded ditching of a Privateer in a combat zone, and the third in the model's short operational life. Running low on fuel in Privateer Bureau Number 59442, Lieutenant Hazlett ditched the aircraft in rough seas after he and his crew became lost while returning from a patrol to the Bonin Islands on 8 April. The aircraft broke in two upon impact but remained afloat for approximately two minutes, enabling the crew of 13 to man the life rafts. Hazlett and his men spent nearly four days adrift while planes from their squadron, along with others from VPB-102, 106, and 118, conducted an intensive search. They were finally picked up in the early morning hours of 12 April by the submarine U.S.S. *Queenfish* after being spotted by a plane from VPB-102.[10]

An interior view showing the 20-millimeter cannons installed on a VPB-108 Privateer. It took a considerable amount of work to install but according to a VPB-108 veteran, there was not anything else to do on Iwo Jima in between patrols. (The contributor of this photograph wished to remain anonymous)

Losses for VPB-118

Venturing close to Japan was always a dangerous undertaking for American patrol aircraft due to armed shipping sailing off the coast, the presence of enemy fighters, and the distance required to reach the mainland from Iwo Jima and Tinian. VPB-118's Crew 12, with Lieutenant Keiser at the controls of *Modest' O-Miss II* (Bureau Number 59448), had a rough day on 12 April during an engagement with an enemy freighter off Honshu. Keiser and his men encountered stiff resistance, and the plane received a hit by a 20-millimeter shell that severely wounded the bow turret gunner, W.A. Van Thiel. Lieutenant Keiser brought *Modest' O-Miss II* back to Iwo, where the wounded gunner was transported to the hospital, and the remaining members of the crew borrowed another plane and flew back to Tinian.[11]

This photograph shows the 20-millimeter cannon modification on a VPB-108 Privateer. The bombsight became useless because of this modification but, according to one patrol plane commander, the sight wasn't needed because bombing took place at altitudes of 300 feet or less. Two crewmembers scrounged the cannons for this particular aircraft from a wrecked plane. According to the patrol plane commander, he only fired it once at the enemy off Japan and missed. (The contributor of this photograph wished to remain anonymous)

Two days after Crew 12's encounter, another VPB-118 crew took to life rafts after ditching their plane (Bureau Number 59401) a few miles off Iwo Jima. After sinking a small freighter off O-Shima, Japan, Crew 2, led by the *Old Crows* Executive Officer, Arthur F. Farwell, landed their Privateer on Iwo, refueled, and took off again for Tinian. Minutes into the flight, the number three engine suddenly cut out; the engines were immediately shifted to the fuel cross-feed system, but then all engine power was lost. Gliding the powerless Privateer down, Farewell made a water landing and the crew exited the floating plane unharmed, climbed into a life raft—except for Farwell, who remained in the water—and waited for rescue. While treading water and unable to climb into the overcrowded life raft Farwell uttered the immortal words, "My first command at sea, and I can't even get in the damn boat!" It wouldn't be the last time Farwell and his crew had to take to the water.[12]

Iwo Jima Detachments

Iwo Jima, a small volcanic island with an area of some eight square miles and only 650 miles from Tokyo, was one of the Second World War's bloodiest battles. During the 36-day battle that began on 19 February 1945, American forces suffered 25,000 American dead, wounded, or missing, while nearly all of the island's 22,000 Japanese defenders perished. Detachments of Privateers from VPB-106 and 108, and Liberators of VPB-102 began arriving on Iwo Jima during the second week of April 1945 to cover search sectors, which extended from Kyushu to Honshu, Japan. The arrival of Navy land-based patrol bombers with the capability to conduct anti-shipping and reconnaissance sweeps of the Japanese home islands provided the Americans with a small but vital means to degrade Japan's ability to wage war.

Operations for the Iwo Jima detachments taxed both man and machine, as unpredictable weather interfered with normal air operations, and the island's fine volcanic ash penetrated everything, including aircraft engines, which invariably caused a number of mechanical problems. The weather was constantly bad during the first few weeks of operations, and often searches were cut short so that aircraft could have enough fuel to make Tinian if Iwo was closed in. Many of the aircrews viewed unpredictable weather as a greater hazard than the threat of Japanese fighter interception or anti-aircraft fire. To make matters worse, heavily loaded Privateers had to take off often in undesirable weather from a short and bumpy airstrip named Central Field. The issue of departing from a short runway was solved by June 1945, when the airstrip was paved and extended to a length of 9,800 feet, enabling B-29 Superfortress heavy bombers to use it as an emergency landing strip after conducting bombing missions on Japan.

Iwo Jima-based PB4Y-2s belonging to the *Wolverators* of VPB-106 inflicted serious damage to shipping and ground installations in and around Kyushu, Honshu, and Shikoku during the last two weeks of April 1945. Lieutenant Schultz scored first when his gunners strafed a 100-ton freighter off Kyushu after the plane's bomb release mechanism failed. Two days later, Lieutenant Commander Howard F. "Pappy" Mears hit targets in Japan, resulting in the destruction of a warehouse and the damaging of two small freighters. A week later on the 23rd, Lieutenant Jerry M. Barlow, patrolling approximately 80 miles southeast of Honshu, found two Japanese patrol vessels and sank them with combined bombing and strafing attacks. Lieutenant Benjamin F. Calwell followed up by sinking a 100-ton freighter after completing four bombing and strafing runs. Before the squadron moved to the Phillippines, *The Wolverators* conducted a pair of single-plane missions on the 29th. Commander Sampson hit shipping off Shikoku, leaving three 100-ton vessels severely damaged, while Lieutenant Leik, outbound from Iwo Jima to Honshu, attacked a picket boat from an altitude of 100 feet. While the Privateer's gunners swept the vessel's decks clear of personnel, Leik's bombardier dropped a salvo of 10, 100-pound bombs that completely enveloped the ship, leaving it seriously damaged and dead in the water. A couple of days later, on 3 May 1945, the men of VPB-106 on Iwo Jima and Tinian began packing their bags after the squadron was issued a directive ordering them to Palawan Island in the Philippines for duty with Fleet Air Wing Ten (FAW-10).

While *The Wolverators* wrapped up its tour in the Central Pacific, Lieutenant Commander Muldrow's VPB-108 began operations from Iwo Jima in mid-April 1945, and would remain on the volcanic island for the remainder of the war, with the exception of a three-week period (8 May to 3 June) when the squadron moved back to Tinian. While operating from Iwo, between 15 April and 8 May 1945 VPB-108 conducted 24 strikes resulting in the destruction of nearly 90 enemy vessels, consisting primarily of fishing vessels and small freighters weighing less than 200 tons. Strafing and bombing attacks by Navy patrol aviation against seemingly innocuous Japanese fishing boats were viewed by patrol plane commanders as legitimate actions, since such vessels were viewed as a possible, if not probable, means of communicating to the mainland the type, number, and heading of allied aircraft approaching Japan.

Privateers and Cannons

One of the Iwo-based patrol plane commanders, Lieutenant Commander Robert C. Lefever, is reported to be the first to order the installation of two externally fixed, forward-firing, 20-millimeter cannons on a PB4Y-2. Lefever's first Ordnanceman, W.E. Maxwell, conducted installation of the cannons with the aide of other crewmembers while the squadron was based at Kaneohe, Hawaii, and later Peleliu. Combat testing of the cannons occurred on 26 April 1945 when Lefever sank a picket boat and five fishing boats

Lieutenant Donald Hartvig (center) and his crew served together for two years with VPB-108 and took part on the Raid against Marcus Island on 9 May 1945. According to Hartvig, "It was a good crew, no prima donnas, just good solid mid-American guys who really knew what they were doing." (Courtesy: Donald Hartvig)

ff Honshu, Japan, with a combination of 20-millimeter cannon and .50-caliber machine gun fire. Testing the weapon on enemy vessels proved successful enough that ComAirPacSubComForward endorsed the project, with ComAirPac forwarding the idea to the Bureau of Aeronautics (BuAer), and by August 1945 the cannons were installed on most VPB-108 aircraft, as well as a number of Privateers in other squadrons, most notably VPB-121.[13]

Lieutenant Ebright's Ditching

An encounter with an enemy APD, a destroyer-type transport, nearly resulted in a fatal disaster for VPB-108's Lieutenant Ebright and his crew. Shortly after starting a routine sector search northeast of Iwo Jima on 5 May 1945, Lieutenant Ebright was ordered to locate an APD that was reported to be northeast of the Bonin Islands. The enemy ship was soon located and kept in sight while he homed in six P-51 Mustang fighters that had taken off from Iwo Jima as soon as the Privateer's contact report had been received. Arriving on scene, the Mustangs proceeded to make rocket attacks on the APD, without much success, but since their strafing seemed to clear the decks, Lieutenant Ebright decided to follow the last of the fighters in for a low-level bombing and strafing run.

Approaching the ship, the Privateer's crew poured a concentration of 20-millimeter cannon and 50-caliber machine gun fire at the ship but, as the patrol bomber passed over the APD at masthead height, it was hit between the number three and four engines by a 4.7-inch cannon shell. The number four engine was put of operation immediately, the number three engine was damaged, and later the propeller had to be feathered. One hour after the attack, finding that he could not maintain course and altitude with two engines out on the same side, Lieutenant Ebright was forced to ditch the plane.

Fortunately the sea was calm, and the ditching was successfully carried out, although the plane was difficult to control with only two engines on the port side functioning. Most of the crew sustained minor injuries, but all escaped from the plane easily into

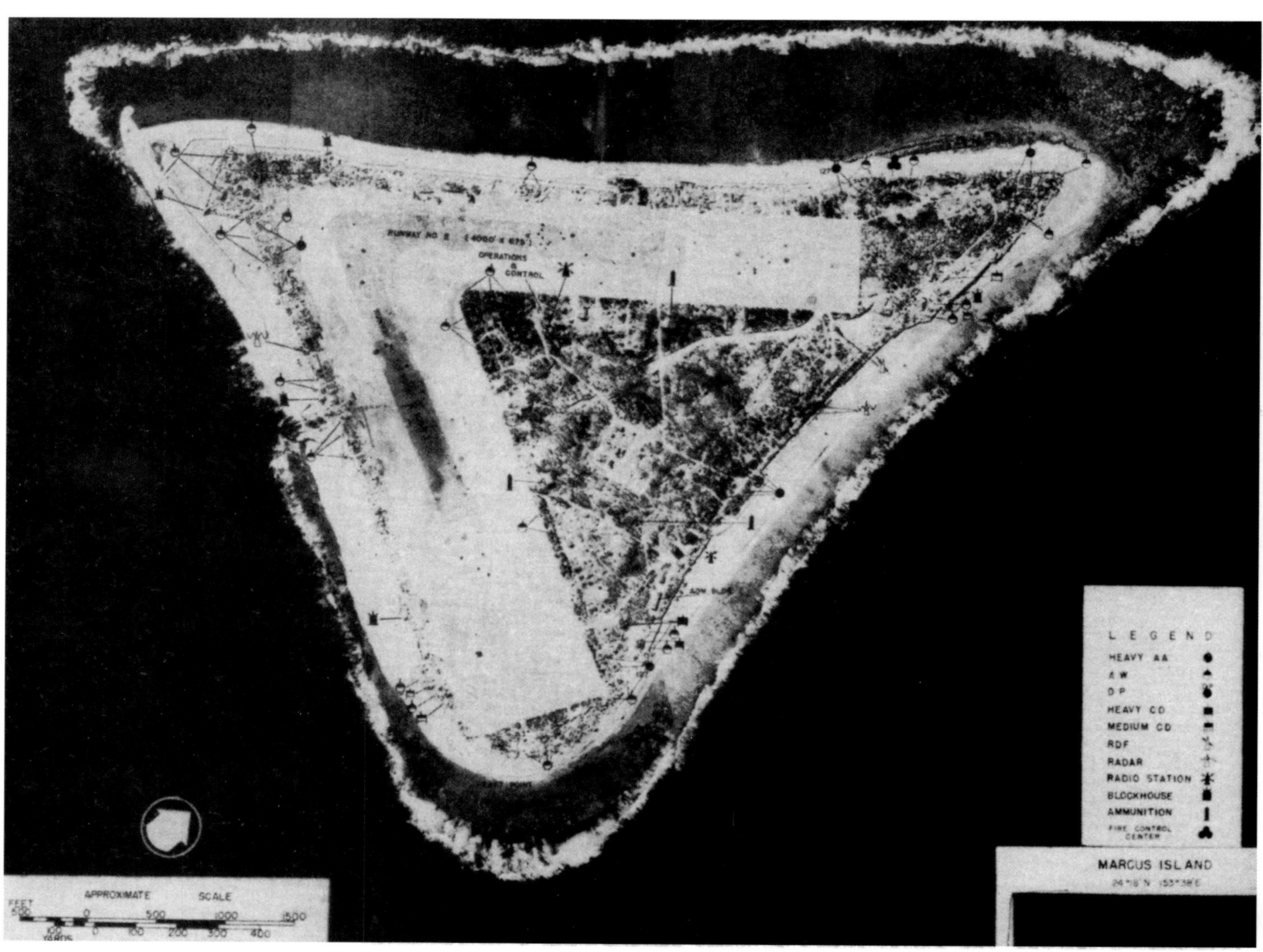

An aerial reconnaissance photograph taken of triangular-shaped Marcus Island by a PB4Y-1 Liberator of Navy Photographic Squadron One (VD-1). Ringed by a series of anti-aircraft defenses, the island posed a formidable opponent to attacking allied aircraft. (Source: Navy Photographic Squadron One Cruise book)

two life rafts. Another VPB-108 Privateer contacted Lieutenant Ebright soon after the latter's plane was hit, and orbited the rafts until relieved by a B-17 and a B-29 Dumbo from Iwo. After some four and half hours in the rafts, the men were picked up by destroyer and returned to base. Aviation Machinist Mate First Class (AMM1c) E. F. Vodicka was out of action for several weeks, but the rest of the crew, whose injuries were minor, returned to the squadron before the end of the month.[14]

Raid on Marcus Island

VPB-108 returned to Tinian on 8 May in response to intelligence reports suggesting that the Japanese were preparing to stage aircraft through Truk and Marcus Island to hit B-29 bases in the Mariana Islands, with the final objective of attacking the American Naval Base at Ulithi Atoll. Responding to this perceived threat, three Privateers of VPB-108, led by Lieutenant Commander Muldrow, and six PB4Y-1 Liberators of VPB-102, led by Lieutenant Commander Pressler, conducted a raid on Marcus Island, with the primary purpose of hitting enemy aircraft on the runways or in nearby revetments and parking areas. The striking force would meet with unexpected resistance from the Japanese defenders on the triangular-shaped island, located between Iwo Jima and Wake, which subsequently resulted in the loss of two aircraft and the lives of nearly 20 men.

During the planning stage of the operation VPB-108 was instructed to cover the east-west runway at Marcus, while VPB-102 was given the north-south runway, with the primary targets being enemy aircraft on the runways or in nearby revetments and parking areas. All planes carried 3,100 gallons of gasoline and 20, 100-pound bombs with 4-5 second delayed action fuses that would allow the attackers to fly in low, drop the ordnance, and get away without becoming a victim of their own exploding bombs. The original intention was for both sections to join up and hit Marcus as one group. However, on the outbound leg, according to one member of VPB-108 who participated in the raid, communication was never established with the VPB-102 Liberators and the two groups failed to join up. The failure to join up or establish communication resulted in disaster for Muldrow's section.

Between 0200 and 0209 hours on the morning of 9 May 1945, three planes from 108 piloted by Lieutenant Commander Muldrow, Lieutenant Hartvig, and Lieutenant (jg) Panther, and three PB4Y-1 Liberators from VPB-102 flown by Lieutenant Commander Pressler, Lieutenant Barnes, and Lieutenant Halahan departed West Field, Tinian, for Marcus. Three additional planes of VPB-102 followed within another 40 minutes.[15]

Weather conditions for the takeoff were terrible, with heavy rain making visibility almost zero. Lieutenant Commander Muldrow, who was the first to be airborne, circled soon after takeoff and turned on his landing lights in order to give his two other Privateers, piloted by Hartvig and Panther, an opportunity to rendezvous with him. The three planes stayed together, in a loose V formation, all the way to the target, flying first at 12,000 feet and then down to 1,000 feet. Conditions continued to improve all the way, with the heavy rain being followed by intermittent squalls and low clouds. High power settings were used in an attempt to reach Marcus before daybreak. Muldrow led the section with Panther to his port and Hartvig to his starboard. The latter fell slightly behind when a detonation in the number two engine forced him to throttle back to lower power settings.

About 150 miles out the planes descended to 200 feet, and at 70 miles they dropped down to 100 feet in an effort to evade enemy radar. At sunrise, they still had some distance to go. They could see a PB4Y-1, which later was identified as Lieutenant Commander Pressler's plane, 10 miles to the starboard, flying a parallel course. Pressler did not attempt to join them and flew straight toward the island, making his run at about 0715 over the assigned target area (the north-south runway) and destroying two aircraft, which he caught at the junction of the two runways, apparently about to take off.

Muldrow, Hartvig, and Panther proceeded on a course that took them about 20 miles to the west of Marcus. They saw the smoke of the aircraft set on fire by Pressler, so they immediately turned and headed for the island on a bearing that took them directly over the target. About three miles out they were subjected to intense and very accurate heavy anti-aircraft fire, the first burst coming quite close to the trio of Privateers. At this point, each patrol plane commander commenced mild evasive tactics, which became violent during the final approach to and into retirement from the island.

Since the ceiling and visibility were unlimited, they could see the island quite clearly before they passed over it. The only planes they could spot were the two that Pressler had attacked, which were already burning fiercely, dense smoke rising high in the air. Since this smoke offered a chance for partial concealment, they headed directly for it. Unfortunately for them, Pressler's attack had sprung the enemy into action, and air defenses were manned and ready as the PB4Y 2s flew into range.

Billowing smoke rises from Marcus Island during a dawn attack by VPB-102 and 108 on 9 May 1945. Both squadrons each lost a plane including that of VPB-108's Commanding Officer who was killed along with most his crew. (The contributor of this photograph wished to remain anonymous)

Muldrow's plane was soon hopelessly shot up even before it crossed the island's reef. Multiple hits from cannon fire knocked out the number three engine, tore the number four engine completely off the wing, blew away some of the tail surfaces, started fires in the forward section, and one shell tore off the back of the plane captain's head. Out of control, the Privateer swerved to port, passing over the island at an altitude of 100 feet before crashing into the sea about half a mile offshore.

As soon as Lieutenant Panther crossed over the island's reef he increased speed and dropped down to the deck. Passing between the two burning planes to take advantage of the smoke screen, he made his attack at an altitude of 25 feet and a speed of almost 230 knots. Soon after beginning the run, Lieutenant Panther's plane was hit by a 40-millimeter shell that tore an eight-inch hole through the aft fuselage; it struck the ammunition box for the tail turret, blowing it to pieces, and causing some of the .50-caliber ammunition to explode. The exploding ammunition started a fire in the after section, but due largely to the prompt actions of the Plane Captain, Vern S. Hartgraves, the fire was soon extinguished. A moment later, the Privateer was over the target and Lieutenant Panther dropped eight 100-pound bombs by pickle switch on gun positions, installations, and personnel along the south side of the East-West runway. However, his remaining bombs became hung up inside the bomb bay, and they were later jettisoned on the return trip to Tinian. Because of the obvious damage to his plane, Panther broke off about half way down the island, turning to starboard and flying on a northeasterly course until he was out of range of the intense anti-aircraft fire.

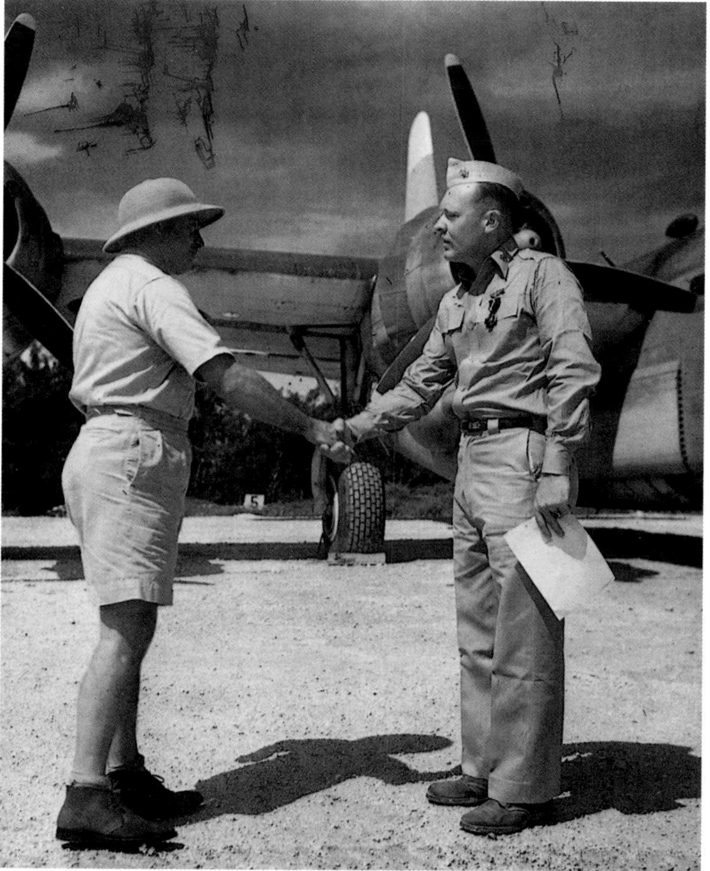

Lieutenant Donald Hartvig being awarded the Navy Cross for his service during the Marcus Island Raid by Rear Admiral Leslie Genres. Lieutenant Hartvig was only 23-years-old at the time. (Courtesy: Donald Hartvig)

Lieutenant Hartvig hit the target a few seconds after Panther, making his run from an altitude of only 75 feet and a speed of 190 knots. Flying through the smoke of the burning planes and along the southern side of the airstrip, he dropped a string of 16, 100-pound bombs on the personnel and installations in that area. Although his plane was hit several times by light anti-aircraft and small arms fire there was no major damage, and he continued on the same course until he was out of range of the island's air defenses. The remaining three aircraft of VPB-102 hit the island soon afterwards. The Japanese defenders shot down one of the Liberators, piloted by Lieutenant Halahan, in flames, and it went down not far from the scene of Lieutenant Muldrow's crash. Another PB4Y-1 Liberator was so badly damaged that it had to be surveyed after returning to Tinian, while a third, hit repeatedly by the island's air defenses, was brought back to base with a considerable amount of difficulty by its pilot and co-pilot.

Immediately after the attack, Hartvig and Panther rendezvoused near Muldrow's crash and began to circle just out of anti-aircraft range. They were on the alert for a possible aerial attack, since Pressler contacted the other aircraft that he thought enemy fighters were following him. Pressler was circling the island, waiting for the other planes of his squadron to come in for the attack. Since he was the senior officer present, and since one of his planes, piloted by Lieutenant Holahan, had crashed into the sea in flames in the same general vicinity, he took charge of the reports and search operations.

After remaining in the area for another half-hour, Panther and Hartvig climbed to 6,000 feet and headed back to Tinian. Lieutenant Panther's Privateer was low on fuel, so Hartvig decreased his power settings and fell behind the other plane. On the way, he was in constant contact with Barnes and Goodman of VPB-102, whose planes had been badly damaged in the Marcus attack. Since both men were having communications difficulties, he relayed messages from them back to base and assisted them in staying in contact with the lifeguard submarine U.S.S. *Jallao* that was in the area.

Five men managed to get out of the twisted wreckage of Lieutenant Commander Muldrow's Privateer; Muldrow was not among them. Lieutenant M.R. Wallace recalled finding himself 15 to 20 feet under water and swimming toward a bright spot above that proved to be the surface. Seaman First Class R.L. Livesay locked himself in the tail turret just before the crash and had no idea how he escaped. When he came to, he discovered that he was caught on a piece of the wing that was floating upright.

Somehow, one of the plane's life rafts became dislodged during the crash and was floating to the surface. Wallace swam to the raft, inflated it in an inverted position, and with the help of Ensign Palma, who was severely injured, managed to turn it over. The survivors either climbed or were hauled into the raft, and the less seriously injured men broke out the oars and began rowing away from the island. The men spent seven hours in the raft awaiting rescue,

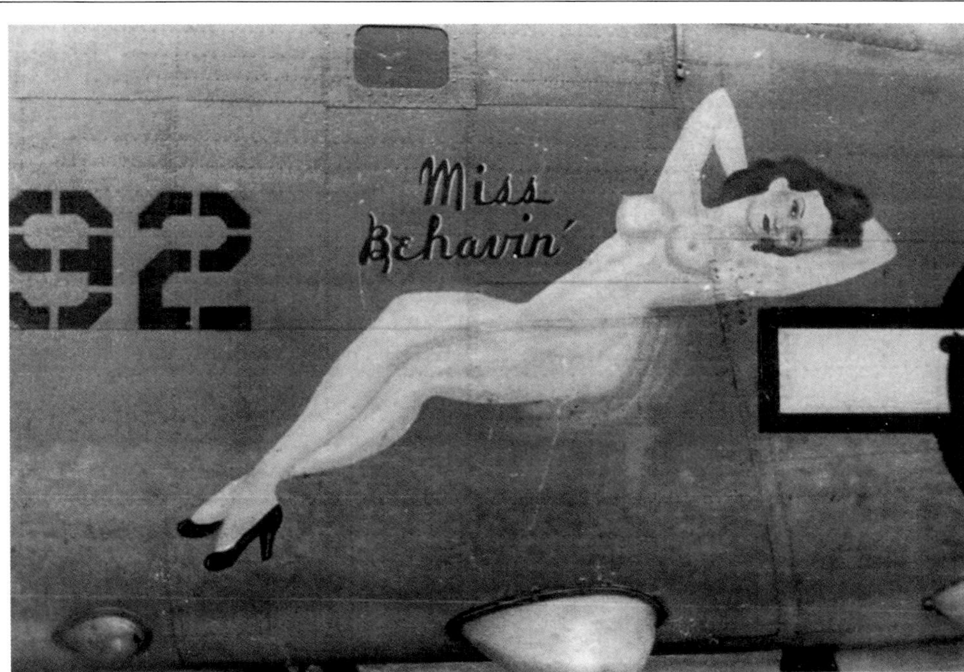

VPB-118's *Miss Behavin'* (Bureau Number 59392) was assigned to Crew 14 commanded by Lieutenant August M. Lodato. According to squadron records, this aircraft was damaged beyond repair at Tinian on 25 May 1945. (Courtesy: Earl Mann)

narrowly escaping capture and possibly certain death when a sampan, sent out from Marcus to search for them, came dangerously close, and an enemy plane flew directly overhead without sighting them. As they were being transferred to the submarine *Jallao*, shore batteries on Marcus opened fire and one shell landed exactly on the spot where the submarine had been a few seconds before crash-diving.[16]

At Saipan, the commander of the Air Sea Rescue Unit ordered a B-17 rescue plane equipped with a motor whaleboat, along with a PBY-5A Catalina Dumbo plane, to proceed to the scene of the reported sighting of Lieutenant Commander Muldrow's men. Meanwhile, Lieutenant Charles Baumgartner of VPB-108 was sent out from West Field, Tinian, to orbit the rafts and cooperate in rescue work, if necessary. At 1830 he reported that the submarine had rescued two officers and three enlisted men identified as Lieutenant M.R. Wallace, Ensign J. Palma, Aviation Radioman Second Class E.J. Lassiter, Aviation Radioman Third Class H.J. Henders, and Seaman First Class R.L. Livesay. A dispatch from the *Jallao* at 0407 hours on the tenth confirmed this statement, giving further information that all five survivors were wounded—two seriously.

After the death of Commander Muldrow, Lieutenant Commander Lefever became 108's new commanding officer. VPB-108 remained on Tinian until 3 June, primarily conducting reconnaissance flights over Truk, when the squadron returned to Iwo Jima. Nearly 60 years after the raid on Marcus Island, some VPB-108 veterans blamed the deaths aboard Muldrow's plane on VPB-102's Commanding Officer, whose actions, they believe, were driven by his desire to win recognition and thus advance his military career. Muldrow, Hartvig, Panther, and Hartgraves were all awarded the Navy Cross, every man who participated in the raid was awarded the Distinguished Flying Cross, and 13 Purple Hearts were awarded, eight posthumously.[17]

3

Privateer Operations in World War II: Iwo Jima (June-August 1945)

VPB-108 returned to Iwo Jima in early June and resumed armed reconnaissance and anti-shipping patrols. Between 8 and 29 June 1945 VPB-108 Privateers, patrolling along the Japanese mainland, continued strikes against enemy shipping, with vessels ranging in size from small fishing boats to 2,000-ton freighters. In addition, harbor facilities and military installations were hit. Enemy aircraft were encountered on several occasions, with Lieutenant Commander Rogers and his crew damaging an Aichi E13A1 Jake floatplane off Tokyo Bay on the eighth. Nine days later, three Mitsubishi A6M Reisen Zeke fighters intercepted Lieutenant Idle's plane south of Choshi Point and, during a 20-minute engagement, his gunners shot down two of the Japanese interceptors. The next encounter with enemy aircraft occurred when a pair of two-plane sections, consisting of Lieutenants Baumgartner and Hazlett and Lieutenant Commander Rogers and Lieutenant Hartvig, engaged Japanese fighters in separate encounters on the 20th. Lieutenant Baumgartner and Hazlett shared credit in the destruction of one Nakajima Ki-43 Hayabusa Oscar and the damaging of two others after a running battle along the southern coast of Honshu, while Lieutenant Commander Rogers and Lieutenant Hartvig fought off two Zekes south of the Chiba Peninsula.

This photograph taken by a VPB-118 PB4Y-2, possibly during February 1945, shows the American invasion fleet anchored off Iwo Jima during the island's invasion. (Earl Mann)

Rugged and Sturdy

The PB4Y-2's sturdiness and its ability to sustain severe damage was tested again on 11 June when Lieutenant Hazlett, flying *Lady Luck II* (Bureau Number 59446), and another Privateer piloted by Lieutenant (jg) Hill encountered a ship off Honshu that exploded while his aircraft flew over it. *Lady Luck II* was directly over a medium-size cargo ship on a second bombing and strafing run when the vessel suddenly blew up, engulfing the Privateer in a wall of fire and cascading debris. The force of the explosion caused the plane to be hurled nearly 500 feet into the air. The plane captain was thrown violently across the bomb bay's catwalk from the con-

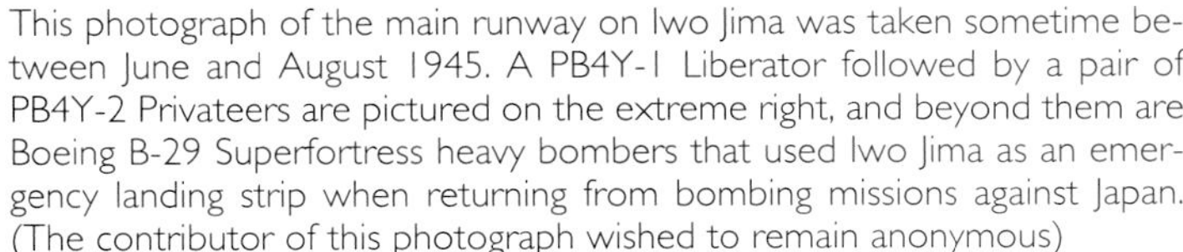

This photograph of the main runway on Iwo Jima was taken sometime between June and August 1945. A PB4Y-1 Liberator followed by a pair of PB4Y-2 Privateers are pictured on the extreme right, and beyond them are Boeing B-29 Superfortress heavy bombers that used Iwo Jima as an emergency landing strip when returning from bombing missions against Japan. (The contributor of this photograph wished to remain anonymous)

This aerial photograph of Iwo Jima taken between June and August 1945, shows the island when it was a fully developed American airbase. The island's main runway is in the middle. (The contributor of this photograph wished to remain anonymous)

cussion, and three of the four bombs in the aft bomb bays were blown out of the plane. However, none of the crew sustained injuries, and although the number three engine was vibrating considerably and the controls were sluggish, Hill and his co-pilot kept the plane in the air without much difficulty. In fact, immediately after this narrow escape Hazlett joined Lieutenant (jg) Hill in two coordinated attacks on four small vessels before flying 600 miles back to Iwo Jima. After getting his landing gear down with some difficulty, Hazlett brought the battered plane down safely. After exiting the plane the crew realized the extent of the damage. Walking around the plane, they counted 98 dents and holes and found pieces of plank, rope, a couple of spikes, and a large section of wire cable from the ship lodged in the fuselage and wings. *Lady Luck II* had made her last flight, and she was immediately surveyed.[18]

The last offensive strike by VPB-108 against the Japanese occurred on 12 August 1945, when Lieutenant Commander Lefever and Lieutenant Hubbard hit ground installations on Miyake Jima. On 1 September 1945, all available squadron aircraft moved to Tinian to join VPB-117 and -124 in a demonstration of airpower over Truk during its surrender ceremony onboard the U.S.S. *Portland*. VPB-108 remained active in the Pacific after the end of World War II and served under the designations VP-108, VP-HL-8, and VP-28. VPB-108, between 16 March and 31 August 1945, flew 731 combat missions, sunk or destroyed 118 enemy ships and damaged another 159, shot down 3 enemy aircraft and one probable, and damaged three more.

The living area for VPB-108 personnel on Iwo Jima shown here consisted of Quonset huts with dirt floors and one light bulb provided interior lighting. The two water towers behind the huts (right center) stored fresh drinking water. (The contributor of this photograph wished to remain anonymous)

Shown here is a supply depot and living/working areas for Navy personnel on Iwo Jima taken between June and August 1945. (The contributor of this photograph wished to remain anonymous)

This hut area on Iwo Jima with Mount Surabachi in the distance possibly housed enlisted members of VPB-108. (The contributor of this photograph wished to remain anonymous)

VPB-121 Arrives

VPB-121, led by Commander Raymond Pflum, began deploying to Tinian and Iwo Jima starting on 3 July 1945 after operating from Eniwetok, in the Marshall Islands, for five months, harassing bypassed Japanese garrisons on Wake and Ponape Atolls. By 8 July most of the squadron—nine PB4Y-2 aircraft and their crews—were operating from Iwo Jima. Soon after arriving, Lieutenant Commander Pflum's personal aircraft *Lotta Tayle* (Bureau Number 59447) and at least one other squadron plane were fitted with the forward-firing 20-millimeter cannons that had become standard armament on most VPB-108 Privateers.

Before VPB-121 transferred to Iwo Jima, the squadron experienced first-hand the tenacity of the bypassed Japanese garrison on Wake Island when four of the squadron's Privateers, led by Commander Pflum, encountered unexpected resistance while conducting a bombing mission against the island on 7 March 1945. The patrol bombers hit the island just before dawn and roared over the island, dropping 500-pound bombs among barracks that dotted the shoreline between Peale and Wake Islands. The Japanese did not open fire until one of the Privateers (Bureau Number 59474 piloted by Lieutenant William McElwee Jr.) came back around to drop a load of fragmentation cluster bombs. The island's guns were highly accurate this time, and the PB4Y-2 received hits from 25-millimeter cannon fire, causing the plane to crash into the lagoon off Wilkes Island and killing Lieutenant McElwee and his entire crew.[19]

Air Sea Rescue

Air Sea Rescue missions became an integral part of PB4Y operations on Iwo Jima beginning in June 1945, as the air campaign against Japan from carrier and shore-based units increased. PB4Ys

This hut area near the airfield on Iwo Jima with PB4Y-2 Privateers in the background served as a living and maintenance area. (The contributor of this photograph wished to remain anonymous)

A person identified as Tom Cook stands next to VPB-108's *Accentuate the Positive* (Bureau Number 59441). The artist for this particular PB4Y-2 was Hal Olsen, who produced a considerable number of such artwork for Navy and Air Force bombers on Tinian. *Accentuate the Positive* went to the scrap heap after a landing accident on 13 August 1945. (Author's Collection)

Super Snooper (Bureau Number 59498) of VPB-108 on Iwo Jima after the squadron transferred to Tinian in April 1945. (Author's Collection)

often orbited over lifeguard submarines or surface vessels a few miles off the Japanese mainland, within easy range of enemy fighters. In July, Navy long-range patrol squadrons of FAW-18 were assigned the mission of flying barrier patrols off Japan as the Third United States Fleet moved up to the coast of Japan to stage carrier plane strikes and occasional shore bombardments on vital areas of Honshu, Shikoku, and Hokkaido. For this screening job, approximately 60 PB4Y-1s and 2s from VPB-102, 108, 109, and 121 were assembled on Iwo Jima, with barrier patrols beginning on 7 July and lasting until 11 August 1945. Each day, 25 planes became airborne at intervals of 30 minutes to fly patrols 2,200 miles in length, averaging over 11 hours in duration, and often pilots flew on instruments due to bad weather, landing on Iwo Jima with little fuel left in the tanks. Although fleet barrier patrol and Air-Sea Rescue took a considerable portion of overall operations, Navy land-based squadrons continued strikes against enemy shipping and shore installations during July. On one such mission, the skipper of VPB-121, Lieutenant Commander Pflum, and his wingman, Lieutenant R.D. Ettinger, were awarded the Navy Cross and their crews, the Distinguished Flying Cross, for their role in the rescue of a downed American fighter pilot on 3 August 1945. During the rescue effort, the gunners on both patrol planes shared in the shoot down of two Japanese Mitsubishi *Pete* fighters.

The patrol began as a routine anti-shipping sweep of the coast of Honshu, south of Tokyo, when Captain E.H. Mikes, a downed P-51 Mustang fighter pilot, was spotted in a lifeboat. Commander Pflum contacted the lifeguard submarine U.S.S. *Aspro* (SS-309) and advised that he would guide the submarine to the downed pilot. Heading towards *Aspro*, the Privateers encountered a 700-800-ton Japanese transport, and both planes proceeded to attack, strafing and dropping bombs as they crossed over the ship from stern to bow. Lieutenant Commander Pflum missed, but he swung the Privateer around, scored a direct hit with another bomb, and the ship sank in less than a minute.

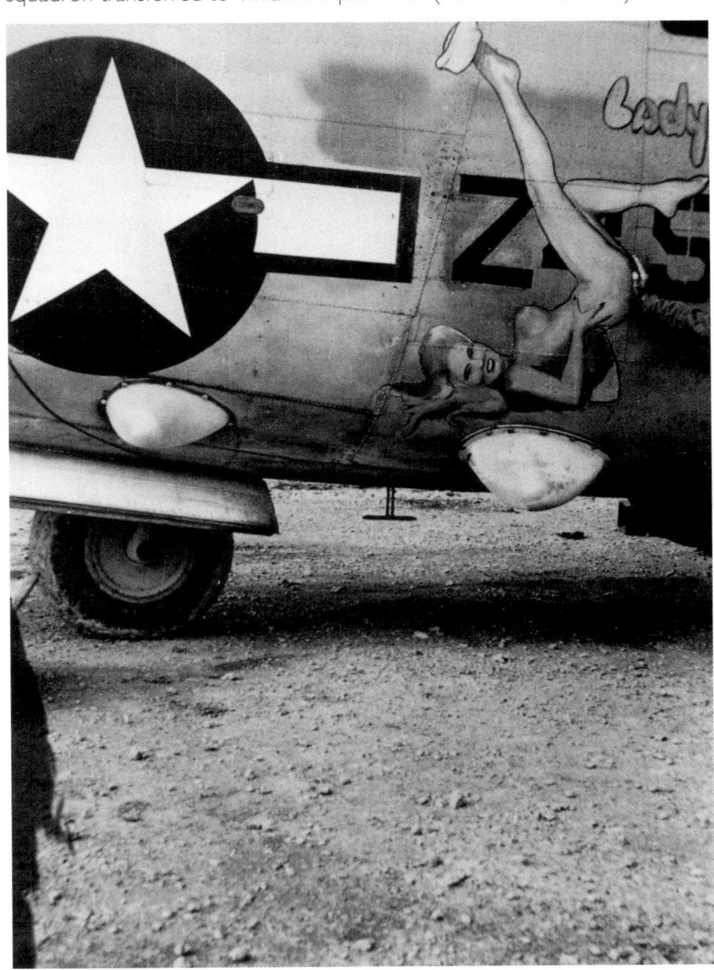

Shown at an unidentified location is VPB-108's *Lady Luck III* (Bureau Number 59459). Her two predecessors were surveyed due to battle damage. (Author's Collection)

A two-plane section of VPB-108 Privateers approaches an island chain, possibly the Bonin Islands, between Iwo Jima and Japan during the summer of 1945. The specks on the water (bottom right) are small shipping. Typically, squadron aircraft on patrol went down to see if any cargo ships were present and if so, attacked them. If they were small fishing craft, they usually left them alone. (The contributor of this photograph wished to remain anonymous)

After sinking the ship, Lieutenant Commander Pflum and Lieutenant Ettinger arrived over *Aspro* and began orbiting low over the submarine while four P-51s, which were low on fuel, flew above at 8,000 feet. As the submarine and her escorts continued towards the downed pilot, five Kawanishi N1K2 George fighters dropped out of the clouds and pounced on the Mustangs, shooting down one of the P-51s. Low on fuel, the remaining Mustangs had to disengage from the dogfight and head for Iwo Jima, leaving the two Privateers alone. One George went after the patrol bombers, coming in from behind, but was driven off by the gunners and left with heavy smoke streaming from its engine nacelle and wing root. The other four fighters then went in for strafing runs on Captain Mikes in the lifeboat.

The Privateers chased after the much faster fighters and broke up the attack, but then the Georges went after the *Aspro*. What went on next could be viewed as comical, if not for the deadly seriousness of the situation. For the next several minutes, the Japanese fighters went back and forth to the *Aspro* and the downed fighter pilot while the Privateers chased them in hot pursuit. The fighters finally gave up and headed home. As the submarine came within feet of rescuing Captain Mikes, three bi-wing Mitsubishi F1M2 floatplane fighters, nicknamed Pete by the allies, appeared. One of

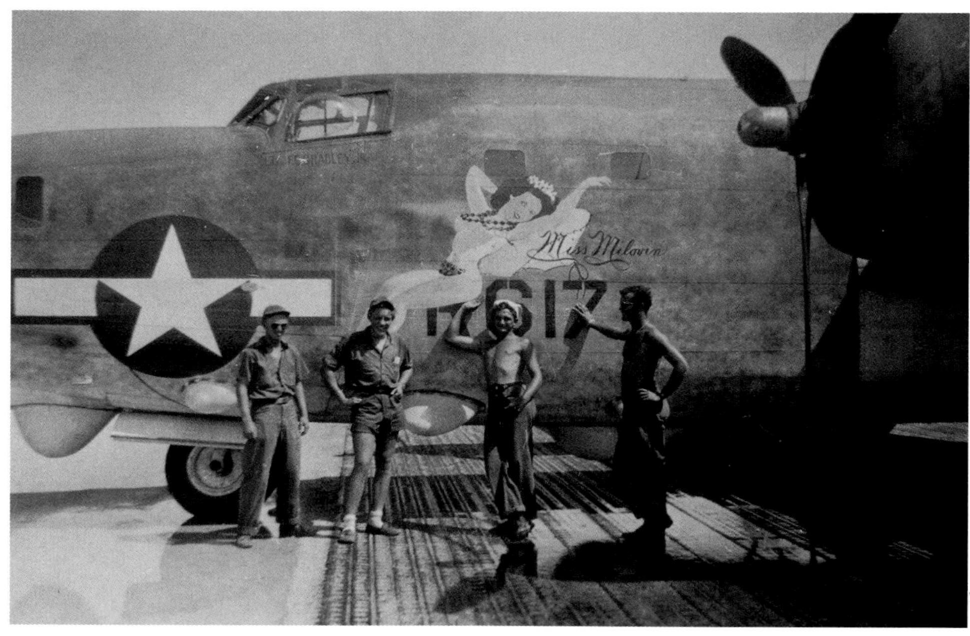

Initially assigned to VPB-121 and possibly VPB-116 in the Central Pacific, *Miss Milovin* (Bureau Number 59617) finally ended up in the United States with Advance Training Unite 12 (ATU-12). She was stricken from the Navy inventory in September 1947. (Courtesy: Richard McMurray via Steve Hawley)

Crewmembers stand next to VPB-121's *'Ol Blunderbuss* (Bureau Number 59564) in the Marshall Islands or on Iwo Jima. (Courtesy: Richard McMurray via Steve Hawley)

the fighters immediately went in for a bombing run on the *Aspro*, dropping two bombs, but failed to score a hit, as the submarine crash-dived. Meanwhile, both Privateers did a 180-degree turn, came up behind the Pete, and shot it down. Then, Lieutenant Commander Pflum and Lieutenant Ettinger conducted another 180-degree turn and came up behind a second Pete starting a bombing attack on the submerging submarine. In a matter of seconds the patrol plane gunners sent the second fighter spiraling down in flames. After the two Japanese fighters went down, the *Aspro* surfaced and hauled in Captain Mikes without any further interference from the enemy.[20]

Sad Distinction for VPB-121

VPB-121 had the distinction of suffering the last World War II combat loss of a PB4Y-2 Privateer when Lieutenants J.B. Rainey and T. Allen took off from Iwo Jima to search the Honshu coast south of Tokyo on 11 August 1945. After making landfall at 1300 hours, they intended to make a reconnaissance of O-Shima Island, located between Okinawa and Kyushu, but that plan fell apart when Allen's top aft gunner spotted enemy fighters approaching. Allen immediately chopped his throttles and started to weave in order to allow Rainey, piloting Bureau Number 59495, to pull up close for mutual

Lieutenant Donald Hartvig of VPB-108 and his crew were on patrol off the Japanese coast near Tokyo when he a poked a camera out of the co-pilot's window and photographed Mount Fuji. Shortly thereafter, a couple of enemy fighters jumped the Privateer, but the Navy patrol bomber managed to escape. (Courtesy: Donald Hartvig)

Bureau Number 59475 named *Louisiana Lil* was another of VPB-121's Iwo Jima-based Privateers. (Author's Collection)

The nose art on VPB-121's Bureau Number 59478 *Buccaneer Bunny* shows a deviation from the typical artwork seen on World War II-era Privateers since the majority sported risqué art of semi-nude women. (Author's Collection)

Above: *Pastime* (Bureau Number 59504) could have flown with either VPB-121, 123, or 124 as it appears in all three squadron cruise books. (Author's Collection)

A three-plane section of VPB-108 Privateers over Iwo Jima runway lined with PB4Y-1 Liberators, PB4Y-2 Privateers, and an R4D transport, a military version of the Douglas DC-3. (The contributor of this photograph wished to remain anonymous)

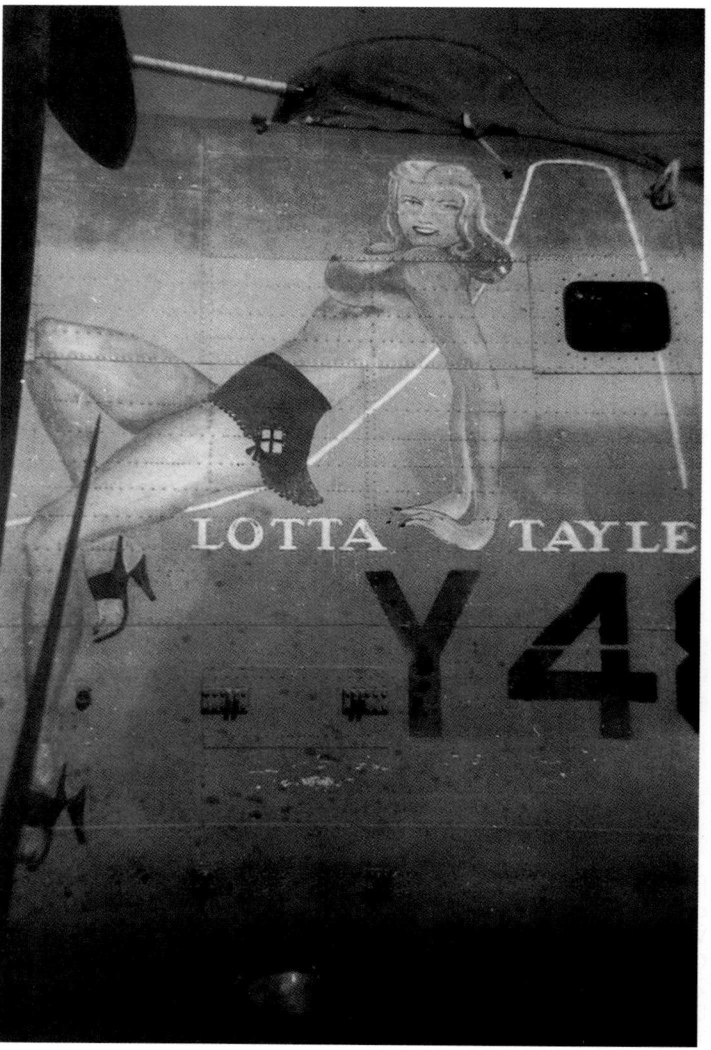

Right: *Lotta Tayle* (Bureau Number 59484) was another VPB-121 Privateer that possibly carried 20-millimeter cannons similar to those installed on some VPB-108 aircraft. (Courtesy: Richard McMurray via Steve Hawley)

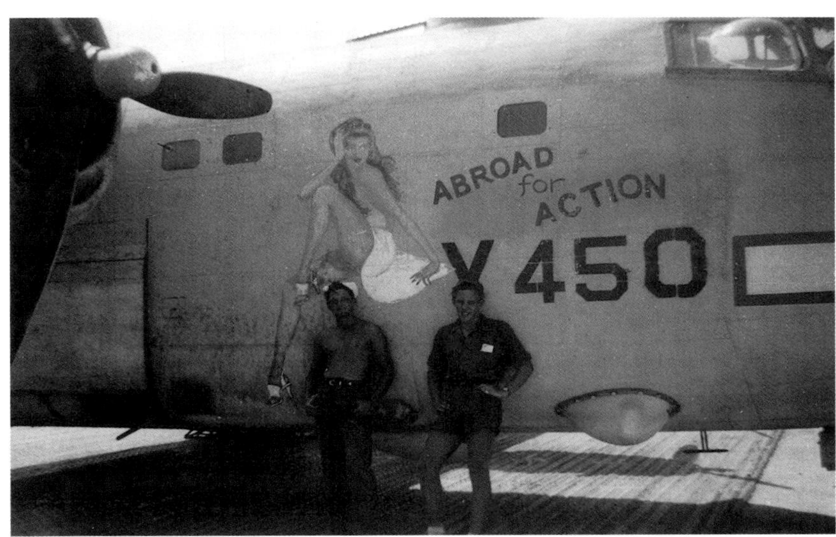

Abroad for Action (Bureau Number 59450) of VPB-121 Eniwetok in the Marshall Islands between March and June 1945. The two men in this photograph have been identified from left to right as Aviation Ordnanceman (?) Gavie and Seaman 1st Class (?) Striker. (Courtesy: Richard McMurray via Steve Hawley)

Pictured is Lieutenant J.B. Rainey's crew from VPB-121 prior to the squadron's departure to the Pacific Theater. While conducting a snooper patrol off Japan on 11 August 1945, enemy fighters intercepted and shot down Rainey's Privateer Bureau Number 59495, the last PB4Y-2 shot down in the Second World War. Back row from left to right: Aviation Machinist Mate 3rd Class (AMM3c) K.C. Gaber, Seaman 1st Class (S1c) C.A. Bremer, Aviation Machinist Mate 2nd Class (AMM2c) R.E. Guth, Aviation Radioman 2nd Class (ARM2c) J. Frashure, Aviation Radioman 2nd Class (ARM2c) R.W. Cox, and Aviation Ordnanceman 2nd Class (AOM2c) A.R. Dugger. Kneeling from left to right are: Aviation Machinist Mate 1st Class (AMM1c) D.W. Mott, Lieutenant (jg) H.H. Whitted, Lieutenant Commander J.B. Rainey, Ensign E.J. Heeb, and Aviation Fire Controlman 1st Class (AFC1c) W.R. Long. Bremer, Guth, Heeb, and Mott were killed in the engagement. (Courtesy: Richard Jeffreys Jr.)

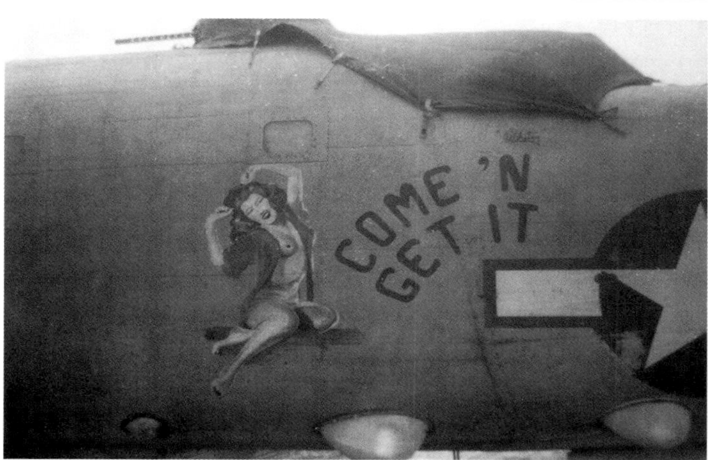

This photograph taken at Eniwetok circa November 1945 is that of VPB-121's Bureau Number 59409 named *Come 'N Get It.* (Courtesy: Richard McMurray via Steve Hawley)

A considerable number of PB4Y-2 squadrons based in the Central Pacific remained on station months after the war; however, when replacements arrived, veteran crews rotated back to the United States. Pictured here is replacement Crew Five of VPB-108 posing by Bureau Number 597664 at Yonabaru, Okinawa in 1946. (Courtesy: Herman Fisher)

support. The Privateers were boxed in, with one group of fighters coming in head on towards Allen, while another group dove down towards Rainey's plane.

On the first run, two fighters went after Allen's plane, knocking out his number one engine and wounding the tail gunner. Meanwhile, his top turret gunners hit one of the incoming fighters, drawing smoke. The Privateer's damaged engine threw the plane into a flipper turn, and it went into a stall as it fell towards the sea. Miraculously, Allen managed to gain control of the four-engined patrol bomber only 75 feet above the water. Meanwhile, Lieutenant Rainey and his men were in serious trouble, as cannon and machine gun fire from the attacking Japanese fighters scored hits on the patrol plane's port wing. Flames erupted from the damaged wing, and the plane turned to the right; the starboard wing suddenly dropped and hit the water. Bouncing once, the Privateer cartwheeled into the water, leaving a patch of flame and smoke. Miraculously, Lieutenant Rainey and seven members of his crew survived the crash and briefly became prisoners of war. After being hit and seeing Rainey's crash, Allen began a mad dash home with the fighters pressing in their attacks for another 30 minutes, before losing one of their own to the Privateer before departing. Six hours later, Lieutenant Allen landed his plane back on Iwo Jima. On the tarmac, the crew inspected the plane and found that it had sustained two 20-millimeter and numerous 12.7-millimeter hits. [21]

The loss of Lieutenant Rainey's plane coincided with the end of combat operations for VPB-121. The squadron claimed 5,260 tons of shipping sunk or damaged while operating from Iwo Jima, with Lieutenant Commander Pflum personally claiming 3,130 tons. After the end of hostilities, VPB-121 flew weather flights until the end of September 1945, when it was ordered back to the United States, where it was disestablished on 1 June 1946.

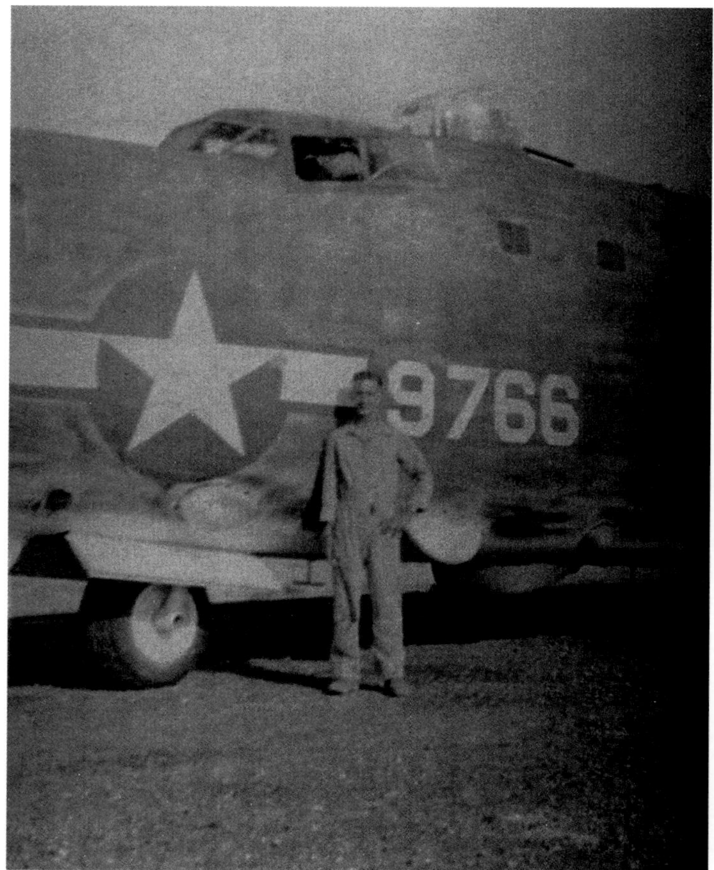

Herman Fisher, an enlisted member of VPB-108, stands next to Bureau Number 59766 circa 1946. The aircraft has the glossy sea blue color scheme. (Courtesy: Herman Fisher)

4

Privateer Operations in World War II: Okinawa (April-May 1945)

Okinawa, 60 miles long and between two and 16 miles wide, is the largest island in the Ryukyu Group, and is situated less than 400 miles south of the Japanese main island of Kyushu. Strategically, possession of Okinawa would provide American forces additional air bases, anchorages, and staging areas for the expected invasion of the Japanese home islands. On 1 April 1945 American forces launched the largest amphibious campaign of World War II with the invasion of Okinawa, codenamed Operation Iceberg. The island was declared secured on 21 June, but mopping up pockets of resistance continued until 2 July 1945. American casualties totaled more than 50,000 wounded, killed, or missing in action, while over 200,000 Japanese and Okinawans perished in the battle.[22]

While the battle still raged, a detachment of six aircraft and crews from VPB-118 left the warmth of Quonset huts and hot food on Tinian for muddy tents and K Rations on Okinawa. Arriving on 22 April 1945, VPB-118 became the first Privateer squadron to operate from Yontan Field; the first American-built airfield on Okinawa, situated east of the invasion beaches. The detachment, led by Lieutenant Commander Farwell, the squadron's new skipper, reported for duty to Rear Admiral John D. Price, Commander of Fleet Air Wing One, Fifth Fleet, with the remainder of the squadron joining them in May. Operations from Okinawa consisted of two to six plane patrols sent out to ferret the southern and eastern coasts of Korea, the west coast of Kyushu, Shimono and Kamino Shima, Goto Retto, and Saishu To of Japan. Such flights were largely anti-shipping, and strikes were permitted wherever the hunting seemed best.[23]

During the last week of April, the Okinawa-based crews inflicted several damaging blows against Japanese shipping. Patrol plane commanders Lieutenants Allan "Tex" Lasater and Harry J. "Horse" Thompson teamed up to damage a large freighter off Korea on 26 April, while Lieutenants Leland P. McCutcheon and Phillip E. Pettes shot down a Japanese D3A *Val* dive bomber the following

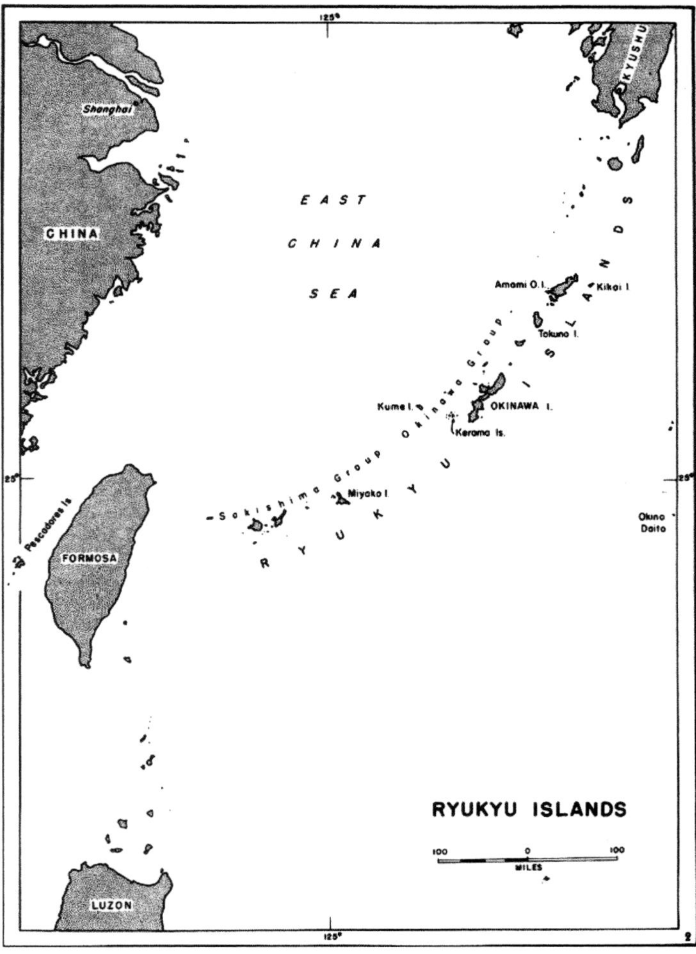

(Source: Roy E. Appleman, et al., *Okinawa: The Last Battle*, Center of Military History)

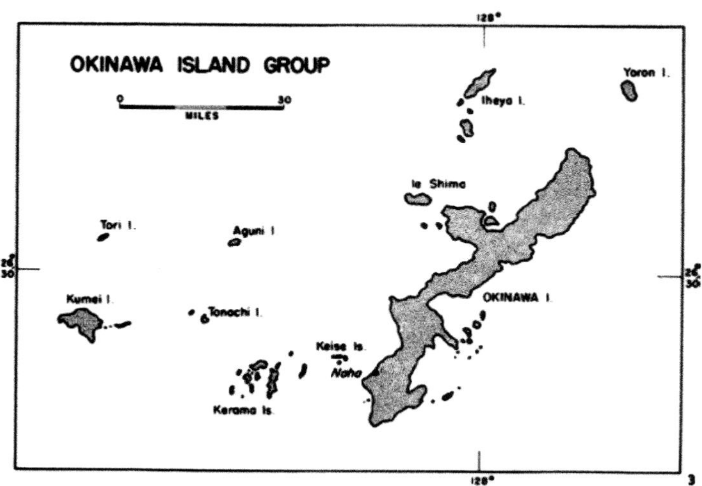

(Source: Roy E. Appleman, et al., *Okinawa: The Last Battle*, Center of Military History)

day off Korea. Two days later Lieutenants Thomas L. Dodson and Robert M. DeGolia found a large merchant ship off southeastern Korea, and after three bombing runs and 14 strafing attacks left the ship burning and settling by the stern. The squadron ended the month with Lieutenant Commander Farwell sinking a 5,000-ton tanker with a pair of 500-pound bombs off Korea on the 30th.

May Sweeps

During May 1945 the Japanese merchant fleet lost approximately 100,000 tons of shipping to Navy land-based aircraft, most of it to one Privateer squadron—the *Old Crows* of VPB-118. The squadron embarked on its most successful anti-shipping campaigns in patrol bombing history beginning on the first, when two Privateers flown by Lieutenant Earl A. Luehman and Lieutenant Lasater conducted a morning patrol along the western coast of Korea and the Yellow Sea. They spotted the 6,800-ton *Kyogyoku Maru*, and after Lieutenant Lasater missed with a pair of 500-pound bombs, he allowed his enlisted bombardier, Robert E. Miller, Jr., to try his luck. Miller's bomb hit 10 feet short of the ship, exploded, and broke the vessel into two pieces.[24]

Two days after Lieutenant Lasater's successful attack on the *Kyogyoku Maru* the squadron staged a two, three-plane strike against Kanoya Airfield on Kyushu after intelligence reports indicated that the Japanese were preparing to unleash a Kamikaze attack against the American fleet anchored off Okinawa. Only half of the original six Privateers reached the target when the others, including Lieutenant Commander Farwell's, had to abort enroute to Okinawa due to engine or electronics failures. The remaining planes, led by Lieutenant Montgomery, hit Kenoya just after dark from an altitude of 200 feet. Flying down the airfield from east to west, the Privateer crews bombed and strafed parked aircraft, barracks, hangars, and a locomotive, leaving in their wake three destroyed planes and more than a dozen fires burning. Lieutenant Mark V. Montgomery earned the Navy Cross for leading the raid, while the Silver Star went to his wingmen, Lieutenants Thompson and Pette; the rest of the flight crews were awarded the Distinguished Flying Cross.[25]

Raids by VPB-118 intensified, with continued anti-shipping strikes around Japan and Korea and stunning attacks conducted between 4 and 6 May 1945. Lieutenants Finley and Duba hit shipping in the harbor of Pusan, Korea, sinking a 2,500-ton tanker and a 2,000-ton freighter, while another freighter and a fishing vessel were damaged. Their success was followed on the fifth by a pair of two-plane sections that sank or damaged an estimated 44,000 tons of enemy shipping off Korea.

The first section, flown by Lieutenants Julian D. Serrill and August M. Lodato, found a convoy of three merchant ships escorted by a pair of destroyer escorts between Kyushu and Tsushima Island. Picking out the last freighter in line, Lieutenant Serrill scored a direct hit with a 500-pound bomb without any interference from the escorts. Continuing on patrol, the Privateers encountered an unescorted convoy approximately 10 miles off Kyushu comprised of three freighters and a small oil tanker. While Serrill and his crew searched for any escorts that might be lurking about, Lodato tar-

Living conditions on Okinawa for VPB-118 personnel were primitive and consisted of tents as shown in this photograph. (Courtesy: Earl Mann)

PB4Y-2 Privateers on Okinawa wait for their load of bombs for strikes against Japanese merchant shipping. (Courtesy: Earl Mann)

VPB-118's Crew 2 commanded by Lieutenant Thomas Dodson, kneeling center, often flew *Miss Lottatail* (Bureau Number 59410). The rest of the crew consisted of Lieutenant (jg) Richard E. Carmelich, Lieutenant (jg) Robert J. Berens, Aviation Machinist Mate 1st Class (AMM1c) Thomas L. Bay, Jr., Aviation Machinist Mate 2nd Class (AMM2c) Paul H. Crowley, Aviation Machinist Mate 3rd Class (AMM3c) Amos A. Price, Aviation Machinist Mate 3rd Class (AMM3c) James K. Wahl, Sr., Aviation Radioman 1st Class (ARM1c) Harold A. Peterson, Aviation Radioman 2nd Class (ARM2c) Walter M. Johnson, Aviation Radioman 3rd Class (ARM3c) John H Seddon, and Aviation Ordnanceman 3rd Class (AOM3c) Joseph C. Tortorice Jr. *Miss Lottatail* made it through the war and was flown back to Hawaii in September 1945. (Courtesy: Steve Hawley)

geted an estimated 6,000-ton merchantman. The Privateer's patrol plane commander sank it with one bomb while his crew shot down a Japanese observation plane, and Lodato's port waist gunner started fires aboard the oil tanker.

The second section of Lieutenant Commander Farwell and Lieutenant Keiser hit shipping along the southwest Korean coast, with Keiser scoring first by damaging a large freighter with two 500-pound bombs; heavy anti-aircraft fire from shore batteries forced Keiser to break off further runs on the vessel. His next target was an oil tanker and, after making one bomb drop and six strafing runs, the ship was left burning. The planes then rejoined and went after a freighter of some 8,000 tons, with Farwell scoring a direct hit with one bomb that sent the ship to the bottom. Out of bombs but with adequate fuel and ammunition, the section flew on to Kunsan Fu airfield, where Farwell's gunners shot down a transport plane coming in to land and a Kawasaki Ki-45 Nick twin engine fighter that tried to intercept the American patrol bombers.[26]

This photograph taken from the bombardier's window of a VPB-118 Privateer commanded by Lieutenant Mark V. Montgomery shows a merchant ship under attack off Korea on 6 May 1945. A moment later, the ship exploded causing severe damage to Montgomery's plane but it and her crew made it back safely to Okinawa. (Courtesy: NARA)

Privateers parked at Yontan Field, Okinawa circa summer 1945 with Bureau Number 59581 belonging to VPB-109 in the left foreground with VPB-123's *Vagrant Verago* (Bureau Number 59487) the nearest aircraft in the right background. (Courtesy: Author's Collection)

Punkie (Bureau Number 59501) preparing to taxi belonged to VPB-109's Crew 15 commanded by Lieutenant Hugh M. Wilkinson Jr. (Author's Collection)

A close-up view of VPB-109's *Punkie* nose art. (Courtesy: Roy Balke)

A SWOD Mk-9 *Bat* is hoisted into position on a Privateer belonging to VPB-109 circa summer 1945. (Courtesy: NARA)

VPB-109's Privateer Bureau Number 59527 preparing to depart from Yontan Field, Okinawa circa May 1945. (Courtesy: Roy Balke)

A World War II Okinawa-based Privateer undergoes maintenance at Yontan Field, Okinawa circa summer 1945. (Author's Collection)

A large Japanese merchant ship encountered by a pair of Privateers flown by VPB-109's Lieutenant Vadnais and Lieutenant Vidal off Korea on 29 May 1945. (Courtesy: NARA)

Enlisted members of Lieutenant Joseph Jadin's Crew 15 of VPB-109 pose next to their aircraft *Miss Lotta Tail* (Bureau Number 59522). From left to right are Isadore Smith, Cecil Lee, Ned Jones, Emory Peterman, Ray Grover, and Roy Balke. (Courtesy: Roy Balke)

Strikes Continue

Anti-shipping strikes on 6 and 7 May earned patrol plane commanders Lieutenants Finley and Keiser the Navy Cross; however, the squadron's luck ran out when one of its aircraft was lost, while another was heavily damaged. On the sixth, a pair of two-plane sections comprised of Montgomery-Lasater and Finley-Thompson hit shipping along the sea lanes between Japan and Korea. The strikes resulted in the destruction of several enemy vessels but, in the process, Lieutenant Montgomery's plane (Bureau Number 59378) was heavily damaged and his co-pilot was wounded, while Lieutenant Lasater and crew went missing in action while flying *Vulnerable Virgin* (Bureau Number 59449). The incident unfolded when Lieutenant Montgomery and Lieutenant Lasater hit enemy shipping off southern Korea.

After damaging a tanker in the mouth of a harbor with a 500-pound bomb, Montgomery and Lasater went after a large transport. Lieutenant Lasater attacked first, dropping two bombs that missed. As Lieutenant Montgomery headed in for a run, the ship suddenly exploded in a mass of flames, possibly caused by strafing from Lasater's gunners. Too late to turn away, the Privateer was hit by flying debris that wounded the co-pilot and caused serous damage to the plane. Pieces of the ship knocked out an engine, severed the main cable to the starboard batteries, broke a fuel line in the bomb bay, and an eight-foot piece of the ship's rigging became imbedded in the leading edge of the port wing. Although the plane was badly mauled by the exploding ship, Lieutenant Montgomery flew his crippled plane safely back to base. Lieutenant Lasater remained behind to continue with the attack; however, he and his crew of 11

Lieutenant Howard M. Turner and his Crew 2B of VPB-109 Bureau Number 59544 was named *Shanghai Lil*. (Author's Collection)

Bachelor's Delight (Bureau Number 59521) assigned to VPB-109's Crew 6A, with Lieutenant John D. Keeling as Patrol Plane Commander, was shot down on 5 August 1945. (Author's Collection)

Redwing (Bureau Number 59505) belonged to VPB-123 during the war and afterward, went on to serve with ATU-12. (Author's Collection)

Redwing after being renamed *Indian Made*. (Author's Collection)

went missing after later sending two contact reports of enemy destroyers and a transport.

The second section on patrol on 6 May, consisting of Lieutenant Commander Finley and Lieutenant Thompson, hit shipping off the southeastern coast of Korea. Their first victim was a tanker in the 5,000-ton range that went to the bottom after Finley placed a bomb that exploded near the ship's waterline, aft of the superstructure. Approximately five miles from the tanker, the Privateers targeted a 4,000-ton freighter, with gunners from both planes firing 3,000 rounds of ammunition at the ship during a series of strafing attacks. Unable to sink the vessel with strafing alone, Thompson finished her off with a 500-pound bomb. The section's last score was a tanker of some 10,000 tons that exploded after being subjected to strafing and bombing by Finley and his crew.

On the seventh Lieutenants Serrill and Lodato damaged two freighters off southern Korea while Keiser and his crew, patrolling the southwestern tip of Korea and without a wingman, sank or damaged three ships, including a 10,000-ton freighter. However, a sec-

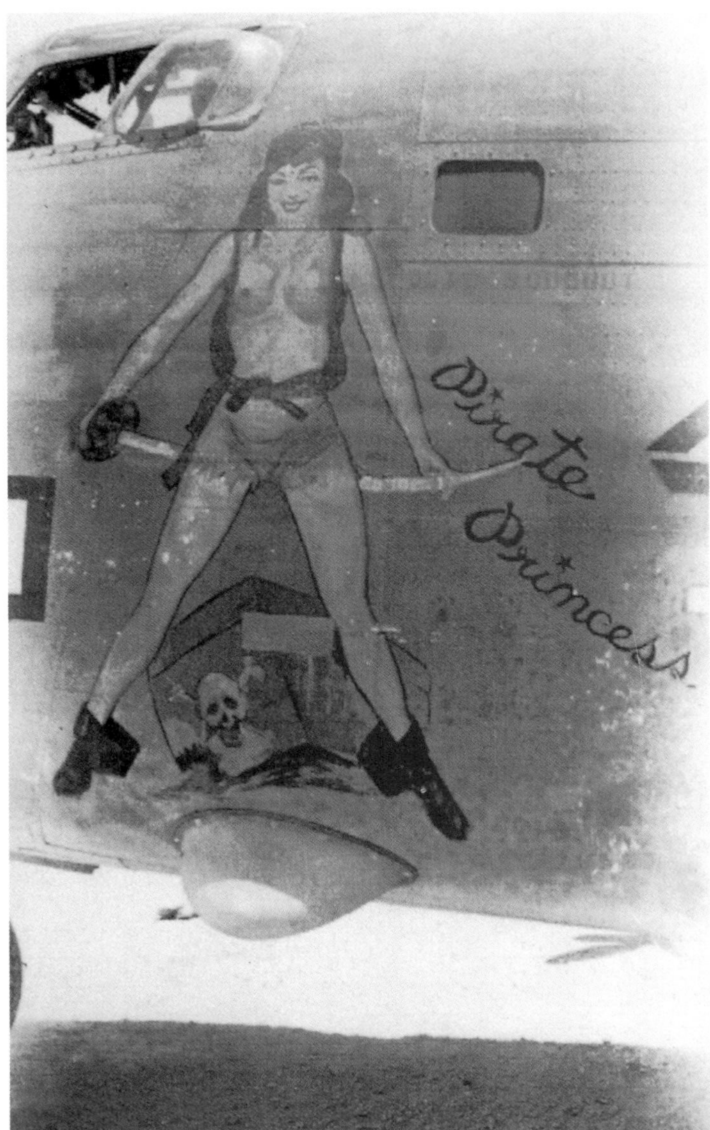

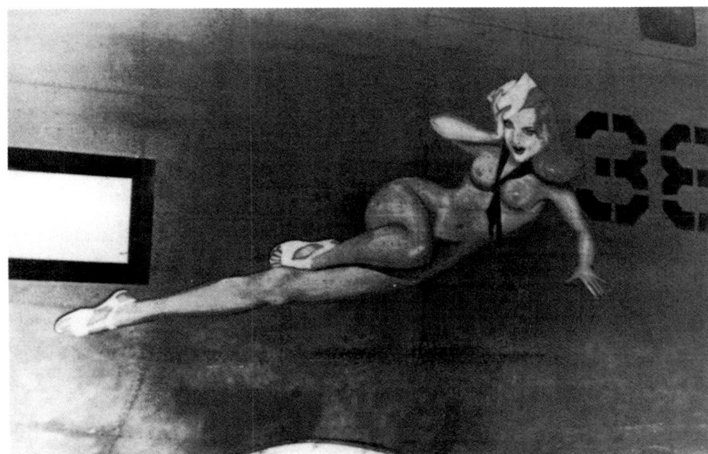

Pictured here is Bureau Number 59382 named *La Cherrie*, she served with VPB-123 on Okinawa between May and August 1945. (Author's Collection)

Nose art of a woman swashbuckler with the corresponding name of *Pirate Princess* appeared on several PB4Y-2s. This example (Bureau Number 59404) was assigned to VPB-118's Crew 16, Lieutenant Nolan W. Weller, Patrol Plane Commander. (Author's Collection)

A row of PB4Y-2 Privateers stand ready for take off from Yontan Field, Okinawa for strikes against Japanese shipping on 13 June 1945. (Courtesy: NARA)

ond section flown by Lieutenant Commander Farwell and Lieutenant Duba ran into trouble while attacking a tanker along the western coast of Korea. The section first spotted an Aichi D3A Val dive-bomber, and Farwell's gunners made quick work of it and shot it down. Afterward, Farwell sank a tanker in the 2,000-ton range after making two bombing runs. Afterward, off Seoul, they spotted a small tanker under the protection of a destroyer escort. Farwell's Privateer *Soaring Fin* (Bureau Number 59388) was hit under the starboard wing by a three-inch shell just as he dropped a load of bombs on the tanker. With the hydraulic and electrical system destroyed and the number three and four engines knocked out, Farwell ditched the plane, which broke into several pieces upon hitting the water. While three of the squadron's Privateers provided cover, Farwell and his entire crew, plus a Navy photographer, were picked up by a Martin PBM Mariner after being subjected to a strafing run from a Japanese fighter.[27]

Between 4 and 7 May 1945, VPB-118 is credited with sinking or damaging over 70,000 tons of shipping, shooting down four enemy aircraft, and inflicting serious damage to a considerable number of shore installations. However, the squadron had to suspend operations for three days, as two planes were lost, three were damaged beyond repair, and another three required major overhaul. Operations resumed on 11 May, with Lieutenant Commander Edward Binning and Lieutenant Nolan Weller teaming up for a patrol off southern Korea. After sinking a 5,000-ton freighter, Binning and Weller went for a 7,000-ton transport that put up heavy resistance. Weller's plane took 25 hits from the ship's 40-millimeter cannons that knocked out an engine and one of his gunners—Aviation Ordnanceman Second Class Donald Berger was wounded, but the Privateer made it home.

AOM2c Robert J. McKay stands next to *Flying Tail* (Bureau Number 59379). This aircraft was assigned to VPB-118's Crew 12, commanded by N. Michael Keiser. (Courtesy: Earl Mann)

Arrival of VPB-109

VPB-118 had an impressive combat record for the period 24 April to 16 May 1945, with 100,000 tons of enemy shipping sunk or damaged, seven aircraft shot down, and three aircraft destroyed on the ground. Relief for the *Old Crows* began to arrive when the first three Privateers of VPB-109, the *Reluctant Raiders*, reached Yontan Field on 10 May 1945 after flying across the Pacific from Palawan, Philippines. Led by Commander George L. Hicks, the squadron was specially trained and specially equipped with PB4Y-2Bs and the SWOD Mk-9 *Bat* air-to-surface guided missile. The *Bat* was an air-to-ground radar-guided missile with a 1,000-pound general-purpose bomb encased in a plywood shell. Some of the squadron aircraft were modified to carry two of them under each wing and were designated as PB4Y-2Bs.

VPB-109 arrived at Palawan in April 1945 with the intention of using the missiles in a combat situation. However, large enemy shipping was scarce, and during the few times adequate targets were acquired, the weapon failed. *Bat* tactics were unsuccessful because of the weapon's difficulty in detecting a specific target from long range, or when multiple radar targets were located at the same range. After the dismal results, the squadron was sent to Okinawa in hopes of finding and successfully destroying enemy shipping but, due to lack luster results, Commander Hicks and his men began to believe it wasn't worth a damn, and by June 1945, kept only two aircraft armed with the weapon.

Privateers vs. 343Ku Air Group

Enemy fighters were a constant threat to patrol bombers skirting the coasts of Japan, Korea, and China. A week after VPB-109's arrival, 11 Kawanishi N1K2 George fighters of the 343Ku Air Group jumped Lieutenants William Warren and G.D. Fairbanks off southeastern Korea, and a running battle ensued for the next half-hour. Lieutenant Warren's *Blind Bomber* (Bureau Number 59514) and Lieutenant Fairbanks' *Hogan's Goat* (Bureau Number 59515) were heading back to Okinawa after sinking an oceangoing tug when Fairbanks' port waist turret gunner spotted enemy fighters as the patrol planes cruised along at an altitude of 1,200 feet. The Japanese fighters were composed of three, four-plane sections flying at

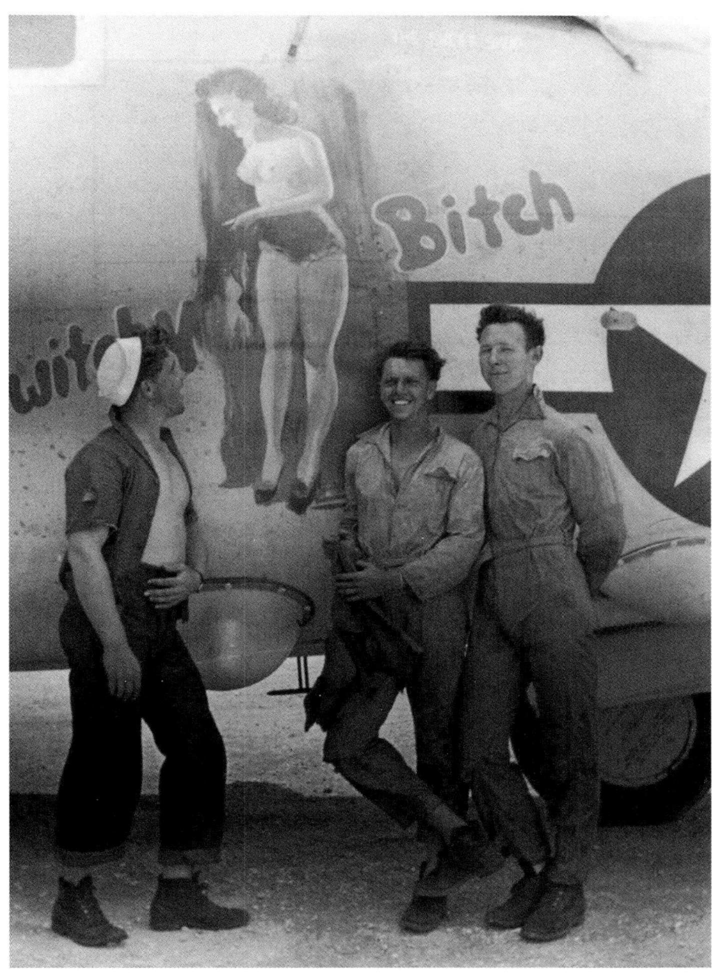

Unidentified members of VPB-118 standing next to *Twitchy Bitch* (Bureau Number 59430) on Okinawa sometime after May 1945. This aircraft was assigned to Crew 13/7 commanded by Lieutenant Commander Edward G. Binning. (Courtesy: Earl Mann)

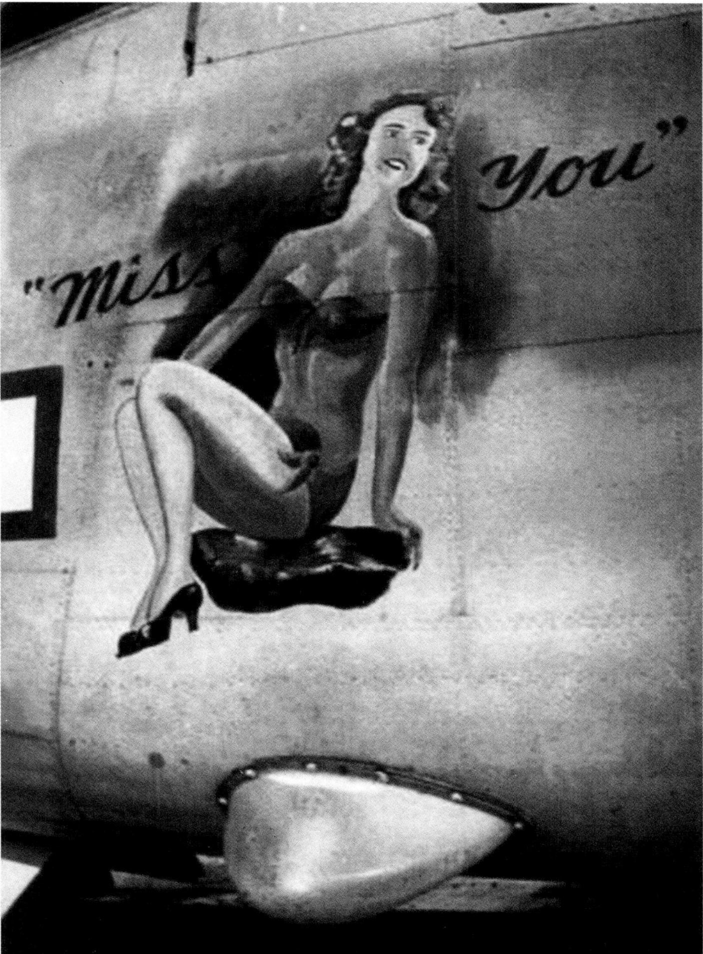

Miss You (Bureau Number 59482) was assigned to VPB-118's Crew 4 commanded by Lieutenant Earle A. Leuhman. (Courtesy: Earl Mann)

VPB-118's *Modest O' Miss II* (Bureau Number 59448) undergoing engine maintenance at Yontan Field, Okinawa. (Courtesy: Earl Mann)

6,000 feet. Seeing their predicament, Fairbanks and Warren nosed the Privateers over and reduced altitude to 400 feet, and throughout the action their altitudes varied between 400 and 700 feet, constantly altering altitude slightly and making gentle turns towards the fighters.

Fairbanks flew close to Warren's starboard wing and remained in position throughout the action. Almost immediately the fighters began attacking by dropping phosphorous bombs. In all, 10 bombs were dropped, three being duds, but the other seven were accurate, with bursting streamers striking the wing surfaces of the search planes. The fighters then broke up into individual attacks, pulling

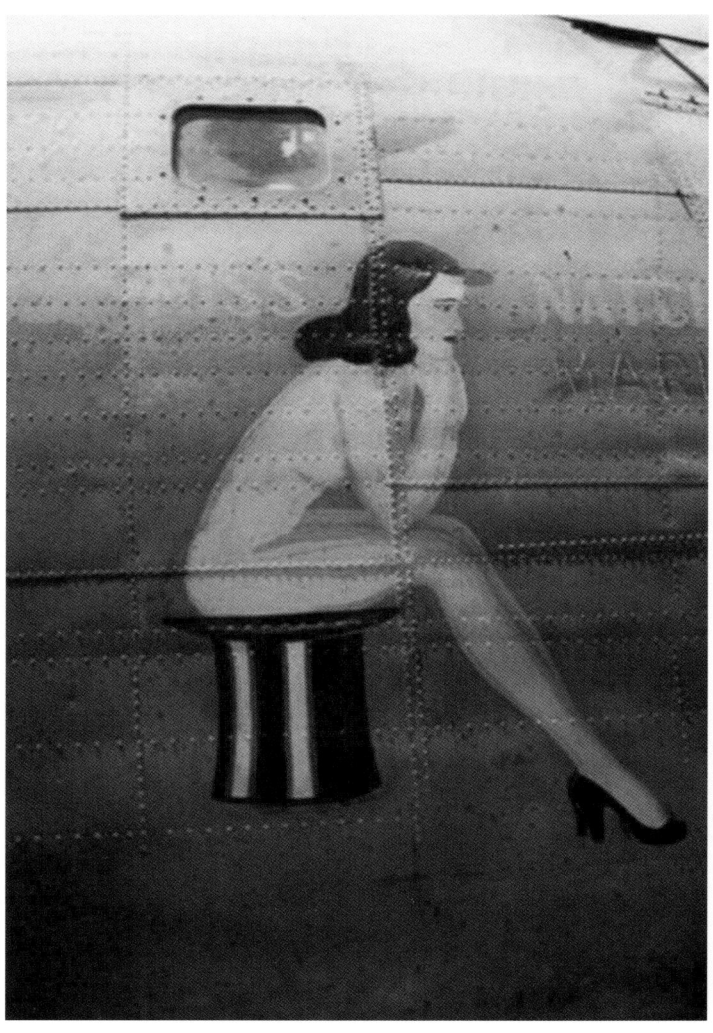

Above: *Miss Natch* (59405 Bureau Number) on Okinawa was assigned to Lieutenant Mark V. Montgomery's Crew 10. Barely visible to the right of the figure are the words "Mark's Farts II." Right: Based on this photograph, it appears that *Miss Natch* sported identical nose art on both sides of the fuselage. (both Courtesy: Earl Mann)

up to within 3,000 feet of the Privateers before starting runs and then breaking to the rear. Single fighters made aggressive runs but, each time, they were driven off by a few bursts from the patrol plane's gunners. The Japanese pilots changed tactics and began attacking in pairs, and both Privateers received damage from machine gun and cannon fire.

Lieutenant Fairbanks' *Hogan's Goat* took hits in the fuselage fore and aft of the number one top turret when a 20-millimeter shell burst inside the plane wounded the gunner and knocked the turret out of commission. Soon afterward, faulty installation of the side plate slides sheared off two ammunition belts and put his aft top turret out of commission. After 15 minutes the ejectors on the starboard waist turret broke, further diminishing the plane's firepower. Meanwhile, *Hogan's Goat* continued to receive damaging hits from the fighters. The plane's radio communication was destroyed, along with the throttle control to the number-two engine, necessitating feathering the engine, and three members of Lieutenant Fairbanks' crew were wounded.

The two Privateers continued to fight back, with Lieutenant Warren's bow, number one top turret, and the tail turret gunners shooting down one George flown by Chief Petty Officer Shiro Hirotome after the fighter was hit in the engine, fuselage, starboard wing, and wing root. A second fighter flown by Petty Officer Second Class Ei Hoshino was hit simultaneously by the bow and the number one top turrets of both planes. Lieutenant Warren's gunners scored hits on the fighter's engine, belly, and starboard wing root, while Lieutenant Fairbanks' gunners hit the port wing root and fuselage. Smoking, Petty Officer Second Class Hoshino's plane crashed into the sea. After losing two of their own, the remaining Japanese fighters broke off the attack, allowing *Blind Bomber* and *Hogan's Goat* to head back to Okinawa without further incident.[28]

VPB-118's Lieutenant Nolan Weller and his Crew 16 were attacking a well-armed Japanese freighter off Korea on 11 May 1945 when their Privateer took multiple hits from the ship's anti-aircraft guns. This photograph shows battle damage from a 40mm shell to the aft portion of the aircraft, which severely wounded the tail turret gunner AOM2c Donald F. Berger. Although suffering from multiple wounds to his left elbow, buttocks, and right calf, Berger climbed out of his turret and tried to put out burning float-flares ignited by the 40mm round. After failing to extinguish the flares, he picked them up and threw them out of a hole in the fuselage made by the exploding cannon shell. He received the Purple Heart for his wounds and earned the Silver Star for throwing the burning float-flares out of the plane. (Courtesy: Earl Mann)

Bat Attacks

VPB-109 continued sweeps along the coasts of China and Korea throughout the last week of May 1945, with a couple patrols attempting to use the SWOD Mk-9 *Bat*. On one such strike, Lieutenants Joseph Jobe and George Serbin, piloting a pair of planes carrying a mixed load of one *Bat* and general-purpose bombs, hit shipping in the Korean Strait on 24 May. Two hours after sinking three small freighters with a combination of strafing and bombing attacks, a 7,000-ton troop transport was spotted and Lieutenant Serbin launched his *Bat* from 10 miles out from an altitude of 4,000 feet. The missile traveled nose high, and approximately three miles short of the intended target dove vertically into the sea. Moments later, Lieutenant Jobe released his *Bat* from eight miles out at an altitude of 5,000 feet, and the missile appeared to function normally, but it struck the water about a quarter mile short of the transport. One of the few instances where the *Bat* actually fulfilled expectations occurred three days later when Lieutenant Commander Hicks scored a hit on a Japanese destroyer-type escort.

Commander Hicks and his wingman, Lieutenant Kennedy, after sinking a 3,000-ton merchant ship and six smaller freighters along the southeast tip of Korea using standard strafing and bombing tactics, were on their homeward trek when two more ships were picked up on radar. The vessels—single-stack destroyer escorts of approximately 2,300 tons—were sighted by radar from 20 miles, cruising at 15 knots, and identified visually at 15 miles from 2,000 feet. Range was closed to six miles as the planes began their *Bat* attack, and as both warships started sending up heavy but inaccurate anti-aircraft fire. The planes made a 180-degree turn, with Lieutenant Kennedy climbing to 8,500 feet, while Commander Hicks, at 6,000 feet, followed two miles behind. Anti-aircraft fire, which was intense and increasingly accurate as the planes neared, ceased as Lieutenant Kennedy began his run. Three miles from the target the missile was released from 6,000 feet, and this time the weapon traveled true, hitting the warship directly on the bow above the water line. As soon as the *Bat* detonated, the undamaged escort, originally a mile away, moved to a position 100 yards from her damaged sister ship, turned broadside, and started throwing accurate anti-aircraft fire. Both planes circled at 5,000 feet to assess the damage before anti-aircraft fire from the undamaged warship forced a withdrawal. Hicks and Kennedy headed their planes towards Okinawa, leaving behind them 11 ships sunk or damaged. At best, the Japanese warship was damaged, since no records document the destruction of such a ship.[29]

Enemy Fighters and Armed Merchant Shipping

A week after Lieutenants Warren and Fairbanks tangled with the 343Ku Air Group Japanese fighters intercepted another pair of VPB-109 Privateers. On 24 May, Lieutenants Donald S. Chay and Floyd Hewitt were off the southern coast of Korea looking for enemy shipping when an enemy destroyer was sighted, which immediately opened fire at the approaching American patrol planes. The planes started gaining altitude in preparation for an attack when Lieutenant Chay sighted three Nakajima A6M2-N Rufe floatplane fighters approaching. The Privateers immediately joined up to present their firepower for whatever aggressiveness the enemy cared to show. Evidently waiting for additional help, the fighters began bracketing Chay and Hewitt's planes, with one coming to port at 5,000 feet, one to starboard at 4,000 feet, and the remaining astern at 2,000 feet, outside the range of the bomber's gunners. Japanese reinforcements appeared moments later in the form of three fighters, consisting of a Kawasaki Ki-45 Nick, Mitsubishi A6M8 Zeke, and a Kawasaki Ki-61 Hien Tony, which represented some of the best fighters the Japanese had in the war.[30]

One Rufe made a head on run on Lieutenant Chay's plane in an apparent attempt to pull away from the patrol bomber's starboard side. Chay's bow gunner scored several hits, causing the fighter to pull up, which presented a perfect target for the forward top turret. The patrol plane's gunners opened fire, and the Rufe began a steep, wobbly glide downward before crashing into the water. The Tony then conducted a frontal attack on Lieutenant Hewitt's plane before pulling away slightly under and starboard of the Privateer. Both the bow turret and forward top turret opened fire, which caused the fighter to join its comrade in a downward journey towards the sea. The Zeke attempted a side run on Lieutenant Chay, who was covering Hewitt's wing, and attempted to pull away to port. The starboard waist and tail guns of Chay's plane opened fire, and the fighter pulled away, leaving a trail of black smoke as it disappeared out of sight. After driving off the nimble enemy fighters, the Privateers headed home just as Lieutenant Chay's plane developed a fuel leak and two of his turrets became inoperative.[31]

The Privateer's 12 .50-caliber machine guns, combined with precision bombing, continued to wreck havoc on enemy shipping. The *Reluctant Raider's* score against merchant shipping rose sharply between 27 and 30 May, but at the cost of losing one of the squadron's veteran patrol plane commanders. Two sections consisting of Lieutenants Davis, Jobe, Kennedy, and Serbin were dispatched to the mouth of the Yangtze River on the 30th after squadron aircraft encountered a considerable amount of shipping a day earlier.

Ten minutes past noon, Lieutenants Clifton B. Davis and George Serbin spotted a 3,000-ton attack transport and two small picket boats traveling slowly off the coast. While Lieutenant Serbin prepared for a *Bat* attack Davis began a low-level strafing run, but his plane immediately received damage from 20-millimeter and 40-millimeter guns that wounded the co-pilot and plane captain. His aircraft also suffered considerable damage to the numbers one and three engines, rudder controls, and radio communication gear, and the starboard fuselage was perforated. Davis immediately set course for base, where he made a safe landing in near zero visibility. For the next hour, the three remaining aircraft were in constant contact with enemy shipping, with the first target being an anchored 2,300-ton freighter. After one strafing run at 200 feet to silence the ship's anti-aircraft fire, the planes commenced two bombing runs from 100 feet. Two near misses by 500-pound bombs started fires, and the ship listed sharply to port and began sinking.

Jobe and Kennedy were in the process of strafing and bombing a 4,000-ton merchantman when Serbin got on the radio and told them about two large attack transports. Preferring to save his bombs for the transports, Kennedy broke off the attack. It proved to be a costly mistake. Initially, the pilots planned a strafing run on the transports until certain anti-aircraft fire was eliminated before making bomb runs. Lieutenant Jobe's plane went in first, cutting across the bow of the lead ship; with his gunners strafing, he then circled around and flew up the trailing ship from stern to bow, and then crossed to port of the lead ship. Kennedy, a quarter mile behind, bracketed the transport by strafing the length of the starboard side and then fell in behind Jobe as the latter crossed over. Suddenly, the lead transport turned hard to port and, as the planes came around on the starboard side, opened fire.

The first burst from the lead transport caught both planes, and Jobe's plane was severely damaged, with the horizontal stabilizer and vertical stabilizer shot to pieces and a bomb bay door blown off. With loss of rudder control, he was forced to retire and return to base. Meanwhile, a 20-millimeter shell exploded inside Lieutenant Kennedy's cockpit, killing him almost instantly and wounding his co-pilot, Ensign William E. Wassner. Although wounded and with most of his instruments shot away, Ensign Wassner took control of the aircraft and conducted a successful crash landing at Okinawa three hours later.

5

Privateer Operations in World War II: Okinawa (June-October 1945)

VPB-123 arrived at Okinawa on 30 May 1945 under the leadership of Lieutenant Commander Samuel G. Shilling, relieving VPB-109, which was ordered to cease combat operations and return to Tinian for rest and relaxation. Combat operations for Lieutenant Commander Shilling's squadron began immediately, with the first kill being recorded on the 31st when two aircraft piloted by Lieutenants Robert J. Monahan and George W. McDonald joined up to shoot down a Nakajima Ki-84 Hayate Frank fighter along the southern coast of Korea. Three days later, after destroying an Aichi E13A1 Jake floatplane taxiing in the water, Lieutenant Harold M. Sanderson and Lieutenant (jg) Erwin L. Klein damaged a 1,300-ton transport off the southern Korean coast.[32]

VPB-123's Daring Duo

Two of the most daring Privateer pilots of VPB-123 were Lieutenant Al G. McCuaig and Lieutenant (jg) Kenneth F. Sanford. On the morning of 4 June, McCuaig and Sanford teamed up for an anti-shipping sweep around Tsushima Island and proceeded to sink over 11,000 tons of shipping before returning to base. Two hours after take-off, two enemy destroyers were seen moving at flank speed as the Privateers approached just feet off the water. The warships spotted the planes and began sending a thick curtain of anti-aircraft fire so intense that the attack was aborted. Both plane commanders knew their aircraft were no match for destroyers on the high seas, so they decided to look for easier game.

Along the southern coast of Korea, near small islands that dot the area, a 1,500-ton freighter was attacked and, during the course of two bombing and strafing runs from both Privateers, sunk after being hit by one 500-pound bomb dropped by McCuaig. A few minutes later several smaller cargo ships were hit; leaving all severely damaged or sunk. The day was not over for them, as they headed for Kyushu, where a large tanker was spotted. Afterward, Lieutenant (jg) Sanford saw small boats around the tanker and assumed they were fishing boats, but he was wrong; they were well-armed picket boats protecting the valuable cargo within the ship.

Lieutenant McCuaig went in first, and his plane immediately took a hit to its number four engine. Sanford came in behind, 50 feet off the water, all guns trained and firing at the tanker. Puffs of anti-aircraft fire peppered the sky around the attacking plane. Sanford crossed over the ship and released two 500-pound bombs. The first hit in the front of the vessel, at the waterline, and the second hit the superstructure, and the ship started to burn. Suddenly, his Privateer lurched, shuddered, and started going down. The picket boats had hit the Privateer with three 40-millimeter rounds; the aileron controls would not respond, and the plane began heading back towards the picket boats. Sanford's co-pilot, Lieutenant Wally Howison, managed to set the aileron trim tab, and the aircraft gradu-

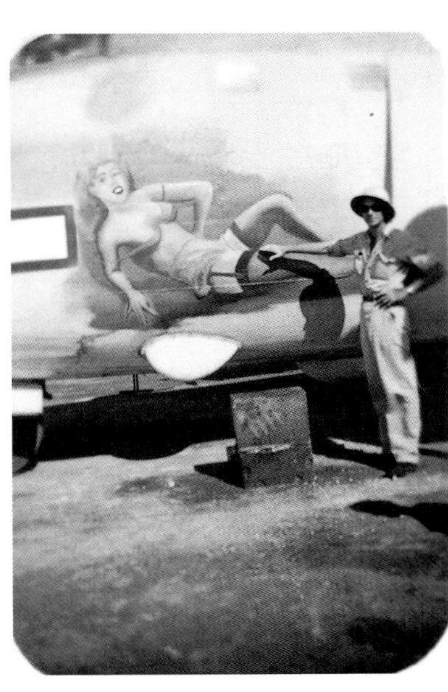

Miss Pandemonium (unknown Bureau Number) probably served with VPB-124 since it appears in the squadron cruise book. (Author's Collection)

ally straitened out just out of range of the picket boats. The crew began jettisoning everything except for the survival gear to lighten the plane and gain altitude. Miraculously, four hours after the planes had been hit both Privateers reached Yontan and landed safely. For their work in getting the plane back to base and sinking a large oil tanker both pilots received the Silver Star Medal, and their crews the Distinguished Flying Cross. During the course of VPB-123's tour, those two Privateer crews would sink 13 ships, damage seven more, and shoot down two enemy aircraft.[33]

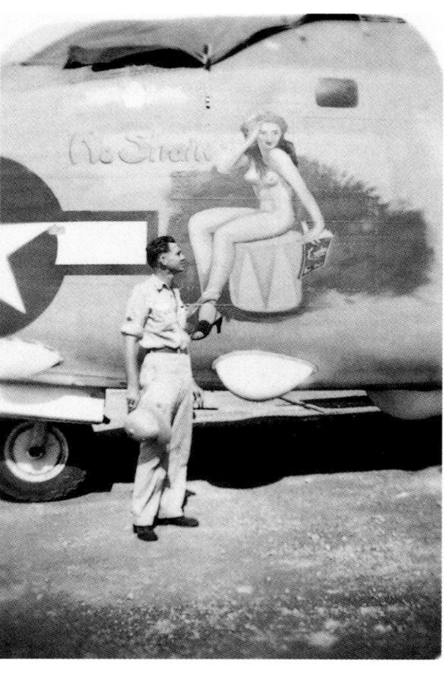

No Strain (unknown Bureau Number) is another PB4Y-2 that appears in the cruise books of VPB-121 and 124. (Author's Collection)

VPB-124

VPB-118 resumed operations from Okinawa on 1 June 1945 after three weeks of R&R on Tinian with an aerial mining campaign in Korean waters that took place between the ninth and 30th. At the campaign's peak, the squadron sent out six planes carrying 12 mines with a total weight of 24,000 pounds. Aerial mining operations did not interfere with the squadron's quest for enemy shipping, as various aircrews succeeded in sinking or damaging an estimated 26 ships totaling some 16,000 tons.

VPB-109 Privateer Bureau Number 59512 piloted by Lieutenant Joe Jobe, Patrol Plane Commander of Crew 8, shows extensive battle damage caused by antiaircraft fire during a raid on enemy shipping along the Yangtze River near Shanghai, China. Pictured from left to right are: Don Chapman, Robert Sims, Don Derham (head in damaged area), Larry Boucvalt, Gustave Greve, and Joe Jobe. (Courtesy: Don Derham via Roy Balke)

In mid-June 1945 Commander Charles E. Houston's VPB-124 arrived at Yontan Field after a brief two-week stay on Tinian under FAW-18, where it conducted harassing raids against Truk before transferring to Okinawa. Lieutenants Jack E. Vincent and Robert D. Johnston conducted the squadron's first patrol during the morning hours of 18 June, with both claiming the destruction of six fishing boats and a small cargo ship in the Sea of Japan. The following day Lieutenant Robert J. Brower and Lieutenant (jg) Osborn joined up to sink an 800-ton cargo ship.

VPB-124's first encounters with enemy fighters occurred the following day while on a joint aerial mining operation with VPB-118. While assisting in the mining effort, Lieutenants Gilbert Miller and J.E. Sanders ran into two small ships and a large coastal passenger steamer in Rakuti harbor, located on the southeast tip of Korea. Miller scored two direct hits on the steamer while the gunners on Sanders' plane strafed the two smaller ships. Just before Miller made his third run, Miller's gunners spotted eight Nakajima Ki-44IIB Shoki Tojo fighters coming down towards them. Seeing the trouble he was about to get into, the Privateer pilot headed the bomber out to sea and away from the pursuers. However, the slower patrol bomber was no match for the speed of the Japanese fighters and, for the next 15 minutes, Miller and his crew fought off eight attacks, as both attacker and attacked dove down to within 50 feet of the water. The Tojos tried the tactic of dropping phosphorous bombs on the Privateer to no avail before deciding to peel off and attack with cannon and machine gun fire. Two of the fighters were hit repeatedly by the Privateer's bow, top, and waist guns, forcing one fighter to break off the attack with smoke pouring out of its engine area. Meanwhile, the Privateer's aft upper turret and tail turrets scored hits on the second Tojo's cockpit area, and it flipped over on its back and plunged into the water. The remaining Tojos, seeing one of their brethren shot down and another damaged, broke off the attack, allowing Miller to rejoin Sanders.[34]

Fishing trawlers suspected of acting as an early warning system for the Japanese often became targets for patrolling USN patrol aircraft. Here are two under attack by two Privateers from VPB-124 commanded by Lieutenants Griffin and Preis on 29 June 1945. (Courtesy: Ted Rowcliffe)

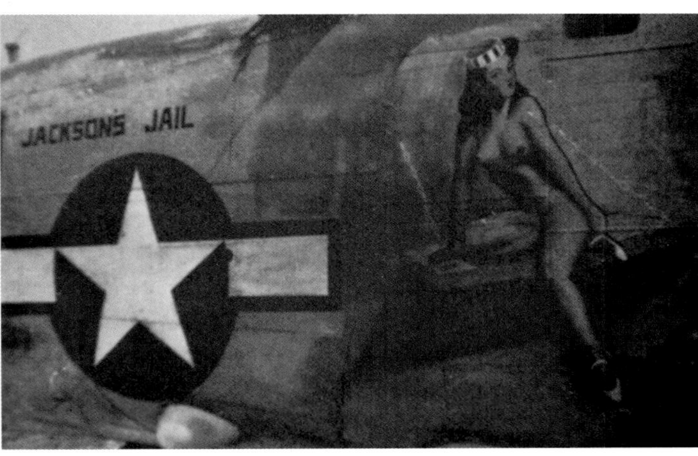

Pictured here is *Jackson's Jail*, an Okinawa-based Privateer of unknown ownership, but it probably served with either VPB-123 or 124 as it appears in the VPB-124 squadron cruise book.

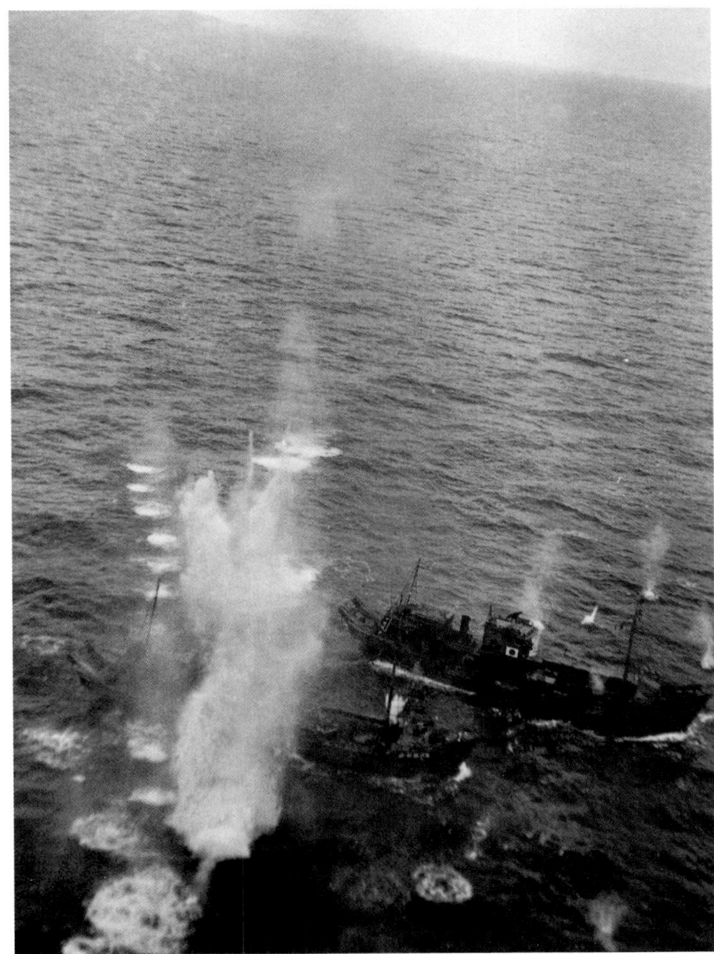

Low-level tactics were the norm for Privateers, with attacks often conducted at altitudes of 100 feet or less. This photograph shows a small cargo vessel under attack by VPB-124 circa June-July 1945. (Courtesy: Ted Rowcliffe)

VPB-124 tried to use their SWOD MK-9 *Bats* on the 23rd and 25th of June 1945, but both attempts failed to record a kill against enemy shipping. One of the attacks occurred when Lieutenants Preis and Griffin spotted three patrol boats sailing in line above the Tsushima Straits, between Korea and Japan. Lieutenant Preis' *Bat* locked onto the lead ship from an altitude of 8,000 feet and a distance of eight miles as the ships began sending up anti-aircraft fire, which exploded close to the Privateer's wings. The weapon traveled true but missed its intended target and exploded between two of the patrol boats. Preis turned away and headed home with Griffin, thus ending the squadron's use of the weapon.

Failed to Return

During a two-plane patrol along the Chinese coast on 26 June, VPB-124 lost two crews, including the Commanding Officer's, when Commander Houston and his wingman, Lieutenant (jg) Jack R. Crist, ran into trouble while flying a sweep north of Shanghai. It was a routine patrol, as Houston dropped his aircraft Bureau Number 59557 through a cloud layer and spotted a convoy of five ships consisting of freighters in the 7 to 10,000-ton range being escorted by two destroyers. There was no indication that the Privateers had been picked up visually or by radar as Houston came in at 150 feet with a 10,000-ton freighter as his target; however, two miles from the target, every ship opened fire. Houston pressed home the attack from an altitude of 100 feet and dropped seven 250-pound bombs as the bomber crossed over the ship's stern, with one hitting the deck and a second exploding along the water line. Jack Crist, following behind the Commanding Officer's plane in Bureau Number 59532, crossed over the ship's bow and scored a direct hit, but what happened next remains a mystery. Members of Houston's crew saw Crist's number three engine smoking as the plane turned away from the ship and appeared to be heading for the China coast, but the

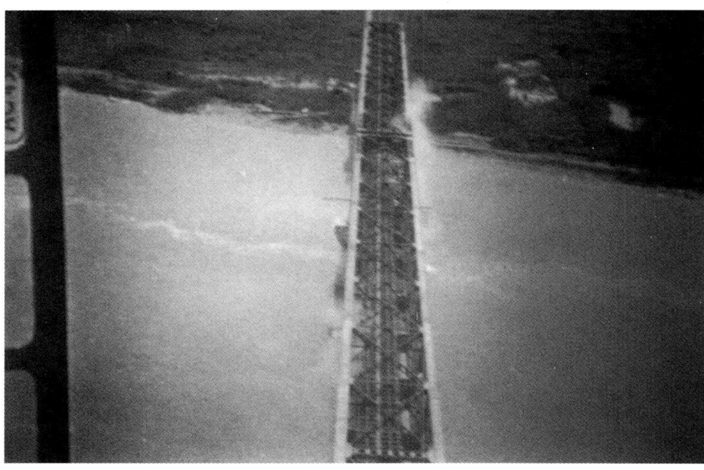

Smoke from the impacts by a VPB-109 Privateer .50-caliber machine gun fire in this image can be seen along the top portion of the rail bridge on the Seisin K River in Korea on 31 July 1945. The raid was a combined effort consisting of Privateers from VPB-109, 118, and 123. (Courtesy: NARA)

VPB-124's *Supreme Zu Zu* was often piloted by Lieutenant John B. Ramsey. (Author's Collection)

Privateer's crew were not heard from again. A few seconds later Houston's plane was subjected to heavy anti-aircraft fire.

The Privateer's path took it over a second ship, and the plane took hits to the port wing and bow turret, killing both the radioman and bow turret gunner. With his number two engine out and his number one on fire, Commander Houston still managed to pickle off two bombs alongside a 7,000-ton ship. The bomber was in serious trouble, losing power and altitude as Houston called his men to prepare for ditching. The stricken bomber flew on for another eight miles before it ditched, breaking into three pieces. From the fractured aircraft, eight of her injured crew managed to get out before it sank. Houston and his men were soon spotted and picked up by a Japanese destroyer, where they were subjected to interrogation and severe beatings that lasted until they were taken off the ship at Shang-

Smoke rises where Privateer Bureau Number 59535 of VPB-124 crashed while attacking a Japanese destroyer-escort on 27 June 1945 killing Lieutenant (jg) Jack Vincent and his crew. (Courtesy: Ted Rowcliffe)

While attacking a Japanese merchant ship in July 1945, Lieutenant Miller of VPB-124 flew Bureau Number 59534 a little too low, and a 45-foot long hole was ripped into the aircraft's belly. Miller and his crew safely returned to Okinawa, but their Privateer was a total loss. (Courtesy: Ted Rowcliffe)

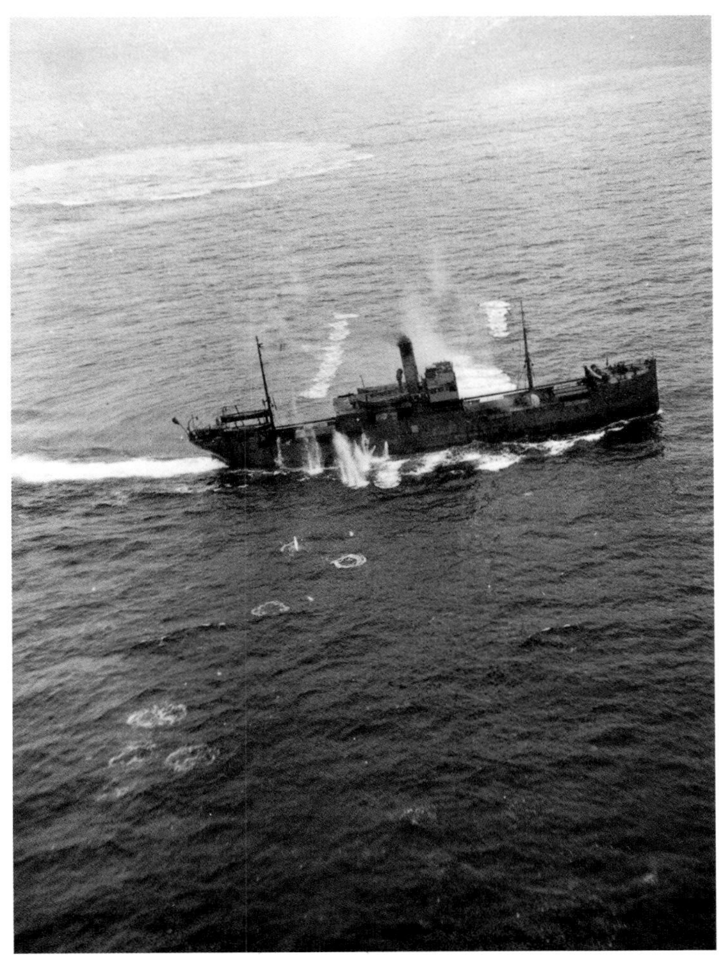

Machine gun fire rake a small Japanese cargo ship as it attempts to flee from an attacking VPB-124 Privateer. The residue from one of the aircraft's exploding bombs can be seen in the water at the upper left. (Courtesy: Ted Rowcliffe)

hai the following day. After undergoing additional interrogations and beatings, Houston and two others of the crew were flown to Ofuna Prison Camp, where they remained until they were liberated on 1 September 1945.[35]

Lieutenant Commander John M. Miller assumed command of the squadron, as VPB-124 continued to hit the enemy on land and sea, only to lose more men and planes in the coming weeks. While Houston and his men endured the beatings on board the Japanese ship, two Privateers from VPB-124 belonging to Lieutenants Jack Vincent and Bob Johnston took off in their planes and headed for a patrol sector that would bring them near Korea. As they neared the southeast coast of Korea on 27 June 1945, a heavy fog hid the sea below. Through it, Lieutenant Johnston briefly made out a ship a quarter of a mile ahead. He called Lieutenant Vincent, flying Bureau Number 59535, about the ship, and then changed course to intercept. Closing in, he identified it as a destroyer escort. Already Vincent was approaching the warship, and Johnston could see puffs of anti-aircraft fire following the incoming Privateer. A few moments later Johnston and his crew saw Vincent's plane take hits to the bomb bay area and the port wing near the engines. The damaged Privateer climbed for an instant, smoke pouring from the port engines, then crashed into the water with a horrendous explosion. Smoke billowed some 1,500 feet into the air and, at the scene of the crash, flames and a few pieces of floating wreckage, but that was all—there were no survivors. VPB-124 would lose three more aircraft and their crews during July 1945, which ended the squadron's ability to sustain combat operations.

PB4Y-2 Hits Mast and Limps Home

The Privateer's ability to withstand major battle damage and still bring her crew home was exemplified again on 2 July 1945 when Lieutenant Gil Miller and Lieutenant (jg) D.E. Ellis spotted a small merchant ship in the Tsushima Straits. Initial strafing by both Pri-

VPB-109 Privateers piloted by Lieutenants Jobe and Turner attacking a Japanese merchant ship on 30 July 1945. (Courtesy: NARA)

vateers caused the ship to explode, and black smoke from the fiery inferno enveloped Miller's plane, Bureau Number 59534. Unable to pull up in time, the Privateer hit the ship's main mast, ripping out the plane's belly. It took the efforts of both Miller and his co-pilot, Lieutenant (jg) R.H. Hepworth, to regain control of the aircraft and prevent it from crashing into the sea. While the pilots struggled to maintain control of the PB4Y-2, a couple of the crew went aft to inspect the damage while others took care of three injured shipmates and a Marine Corps aerographer. Damage to the plane was extensive. A hole along the bottom of the plane 45 feet in length and between five to seven feet wide had ripped away the bomb bay doors, hydraulic system, radar, and radio equipment. For an hour and a half, standing in the oily catwalk, the plane captain, Aviation Machinist Mate First Class (AMM1c) O.M. Osborn, cut away bomb bay tanks, bomb racks, and other loose equipment that had been smashed inside the bomb bay. After a four hour trip, in which the only communication between Lieutenant (jg) Ellis' plane and Miller was by flashlight and Morse code, the pilot made a wheels-up, belly landing at Yontan. The plane was immediately surveyed.

Flying Sieve

Ten days after Lieutenant Gil Miller's close brush with disaster, Lieutenant Arnold's crew experienced first-hand the PB4Y-2's toughness while on a sweep with another Privateer piloted by VPB-124's new skipper, Lieutenant Commander John Miller. After a negative search for shipping, both patrol plane commanders decided to look for targets of opportunity along the coast of Kyushu, Japan. They soon found a village and, in the process, destroyed factory buildings, one span of a railroad bridge, a locomotive, and a passenger train. However, on the third attack run both planes encountered heavy anti-aircraft fire. Arnold's plane was hit by a 40-millimeter shell that exploded inside the plane, punching 200 holes in the fuselage, causing an electrical fire, and wounding the radioman. Meanwhile, Miller's plane received several hits from 7.7-millimeter machine gun fire that knocked out the number three engine, punctured the main landing gear, and severed the pilot's rudder cables. However, the ruggedness of the PB4Y-2 to sustain battle damage and keep flying paid off again, as both planes landed safely on Okinawa some three hours later.[36]

Maximum Effort

Individual squadrons continued patrolling off the coasts of China, Japan, and Korea throughout July and into August 1945, resulting in the destruction of Japanese installations, transportation facilities, and shipping, but such missions resulted in the loss of six Privateers and their crews. Multi-plane and multi-squadron strikes

VPB-124's *Gear Down and Locked* was lost in action along with Lieutenant John Ramsey and his crew on 24 July 1945. (Courtesy: Ted Rowcliffe)

A VPB-109 "Bat" carrying PB4Y-2B Privateer on patrol during the summer of 1945. (Courtesy: Tom Wack via Roy Balke)

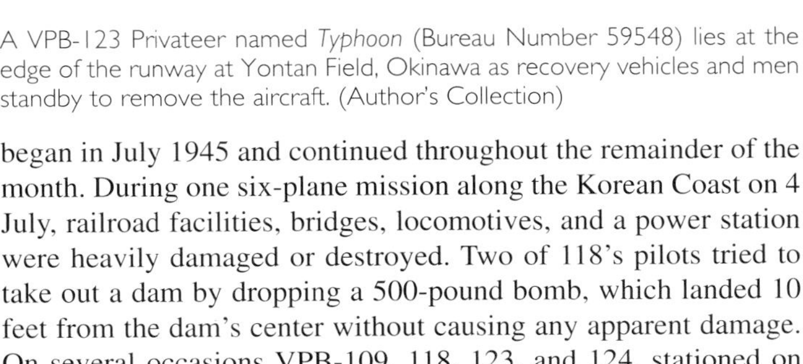

A VPB-123 Privateer named *Typhoon* (Bureau Number 59548) lies at the edge of the runway at Yontan Field, Okinawa as recovery vehicles and men standby to remove the aircraft. (Author's Collection)

This shows another view of *Typhoon* with a crewmember standing atop the aircraft. (Author's Collection)

began in July 1945 and continued throughout the remainder of the month. During one six-plane mission along the Korean Coast on 4 July, railroad facilities, bridges, locomotives, and a power station were heavily damaged or destroyed. Two of 118's pilots tried to take out a dam by dropping a 500-pound bomb, which landed 10 feet from the dam's center without causing any apparent damage. On several occasions VPB-109, 118, 123, and 124, stationed on Okinawa, coordinated multi-plane strikes against targets in China, Korea, and Japan, with probably the most ambitious undertaking occurring on 14 and 15 July 1945. Three separate attack groups totaling 16 planes belonging to VPB-118, 123, and 124 hit shipping and railroad targets along the eastern coast of North Korea in and around Genzan Harbor and Bokku Wan.

A group of two, four-plane sections hit railroad communications in the Genzan Harbor Area, located in north-central Korea, since their primary targets of oil refineries and shipping were obscured due to heavy overcast. During the coordinated bombing and strafing attack locomotives, freight cars, rail lines, and facilities

Above: This photograph taken after the crash shows extensive damage to *Typhoon's* wing section and that the vertical stabilizer has been removed. (Author's Collection)

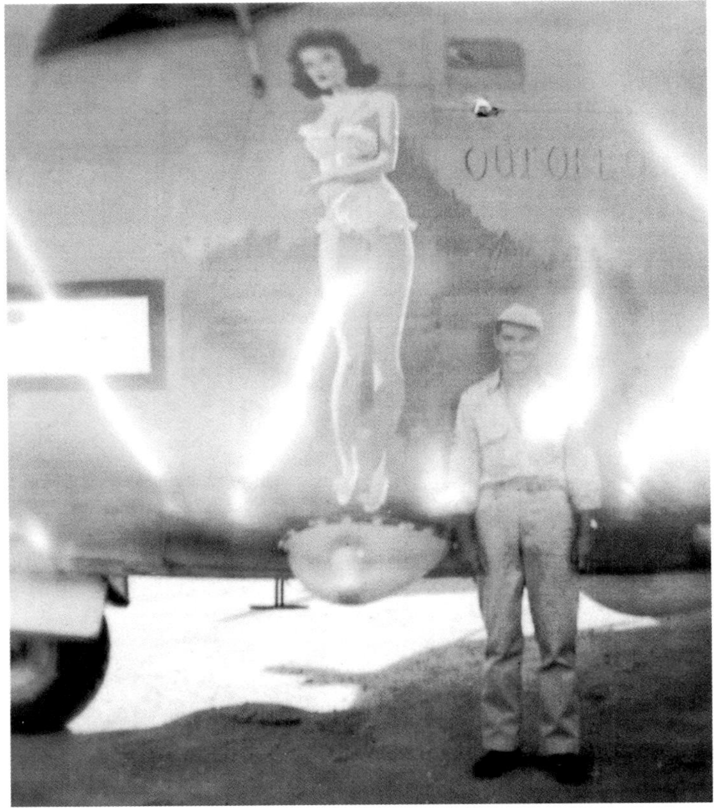

Right: This somewhat overexposed photograph shows an unidentified individual standing next to *Out of Bounds*, a PB4Y-2 Privateer based at Yontan Field, Okinawa circa mid-1945. (Author's Collection)

were destroyed. A second group consisting of four planes from VPB-118 and led by Lieutenant Pettes penetrated a heavy overcast and hit shipping and installations at Bokka Wan from an altitude of 200 feet, damaging a small freighter and a tug in the harbor, as well as destroying gas works, a warehouse, and a locomotive. The section then moved on to a rail junction at Kinsen, where two locomotives, freight yards, rail lines, and a bridge were destroyed. During a bombing run on the bridge, Lieutenant Lodato's port waist gunner, Aviation Ordnance Mate Second Class (AOM2c) Marion L. Marshall, was seriously wounded in the right elbow by a 7.7-millimeter round. The third section, consisting of a pair of Privateers from VPB-123 and 124, executed attacks on shipping in Seika Wan in extremely hazardous flying conditions, occasioned by low overcast and fog, and in the face of anti-aircraft fire from ships and shore installations. In the strike on Seika Wan VPB-123's crews worked over a dozen freighters in the harbor, sinking five and damaging the rest, while Lieutenants John E. Ramsey and Thomas F. Pierce of 124 left four ships sinking and nine more damaged.

Genzan Harbor Striking Force

VPB-123 Section	**VPB-118 Section**
Monahan	Dodson
McDonald	Weller
McCuaig	Duba
Sanford	Park

Bokku Wan Striking Force

VPB-118 Section
Pettes
Lodato
McCutcheon
Thompson

Seika Wan Striking Force

VPB-123 Section	**VPB-124 Section**
Reusswig	Ramsey
Harrington	Pierce

On the evening of the 15th Lieutenant William N. Lloyd led three, two-plane sections from 118, 123, and 124 against shipping and docks on the Huang P'u River near Shanghai, China. Those participating in the strike viewed it as a suicide mission, and they were pretty close in that assessment when the group met with intense anti-aircraft fire upon approaching the target area. Miller swept in along the Huang P'u River, attacking a concentration of ships and from an altitude of 600 feet, and pickled off nine bombs. Ellis, slightly behind Miller, dropped two 500-pound bombs in the area of a power station and gas works, and a pillar of fire shot up into the sky. Meanwhile, Lieutenant Pepe and Lieutenant (jg) Treat bombed shipping and dock installations along the Huang P'u River. Their attack was met with extremely intense heavy anti-aircraft fire and night fighters, the former knocking out one engine on Lieutenant Pepe's plane just as he released his bomb load.

Huang P'u River Striking Force

VPB-118 Section	**VPB-123 Section**	**VPB-123 Section**
Lloyd	Pepe	Miller
Keiser	Treat	Ellis

Casualties of War

In between the multi-squadron strikes the Okinawa squadrons continued with the job of neutralizing enemy merchant shipping, but such strikes cost VPB-118 a plane and most of its crew, while 124 suffered a double tragedy when the squadron lost a pair of planes. The first loss occurred on 7 July when VPB-124's Lieutenant Rob-

VPB-116 operated this Privateer fitted with loudspeakers in the bomb bay during the closing days of World War II and reportedly used it to harass bypassed islands held by the Japanese. (Courtesy: David Smith)

This is a close-up of the nose art on the aircraft discussed in the previous caption showing a semi-nude woman with oriental characters written next to her that in translation means either *Big Snow Propaganda* or *Big Show Propaganda* depending upon the translation. According to Chet Krokoski, a veteran of VPB-116, the plane also went by the name *Dragon Lady* in reference to a character in the *Terry and the Pirates* comic strip that was popular during the 1940s. (Courtesy: Chet Krokoski via Lieutenant Colonel Chip Krokoski, U.S. Army)

ert Brower and Lieutenant (jg) Everett Osborn teamed up for a sweep of the Tsushima Straits between Kyushu and Korea.

The first visual contact was made on two enemy warships that opened fire with their five-inch guns but failed to hit the patrol bombers. Shortly thereafter, a pair of Rex fighters attacked the patrol bombers in a five-minute battle, and the 12 .50-caliber guns of each Privateer proved to be too deadly for the attacking enemy planes. Lieutenant (jg) Osborn's gunners shot down one that spiraled into the sea, while the other turned tail and headed for home with smoke pouring from its fuselage.

Heading for base, the crews made visual contact with a small enemy ship, which was identified after the attack as a subchaser. Lieutenant Brower, leading the section in Bureau Number 59538, started in for the attack, followed closely by Lieutenant Osborn. As Brower's plane flew into range, the subchaser opened fire and caught the incoming Privateer. Just before reaching the ship, Lieutenant (jg) Dave Davis, Brower's co-pilot, called via radio to Osborne, "Get out of the way, Ossie; we're going in!"

Brower's plane, badly crippled and on fire, crashed into the water almost immediately about one and one-half miles from the subchaser, and about six miles offshore from Uki Shima, the northernmost island in the Goto Retto group. Five of the crew escaped from the plane: Lieutenant (jg) Davis, Jack Lewis, George Dacier, Theodore Kalmuk, and Frank Gardner. Osborne circled over the five men in the water, receiving intense fire from the subchaser and from shore batteries. He dropped a life raft, advised base of the situation, and set a course for home, as his fuel supply was running low. Five men escaped from Brower's plane after it crashed, while the others were apparently killed when the big bomber hit the water. A Japanese boat later picked up the survivors, and the men became prisoners of war.

On 22 July, VPB-118's Lieutenant Leland McCutcheon and his crew were shot down in Bureau Number 59458 while attacking what appeared to be an innocuous ferry off Shanghai, China, but it turned out to be a heavily armed ship, with 20 and 40-millimeter cannons. The Privateer was hit hard and mortally damaged. McCutcheon managed to ditch the plane, but he, along with five crewmembers, were killed; a Coronado PB3Y-2 flying boat rescued seven others.

Operating from Tinian with detachments on Iwo Jima, Squadron VPB-116 began receiving PB4Y-2s during the closing days of the Pacific War. Bureau Number 59760, named *Cover Girl*, was among them. (Courtesy: David Smith)

VPB-124 continued to lose men through the end of July when Lieutenant Ramsey, piloting Bureau Number 59519 with the name *Gear Locked and Down*, and Lieutenant Gil Miller aboard Bureau Number 59747 were lost on the 24th while on an anti-shipping sweep along the western coast of Korea. Three hours after take off, a morning contact report from Lieutenant Ramsey stated that enemy aircraft were attacking him. Later in the morning a radioman from another VPB-124 Privateer intercepted a transmission from Ramsey calling Miller that he had made a successful attack on a ship and telling him they had sufficient gas to continue searching. According to squadron records Ramsey's radioman started an enemy contact report, but was told by home base to wait due to other radio traffic. After that, there was nothing. They were never heard from again. The following day, two planes from another unit sighted two beached and partially submerged ships near the vicinity of Ramsey's last report.[37]

VPB-124's active combat duty came to a hasty conclusion on 28 July 1945 when the squadron was sent to Tinian for rest and rehabilitation, as replacement crews were not available, and the remaining PB4Y-2s were in dire need of overhaul. Within a span of a month, six out of 15 crews were either killed, missing in action, or prisoners of war—70 out of approximately 180 men for a loss of nearly 40 percent.

Working on the Railroad

Three days after 124's withdrawal, the three remaining Privateer squadrons joined together for the last combined effort of the war on 31 July with VPB-109, 118, and 123 hitting rail communications in northwestern Korea. Commander Hicks and Lieutenant Hewitt, with two planes from VPB-118 and VPB-123, took off on a special strike against rail transportation and railroad facilities in Northwestern Korea. The target was a bridge works consisting of three parallel sections comprised of a highway bridge to the east; a partially completed railroad bridge in the center, and a completed railroad bridge to the west. The primary target, as selected by Commander Fleet Air Wing One, was the railroad bridge, a steel 2,700-foot long, multiple span, single-track structure on the Seisin K River, just two miles north of the town of Shinanshu. The bridge was vital to the supply of war materials flowing south through Korea to the ports of Fusan and Kunsan and other important shipping areas. To render this important artery useless, it was necessary to cut it off by destroying the bridge.

109 Section	118 Section	123 Section
Hicks	Rinehart	Sanderson
Hewitt	Shortlidge	Klein

Taking off at 0600 hours and leading his planes low and under radar detection, Commander Hicks planned to strike the target so that retirement could be made away from the direction of the towns of Shinanshu and Anshu. As the Privateers approached the primary target Lieutenant Shortlidge's tail gunner worked over a locomotive, while Rinehart's bow turret gunner strafed barges near the bridge complex. The planes hit the bridge at noon, with Hicks' first 1,000-pound bomb entering the water and scoring a perfect hit on the starboard center of the pier. The steel span lifted upward, covered by a geyser of water, immediately causing the northern end of the southernmost span to drop 20 feet below the level of the tracks, while a second bomb was a near miss on the second span pier. Meanwhile, Rinehart and Shortlidge arrived and began their bombing runs; however, the proximity of the 109 planes prevented accurate bombing, and Rinehart's bomb overshot the target and exploded approximately 30 feet from the northern end of the bridge.[38]

Return to base was started over land, looking for targets of opportunity along the railroad bed. A locomotive with 12 cars was spotted and seriously damaged by Hicks. A rail junction yard containing several small buildings was damaged by bombing and strafing by Lieutenant Hewitt, and a coal mine and six buildings, including a hopper elevator, were strafed and left in flames by Hicks' plane. Just as they were leaving the coast, four small power trawlers tied up together at a landing at the mouth of the Gaisan Ho River were strafed and bombed in passing, with bombs scoring direct hits and sending debris flying into the air.

Final Missions (August 1945)

The first few days of August 1945 were relatively quiet, except for the *Reluctant Raiders* of VPB-109, which suffered their final combat loss of the war when Lieutenants Keeling and Albert Vidal went on an anti-shipping patrol off the Korean coast. Spotting a 2,500-ton tanker, the patrol bombers dropped from 1,000 feet to 200 feet, circled the ship to port, and began strafing attacks. Light and medium, but inaccurate anti-aircraft fire was received during the strafing run, and the planes pulled up to 1,000 feet, still circling to port, as Lieutenant Keeling initiated a bombing run. Vidal remained a mile and a half behind with the intention of following Keeling with his own bombing run.

The planes were subjected to intense medium and light defensive fire from the ship, and Lieutenant Keeling's plane was hit in the number three engine immediately after completing his bombing run. Keeling pulled up to an altitude of 500 feet with smoke pouring out of the engine, but the plane gradually nosed over in a slight turn to starboard and crashed into the water two miles west of the ship. Following behind, Lieutenant Vidal broke off his bombing run when he observed Lieutenant Keeling in trouble and headed directly to the scene of the crash. Smoke and flames reached a height of 200 feet after the plane hit the water, and only a few pieces of debris were visible, consisting of an uninflated life raft, a wheel, and a large amount of dye marker floating on the surface when Vidal's plane reached the scene. There were no survivors.

While sister squadrons suffered a number of operational and combat fatalities during the course of combat while operating from bases in the Central Pacific, VPB-123 suffered only one fatality during its 73 days of combat between 30 May and 10 August 1945. The death occurred on 7 August when Lieutenant Sanderson and Lieutenant (jg) Klein teamed up to fly their last combat patrol together. Two stack-aft freighters were sighted off the northwest coast of Honshu and both planes made runs, but the bombs hung up in Sanderson's plane, leaving Lieutenant (jg) Klein to handle the task himself, who subsequently sank both ships. To wind up the patrol they both took passes at two small stack-aft freighters, leaving them in a damaged condition; however, anti-aircraft fire hit Sanderson's plane, and the tail gunner, Joseph H. Farmer, Aviation Ordnance Mate Third Class (AOM3c), was killed.[39]

A day after the dropping of the atomic bomb on Hiroshima, Lieutenant Commander Rinehart and Lieutenant (jg) J.R. Park from VPB-118 went on patrol along the western edge of Kyushu, through Tsushima Straits and the western coast of Honshu. The strategy of attacking at minimum altitude this time would cost the lives of an entire Privateer crew. After successfully sinking a small 100-ton cargo ship in the Sea of Japan, a merchant ship in the 2,000-ton range was spotted heading towards Honshu. Lieutenant Park went in first with his gunners laying down fire on the ship's superstructure, and with the vessel's crew firing back with light machine gun fire. The ship began to burn from Lieutenant Park's strafing attack as Rinehart lined up his aircraft for a bombing run. He pickled off three 500-pound bombs, with one detonating under the ship's stern, and turned back around as Park went in again.

The fire that Park's gunners had started was blazing furiously as the Privateer closed in on the ship. The ship, possibly carrying ammunition, suddenly exploded just as Park's bomber passed over it, and both the vessel and the plane disintegrated in a flash of fire and smoke. Debris from the ship and possibly from Park's Privateer was hurled 1,000 feet into the sky, with a fiery plume of smoke rising another 2,000 feet. Rinehart approached the scene only to find wreckage floating on the water. A fire in the shape of a wing burned where the port side of the ship had been. Nearby, an inflated life raft and a sleeping bag floated on the surface, marking the only remains of a PB4Y-2 and her crew.[40]

The last offensive actions by Okinawa-based Privateer squadrons were conducted on 10 August 1945. Lieutenant George L. King

Military decorations are handed to Lieutenant Bronson (misspelled as Bronstein in the book, *Above an Angry Sea*) and his crew of VPB-116 as they stand next to *Miss Sea-ducer* Bureau Number 59582. (Courtesy: David Smith)

of VPB-118 damaged two small vessels weighing between 80 and 175 tons off southern Korea. Still trying to get some use out of the SWOD-Mk-9 *Bat*, VPB-109's Lieutenants Chay and Moyer made an unsuccessful attack against a 2,400-ton tanker, but conventional bombing and strafing sank two small freighters and left three more damaged. VPB-123 ended its wartime combat operations on the same day with Lieutenants Koontz and Reussing teaming up to sink a small freighter.

Immediately after the cessation of hostilities and for the next several months, some Privateer squadrons conducted various reconnaissance missions over Korea, Japan, and China, flew special weather flights, or participated in a mosquito eradication program by spraying DDT insecticide on countless islands. The *Reluctant Raiders* were transferred to Guam for rest and relaxation at the end of August before shipping back to the United States in October 1945, where the squadron was disestablished. Between April and August 1945, VPB-109 is credited with destroying 16 planes in the air and on the ground, sinking 118 and damaging 87 ships, and conducting 56 bombing and strafing attacks.

The *Old Crows* of VPB-118 were transferred to Awase during the last week of August and later Yonabaru, Okinawa, where they remained until November 1945, when the squadron received orders to return to the United States, where it was disestablished on 11 December. Between January and August 1945, VPB-118 claimed sinking or damaging 205 enemy vessels, destroyed or damaged 16 enemy aircraft, and destroying or damaging numerous ground installations. The personnel cost to the squadron was 31 killed and 16 wounded.

VPB-123 was based at Agana, Guam, Yontan Field, and Yonabaru between 25 August and 19 November 1945 before being transferred to Barbers Point, Hawaii. Between 24 January and 5 February 1946 one crew and plane participated in the nuclear testing at Bikini Atoll, flying photographic reconnaissance over the test site. On 1 October of that year the squadron was disestablished. Between 30 May and 10 August 1945 VPB-123 sank or damaged 105 ships worth 53,250 tons, shot down nine aircraft, damaged three more in the air, and destroyed one aircraft in the water.

In August 1945, after R&R on Tinian, VPB-124 operated out of Yonaburu, Okinawa, and flew air cover for the Japanese surrender of Truk and Marcus Island. During the squadron's combat tour from 6 June to 27 July 1945, VPB-124 Privateer crews conducted 145 missions, attacking shore installations, sinking or damaging 54,296 tons of shipping, shot down two enemy planes and damaged six more. From December 1945 to May 1947 the squadron was based at NAS Barbers Point, Hawaii, with the primary missions of ferrying worn out Privateers back to the United States and operating air-sea rescue from Johnson Island, during which time it was redesignated as VP-HL-3.

Privateers to VPB-102 and 116

Between June and July 1945 Privateers began arriving on Tinian and Iwo Jima to replace the worn out PB4Y-1 Liberators belonging to VPB-102 and 116, as both squadrons had seen more than a year of action and were in need of replacement aircraft. VPB-116's skipper, Lieutenant Commander Walter C. Michaels, became the first American to set foot on Japanese soil after the surrender when he landed his PB4Y-2 on 27 August 1945 at Atsugi Naval Air Base, Japan. VPB-116 continued to operate from Tinian and Iwo Jima until October 1945, when it was transferred to San Diego, where it remained until 22 May 1947, when it was disestablished. While based in San Diego the squadron was redesignated as VP-HL-1.

By September 1945 VPB-102, with the nickname *Reluctant Dragons*, had 15 aircraft on hand consisting of 11 PB4Y-1 Liberators and four PB4Y-2s. With the end of the war, VPB-102 transferred to Agana, Guam, where it continued to serve primarily as a weather reconnaissance squadron flying the PB4Y-2 Privateer with detachments at Peleliu, Naha, Okinawa, and Iwo Jima. During the post-war years, the squadron continued to fly the aircraft under the designations VP-102, VP-HL-2, and then VP-22, with weather reconnaissance and ASW as its primary mission, before transitioning to the P2V-4 Neptune in June 1950.

VPB-102, another Tinian-based squadron, began trading in its PB4Y-1 Liberators for Privateers around the same time as VPB-116. Here is a photograph of R588 Bureau Number 59588 taken on Majuro Atoll circa 1946. According to Naval records, R588 was demolished in a landing accident at Marcus Island on 23 August 1946. (Courtesy: Donald Dirst via Steve Hawley)

6

Privateer Operations in World War II: Clark Field, Philippines (March-August 1945)

In early March 1945, VPB-119 became the first PB4Y-2 Privateer squadron to operate from the Philippines when it arrived at Clark Field, located on the island of Luzon. Commanded by Raymond C. Bales, he and some of the men were combat veterans from a previous tour of duty with VB-106 in the South Pacific. Operating under Fleet Air Wing Seventeen (FAW-17), VPB-119's search sectors ranged from the coast of Mainland China, within 30 miles of Shanghai, to Okinawa, Formosa, the Gulf of Tonkin, and Haiphong. Those sectors were extended 1,050 miles during the American landing on Okinawa in April 1945.

First Blood

Commander Bales' squadron didn't waste any time in searching for enemy shipping. On 2 March 1945 the first blood drawn by 119 was conducted by the commanding officer, which resulted in the destruction of one small freighter and the damaging of another. However, the squadron's first major strikes against the Japanese were the result of two separate patrols on the same day conducted by Lieutenant (jg) Walter Vogelsang and Lieutenant John W. Holt. Lieutenant Vogelsang made a masthead level bombing and strafing attack against a large freighter transport estimated at 5,000 tons, which was later found beached. A second Japanese merchant ship fell victim to a VPB-119 Privateer when Lieutenant Holt picked up a convoy of three merchant ships being protected by three destroyer escorts. During the ensuing masthead attack Holt sank the 1,000-ton cargo ship *Nichirin Maru*. It was the first of 15 Japanese ships totaling over 25,000 tons Lieutenant Holt and his crew would sink or damage between March and May 1945 while flying a couple of Privateers, one with the name *Holt's Patches*, Bureau Number 59413.[41]

(Source: Robert W. Coakley, *World War II: The War Against Japan*, Army Historical Series)

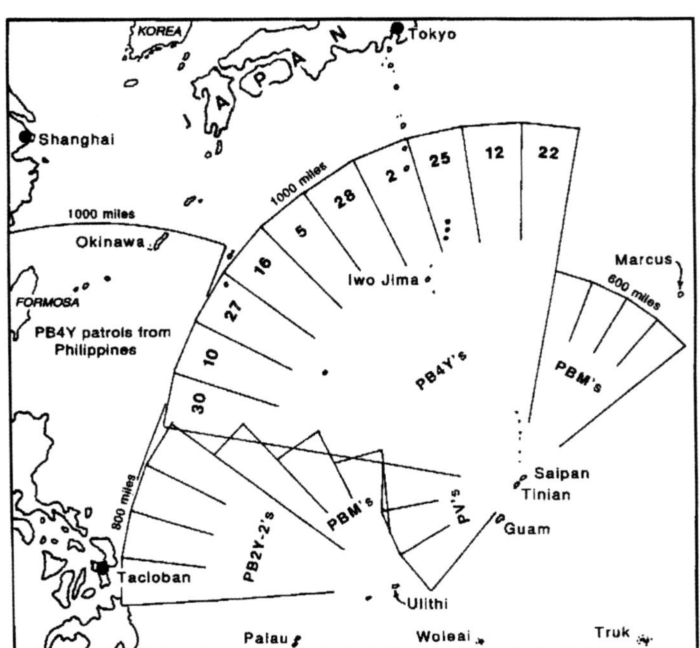

The operational search sectors for U.S. Naval patrol squadrons in 1945 stretched across the Southwest and Central Pacific.

VPB-119's Four-Engined Fighters

Combat aircrews of VPB-119 continued to pound away at enemy merchant shipping throughout March 1945, with 90 vessels being sunk or damaged totaling over 71,000 tons. Interspersed with daily strikes against shipping were a series of aerial duels that took place during March that showed the effectiveness of the PB4Y-2 in engaging enemy fighters. A crew commanded by Lieutenant Virgil J. Evans scored the squadron's first of eight aerial kills on 10 March when their plane was intercepted by Japanese fighters while Evans and his men were in the process of seriously damaging an ocean-going tugboat. While Evans covered another Privateer attacking the vessel, two Nakajima Ki-43IIB Oscar fighters appeared, and one of them made a series of runs on Evans' plane. The Privateer's gunners returned fire, and during the Oscar's fifth run the fighter was set afire, flipped over, and went down in flames. Two more Japanese aircraft went down after tangling with VPB-119 patrol planes on the 12th and 13th. Lieutenant (jg) Aubrey L. Althans overtook a Nakajima B6N2 Tenzan bomber (nicknamed Jill) flying at 1,000 feet, and after his gunners expended 1,200 rounds of ammunition, the enemy plane spun into the water and exploded. The second Japanese plane to fall in as many days went to Lieutenant (jg) Frank Murphy and his gunners when an Oscar was sighted over an airstrip at Swatow. Murphy closed to 200 yards, his gunners opened fire, and the fighter went down in flames in a town adjacent to the airstrip.

Five days after the downing of the Oscar by Lieutenant (jg) Murphy, an aerial battle took place near Formosa that resulted in the downing of two enemy fighters by a single Privateer crew. On 18 March Lieutenant (jg) William L. Lyle of VPB-119 was flying northwest of Formosa when two Nakajima Oscar fighters were spotted 2,000 feet above the Privateer. Lyle then used his four-engined patrol plane as a fighter and pulled up behind the Oscars, who were now racing towards the coast and the protection of anti-aircraft batteries.

It was too late, as Lyle's bow, starboard waist, and both top turrets opened fire on one of the Oscars, which turned over, dove past the PB4Y-2, and exploded 400 yards from the patrol bomber's port wing. The Privateer's pilot then went after the second fighter using full throttle in a slow dive towards the intended victim. All turrets opened fire, and the Oscar went into a dive at full speed, hit the surf near a beach, and exploded. The Privateer headed for home as the shore batteries finally opened up ineffectively at the retreat-

A trio of VPB-119's early model PB4Y-2s with the MPC nose turret. VPB-119 became the first of three PB4Y-2 squadrons to operate from the Philippines beginning in March 1945. (Courtesy: Curt Brownlow)

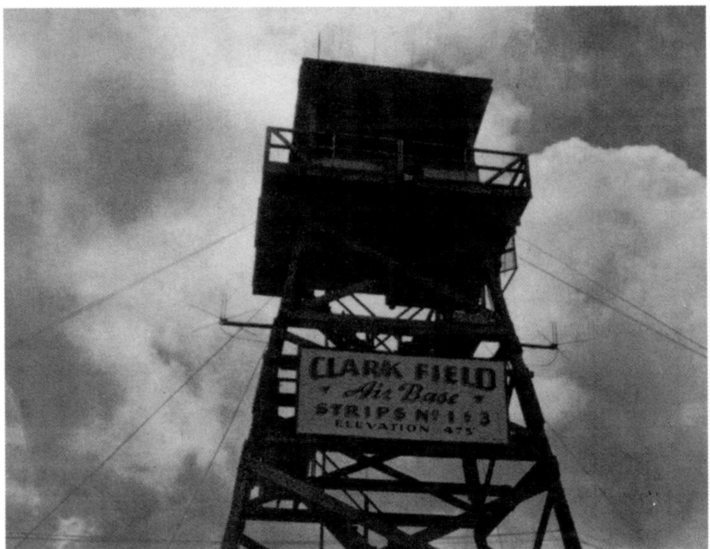

The control tower at Clark Field photographed during the summer of 1945. From this base, Navy Privateers and Liberators patrolled sectors that covered most of the Celebes, Borneo, Malaysia, and Indochina. (Courtesy: Bill Woodward)

VPB-119's Bureau Number 59418 coming in for a landing at Clark Field. (Courtesy: Curt Brownlow)

The remains of W429 (Bureau Number 59429) of VPB-119 in the boneyard at Clark Field after colliding with a PB4Y-1 Liberator from VPB-104 on 8 March 1945. (Courtesy: Curt Brownlow)

ing bomber turned fighter. Three more Japanese aircraft would fall victim to the lethal firepower of VPB-119's Privateers before the squadron's final tally ended at eight.

Losing Battles

Even with the combined gunfire of 12 .50-caliber machine guns, sometimes a Privateer was no match for an aggressive Japanese fighter pilot or a well-trained anti-aircraft crew. On 22 March 1945, 119 suffered its first combat loss when Privateer Bureau Number 59426, piloted by Lieutenant Virgil J. Evans, was shot down two miles north of Amoy, China. He had been one of the squadron's most aggressive pilots, with seven ships and one fighter to his credit in only three missions. Friendly Chinese troops rescued Evans, along with six of the 13-man crew that survived the crash. The downing of Lieutenant Evans turned out to be the first of many losses suffered by VPB-119 in the coming weeks, as several more aircraft and crews were lost to hostile fire.

The number of operational sorties flown by VPB-119 remained the same in April as it did in March (139), and the amount of ships sunk or damaged during April (83) nearly equaled the previous month, but tonnage fell dramatically from over 71,000 to some 14,000 tons. The second month of operations also turned out to be a bloody month for VPB-119, as it lost two aircraft and crews. Commander Bales and his crew, most of them veterans from VB-106,

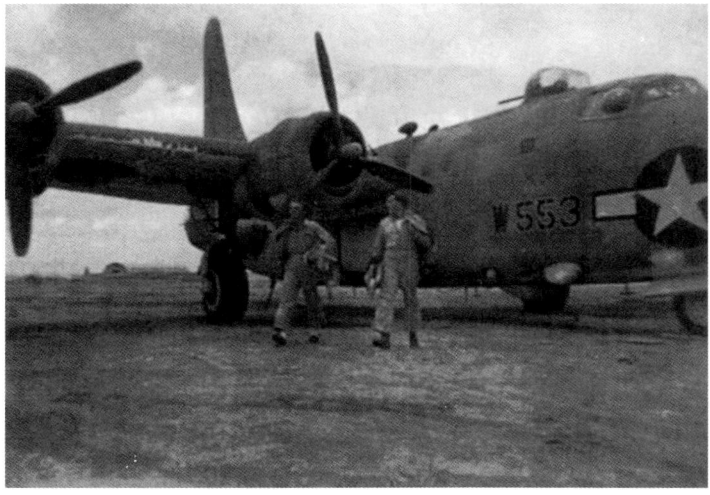

Crewmembers of W553 (Bureau Number 59553) of VPB-119 walk away from their aircraft. On 24 June 1945, she was lost in action along with her entire crew. (Courtesy: Curt Brownlow)

R468 (Bureau Number 59468) coming in to land at Clark Field probably belonged to VPB-119 although it has the letter R call sign that was used by VPB-104 and 117. This aircraft survived the war and went on to serve with ATU-12 in the United States. (Courtesy: Curt Brownlow)

Two members of VPB-119 apparently conducting repairs on a PB4Y-2s vertical stabilizer at Clark Field. (Courtesy: Curt Brownlow)

went out on patrol aboard Bureau Number 59452 on 1 April to China. The aircraft was later seen near Hangchow Harbor, but after that sighting, nothing was seen or heard from Commander Bales again. Command of the squadron went to the executive officer, Lieutenant Commander M. S. Ragan. Ten days after the loss of Commander Bales and his crew, Lieutenant A.L. Althans failed to return from a routine search of Formosa in Bureau Number 59414.

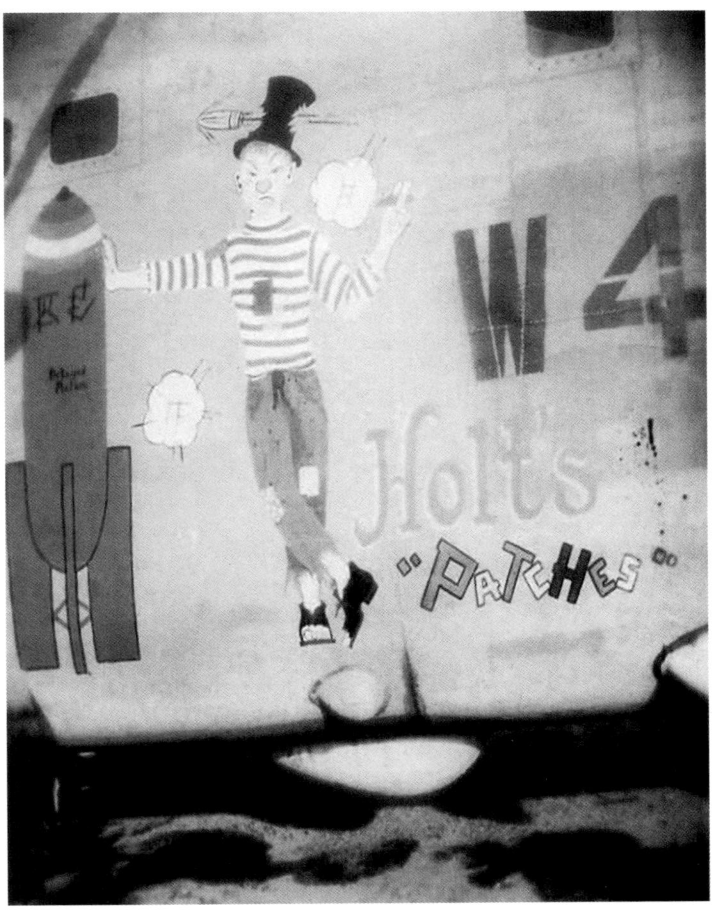

Pictured here is VPB-119's *Holt's Patches* (Bureau Number 59413) was named after a squadron patrol plane commander. (Courtesy: Author's Collection)

Striking Back

The latter part of April through May 1945 marked increased strikes on land targets, including blockhouses, barracks, vehicles, and radio stations. Japanese shipping was now reduced to coastal vessels, as the Empire's merchant fleet was all but destroyed, primarily through American submarines. By this time restrictions against attacking land targets by Navy patrol squadrons (those targets fell

Her engines running, W415 (Bureau Number 59415) of VPB-119 prepares for another patrol from Clark Field. W415 and its crew were lost while conducting a typhoon reconnaissance mission on 1 October 1945. (Courtesy: Curt Brownlow)

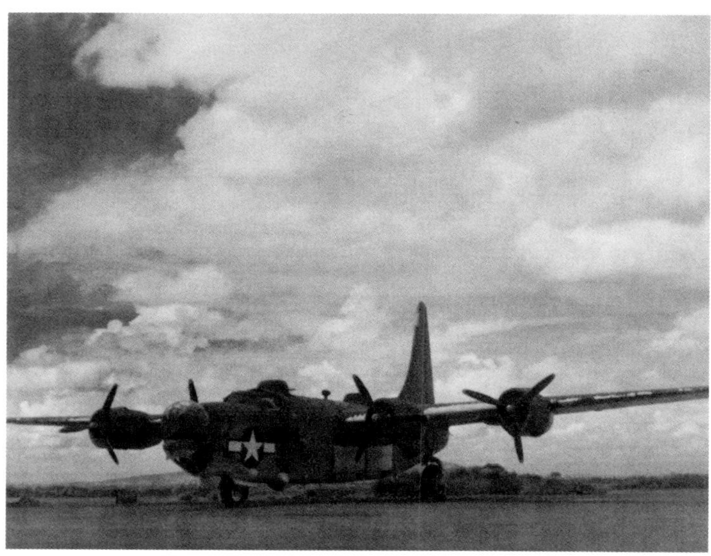

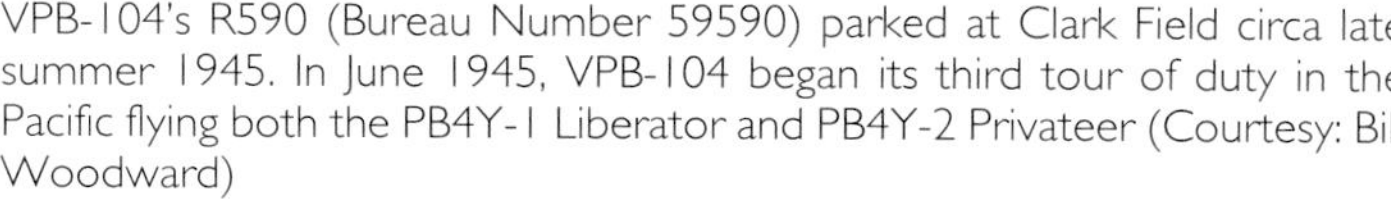

VPB-104's R590 (Bureau Number 59590) parked at Clark Field circa late summer 1945. In June 1945, VPB-104 began its third tour of duty in the Pacific flying both the PB4Y-1 Liberator and PB4Y-2 Privateer (Courtesy: Bill Woodward)

Landing gear down, R551 (Bureau Number 59551) of VPB-104 preparing to land at Clark Field in the summer of 1945 (Courtesy: Bill Woodward)

under the Army Air Force) were lifted. The increased focus on land targets resulted in a continued decline in the number and tonnage of ships sunk or damaged by VPB-119, with 53 vessels engaged totaling less than 10,000 tons. The reason behind such a drastic reduction in total tonnage was due to the combined effort of Army aircraft, submarines, and Navy patrol squadrons, which by the spring of 1945 had reduced Japanese shipping traffic to a trickle. Due to the decline in enemy shipping, Philippine-based PB4Y squadrons began hitting enemy ground installations in Indochina, Korea, and China.[42]

Strikes by VPB-119 Privateers continued unabated, as patrol plane commanders continued to fly their aircraft at extremely low altitudes and subjected the enemy, as well as themselves, to punishing blows. One example on how low the four-engined bombers were being flown during bombing and strafing attacks occurred on 3 April 1945, when Lieutenant (jg) Frank Murphy attacked two merchant ships off Myako Jima. In his first bombing run, one direct hit was obtained with a 250-pound bomb that literally blew the ship into bits. His gunners then began strafing the second ship, but as Murphy passed over the target at an altitude of 300 feet, it exploded with such terrific force that pieces of the debris pierced the plane's aluminum skin. Although the plane had received countless dents and holes from the exploding ship, the Privateer brought Lieutenant (jg) Murphy and his crew safely back to Clark Field.

Lieutenant J.W. Holt, one of VPB-119's best patrol plane commanders, ran into trouble on 7 April when his crew spotted a me-

An unidentified VPB-104 Privateer at Clark Field during the closing days of World War II. (Courtesy: Bill Thys)

A sunken Japanese merchant ship photographed by a patrolling VPB-104 Privateer. (Courtesy: Bill Woodward)

dium sized merchant ship at anchor in a cove at Myako Jima. After beginning a masthead run he discovered that the ship was a beached derelict. However, intense 12.7 and 20-millimeter anti-aircraft fire opened from all sides, and he withdrew towards Myako Jima airfield, where five Oscar fighters were spotted on the field. Strafing from the Privateer destroyed two of the aircraft, while the remaining three were damaged. However, during the run on the Japanese fighters, Aviation Ordnance Mate Second Class (AOM2c) Henry Babe received a slight wound to the arm when the Privateer took numerous hits from enemy anti-aircraft fire, which severed the rudder control cables, shot out one engine, and damaged the number two fuel cell. The crew, by using safety wire and solder, repaired the rudder control cables, which kept the rudder from fluttering. Holt had the bomb bay fuel tanks jettisoned, and the plane returned safely to base. Holt's tenacity and the crew's ability to perform under such conditions saved them on this trip, but on a future patrol they would not return.

On 15 April a pair of VPB-119 Privateers piloted by Lieutenant Willard P. Comstock and Lieutenant (jg) John H. Fette ventured to Amoy on an anti-shipping sweep. Lieutenant Comstock flew in alone and, upon entering the harbor, found a medium sized cargo ship with a displacement between 1,000 to 2,300-tons. On his first run he scored a direct hit on the ship's starboard side and the vessel began to burn. Coming back around, he pickled off another 250-pound bomb for another direct hit on the vessel's deck. The ship blew up, leaving a thick cloud of black smoke drifting in the sky. A few minutes later Lieutenant (jg) Fette arrived on the scene, and both Privateers then went after three power barges filled with enemy troops. Strafing by both planes sank the barges, killing many of the occupants.

Lieutenant (jg) Vogelsang's War

Lieutenant (jg) W.G. Vogelsang began a series of strikes against shipping and land targets in and around China that would make him and his crew experts in neutralizing enemy troops and destroying all means of transporting them. On 28 April, during attack near Hong Kong, his gunners strafed a small wooden ship and an adjacent barracks area. Proceeding towards present-day Shaoguan, strafing destroyed a pair of riverboats and four similar vessels on the Xi Jiang River. Vogelsang's gunners then destroyed a locomotive and six cars, a railroad dockyard, and an unidentified ship mounting a large crane. Going farther into China, a large locomotive with eight passenger cars was blown to bits by three direct bomb hits near Kowloon. The patrol plane commander's final attack of the day was against a Japanese patrol of about 50 men, which was decimated by Vogelsang's aerial gunners as the PB4Y-2 flew past the enemy troop concentration at an altitude of less than 200 feet.

Lieutenant Vogelsang's personal war against Japanese troops continued on 1 May when he flew his Privateer to Hainan Island. On this mission, strafing by his gunners caused two trucks loaded with gasoline to explode. Three more trucks carrying troops were then set on fire, and many of the troops onboard the vehicles were killed. Vogelsang then pickled off three 100-pound bombs in a barracks area, causing numerous small fires, and then a locomotive and eight flat cars were riddled with 50-caliber fire. Lieutenant Vogelsang's gunners continued delivering a deadly hail of .50-caliber machine gun fire by starting fires in a building and barracks area.

The Privateer's crew then set their sights on targets at Fat Law Airfield, where the control tower was strafed, along with administration buildings and a barracks. The next target was a large railroad center, where strafing destroyed a large locomotive and six empty ore cars. Fifteen runs were made on three more locomotives, and they, along with nearby installations, were left in flames. The final target for the day was a large mining operation, where Vogelsang's men expended a thousand rounds of ammunition and left fires burning in buildings near the mine entrance.

A week later, on 7 May 1945, Vogelsang and his aircrew attacked land and shipping targets in the Swatow area. A string of five 100-pound bombs placed lengthwise across a small cargo ship sent it to the bottom. A subchaser was then sighted tied to a large

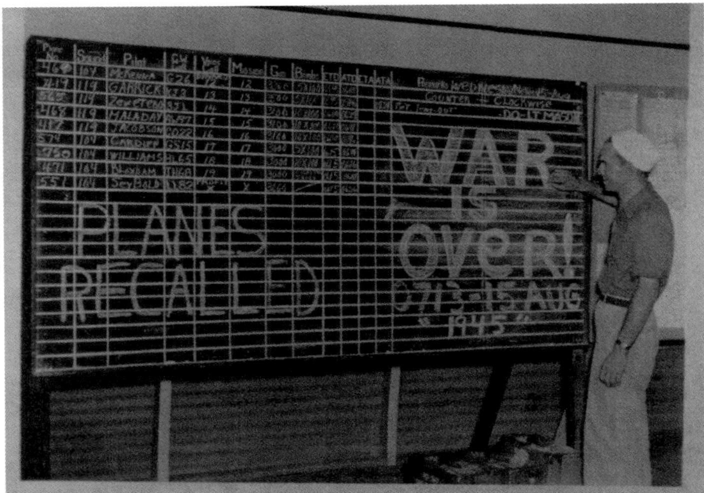

The operations board at Clark Field tells the story. World War II combat operations for Philippine-based Privateer squadrons ended on 15 August 1945. (Courtesy: Bill Woodward)

barge, and three 250-pound bombs were dropped; two of which were direct hits, and the subchaser sank, while the third bomb heavily damaged the barge. While Lieutenant Vogelsang was busy bombing his primary target, the Privateer's gunners damaged two smaller subchasers by expending 2,500 rounds of .50-caliber machine gun fire.

The Privateer's gunners then turned their attention to shore facilities as Lieutenant (jg) Vogelsang began a series of strafing runs. At a waterfront area, a power plant and a water tower were put out of commission. A gun emplacement was the next target; it was strafed with uncertain results, although it ceased firing. The final target was a large artillery encampment, including a considerable number of field pieces. All through this attack, his plane received only minor damage in the bomb bay, tail, port wing, and starboard waist turret.

Three days later, on 10 May Lieutenant Vogelsang inflicted a great deal of damage on Japanese forces located in the Canton Area. A bombing and strafing attack left a riverboat burning and beached, a direct bomb hit blew up a locomotive, and strafing damaged 16 railroad cars. Three riverboats were then thoroughly strafed, and two were left burning. All through these attacks the PB4Y-2 encountered moderate, medium, and accurate enemy fire that resulted in Seaman First Class (S1c) R.W. Wilson receiving a minor wound when a 7.7-millimeter round hit the Privateer's tail turret. Lieutenant Vogelsang then went after another locomotive and seven cars; a direct hit from a 250-pound bomb knocked the locomotive off the tracks. The Privateer's pilot then sighted a series of trucks fitted to operate on railroad tracks, and 14 of them were set on fire. The dock area on the Canton River was then strafed; small fires were started in the warehouse area, and the wooden roof of a large cement storage tank was set on fire. As the Privateer departed the area three unidentified planes took off from Whampoa Airfield, but being low on ammunition, Vogelsang took cover in the overcast and evaded the pursuing Japanese fighters.

Crew 27 of VPB-104 atop Bureau Number 59551 celebrates the end of the war upon landing at Clark Field after being recalled from a mission. From left to right beginning in the cockpit are: Dewey McDonald, William Seybold, Glen Wilcox, Frank Driscoll, Billy Woodward, Byron Gaudry, Joseph Hahn, Paul Murr, unknown weather observer, and Wilfred Villa. (Courtesy: Bill Woodward)

Losses Mount

May 1945 brought additional losses to VPB-119, when two Privateers and their crews went missing in action. Bureau Number 59559, piloted by Lieutenant Holt, went on a search to Hainan Island, in the Gulf of Tonkin, on 1 May and was lost. On the 19th Lieutenant (jg) Vogelsang went on a similar mission to Hainan Island in Bureau Number 59422 and did not return. One man not onboard that last patrol was Seaman First Class R.W. Wilson, who was still recuperating from his wound received on the tenth. The squadron lost another two crews in June beginning on the 17th, when Lieutenant Frank Murphy took off on a routine search patrol of Luichow Peninsula in plane Bureau Number 59427. While on patrol, several enemy trucks were observed traveling along a road and were strafed. As Murphy began another strafing run, small arms fire smashed the cockpit window and temporarily blinded him. The pilot was unable to pull up in time and the plane crashed. The following day special search planes from the squadron sighted the wreckage of the plane on Luichow and established that Murphy, with four enlisted members of the crew, had survived the crash, and rescue efforts began. While flying cover for the rescue on 24 June, Lieutenant W.P. Comstock, in Privateer Bureau Number 59553, crashed and exploded on impact, killing the entire crew. After a failed rescue attempt in which a PBY5A Catalina was forced to ditch and its crew joined Murphy and his crew, the men were finally picked up by another PBY and returned to Clark Field on 30 June.

Finales from Clark Field (July-August 1945)

Although VPB-119 suffered a considerable amount of casualties during May and June, it did not impede the tenacity of combat aircrews, as 75 ships were either sunk or damaged along the coast of China. Daily searches and offensive reconnaissance missions by VPB-119 continued, with strikes against Japanese shipping, land targets, and troop concentrations along the southern Chinese coast and Indochina. During the last full month of the Pacific War, the squadron sank or damaged 59 vessels with a combined displacement of 2,300 tons, while hundreds of enemy troops were killed or wounded.

On 6 July Lieutenant Commander H.D. Allen spotted a converted patrol craft anchored close to shore near Hong Kong. The patrol craft commenced firing immediately as Allen's Privateer approached for a bombing and strafing attack. The patrol craft's crew kept up a steady stream of anti-aircraft fire from guns forward and aft on the ship, but they failed to man a three-inch gun located amidships, which could have caused a considerable amount of trouble for the patrol bomber. On his first run Allen dropped two bombs that did no visible damage, and the ship got underway and began heading for the open sea. On his second run three bombs straddled the ship, and it stopped dead in the water. Two bombs on the third run caused the ship to settle by the bow, but a direct hit by a single bomb dropped on the fourth run blew off the stern, and the ship sank stern first. Throughout the entire attack, Aviation Machinist Mate Third Class (AMM3c) R.G. Friel's port waist gunner

After the cessation of hostilities, PB4Y-2 squadrons were given a variety of missions. Here supplies are being parachuted from a VPB-119 Privateer to a prisoner of war camp somewhere in China. (Courtesy: U.S. Naval Historical Center)

guns were jammed, but determined to get his share of the enemy, he used his .38 revolver on the four strafing runs. He expended nine rounds and claimed slight damage to the ship and enemy personnel before the bombs sank it.

On 12 July, first dividends of a new arrangement between ComNavGroup China Coastwatchers and Fleet Air Wing Seventeen search planes resulted in a substantial number of casualties among Japanese troops in China. Lieutenant (jg) A. L. Lindsell was given a target by voice radio from a naval coast watcher in the Amoy area. Led to the target area by means of markers put out by friendly Chinese, he came upon a formation of enemy troops spread along three miles of a mountain trail and estimated to be approximately 3,000 in strength. Five strafing runs were made, which inflicted substantial casualties among the enemy personnel and many of their horses. Retiring for about one half hour to give the Japanese time to reform its ranks, Lieutenant (jg) Lindsel made another attack from over the top of a mountain, again catching the enemy in formation, which resulted in additional casualties among their ranks. The following day the coastwatcher reported to another search plane that among the injured was a Japanese General who was shot in both legs and had his horse killed from under him.

Formosa started getting the squadron's attention as a profitable area for shipping and land targets during July, with Lieutenant (jg) H.W. Evans wrecking havoc on shipping on the 27th. Coming in at minimum altitude, Evans dropped five napalm incendiary cluster bombs on six wooden coastal ships lined up on the beach at Ryukyu Island. Four of the vessels were enveloped in flames that spread to the remaining two ships. As this attack was completed, a Mitsubishi Ki-21 Sally medium bomber appeared heading in the opposite direction, and Evans pointed his Privateer towards the fleeing Japanese bomber.

The Sally tried to draw the Privateer over anti-aircraft positions, but the Privateer's pilot elected to avoid them, and by the time he was clear of the anti-aircraft positions the Sally had disappeared. Later in the day two small wooden vessels were sighted a half mile outside of Kiirun harbor. Strafing attacks left one of the vessels in flames and the other dead in the water. Fifteen minutes later a large camouflaged 300-ton cargo ship was sighted underway. Having expended his remaining bombs, Evans made 10 strafing runs, using 2,700 rounds and setting the ship on fire, destroying it. Shortly thereafter, Evans made a strafing run over Suo Harbor, inflicting minor damage on six camouflaged cargo ships and two tugs. The final attack of the day was made on three luggers underway in the Yellow Sea. Three strafing runs left two of them in flames and the third dead in the water.

During the first two weeks of August 1945, squadron aircraft engaged and either sunk or damaged 23 vessels and damaged four Japanese aircraft in the air. Combat operations for VPB-119 concluded on 14 August when Lieutenant (jg) S.S. Aichele made the squadron's last kill by sinking a 300-ton cargo vessel. The men of VPB-119 chalked up one of the most impressive combat records for a Navy land-based patrol squadron of World War II. From March to August 1945 it sank 114 ships, damaged 124, shot down eight Japanese aircraft, damaged three in the air, and damaged or destroyed five aircraft on the ground. Through June 1947 VPB-119, later redesignated as VP-HL-9 in November 1946 and VP-ML-7 in June 1947, performed weather reconnaissance and air-sea search from bases at Puerto Princessa, Samar, and Sangley Point, Philippines. In July 1947 the squadron returned to the United States and transitioned to the P2V-2 Neptune patrol bomber.[43]

Privateers for VPB-104

At Clark Field, the battle-worn PB4Y-1 Liberators of VPB-104 began to be replaced by late May 1945 and, by the end of hostilities, the squadron would be fully outfitted with the aircraft. In June the squadron officially began a third tour of duty, with fresh crews

The crash scene of PB4Y-2 Bureau Number 59750 belonging to VP-119 soon after the accident that took place on 30 July 1946. Flying out of NAS Sangley Point, Philippines on a search mission for a lost Army Air Force C-47 and a Navy PBM Mariner the Privateer crashed on Mindoro Island killing the entire crew. (Courtesy: U.S. Army)

coming in to replace the battled-tested veterans. By the end of August VPB-104 had 12 PB4Y-2s and a lone PB4Y-1 on hand, as the squadron conducted supply runs, weather reconnaissance flights, and search missions for lost aircraft before returning to the United States in October 1945.

In April 1946 the squadron was relocated to Edenton, North Carolina, for ASW training, where it was redesignated as VP-104 and then VP-HL-4. During this period crews were provided training on the SWOD ASM-N-2A *Bat* air-to-surface guided missile that earned them the squadron nickname the *Batmen*. In May 1946 VP-HL-4 transferred to Atlantic City, New Jersey. In 1948 the squadron was redesignated as VP-24, and the squadron's primary mission changed to aerial mining, but it continued to conduct ASW, reconnaissance, and antishipping operations. VP-24 operated the Privateer until 1954, when it transitioned to the P2V Neptune. It was the last active duty Atlantic Squadron to fly the Privateer.

7

Privateer Operations in World War II: Palawan and Mindoro, Philippines (April-August 1945)

While VPB-119 conducted missions from Clark Field, the Navy established another base of operations for PB4Ys in the Philippines at Puerto Princessa, Palawan. Palawan is situated in the Southern Philippines between Borneo and Mindoro, and is some two hundred miles in length and up to 30 miles wide. American forces, primarily composed of the U.S. Army's 186th Regimental Combat Team, invaded Palawan on 28 February 1945, and the island was secured five days later, but mopping up remnants of the Japanese garrison continued until April.

The *Reluctant Raiders* of VPB-109 arrived at Puerto Princessa in late April 1945 under the leadership of Commander George L. Hicks (former Executive Officer of VB-109), and as discussed earlier the squadron was outfitted with the SWOD *Mk-9 Bat*. On April 23 Commander Hicks and Lieutenant Kennedy (both veterans of the squadron's first tour of duty) conducted the squadron's first *Bat* strike against Japanese shipping anchored in Balikpapan Harbor, on the southeast coast of Borneo. Fifteen miles from the harbor, a large transport, a 4,000-ton freighter, and five smaller merchant vessels in the 300 to 850-ton range were sighted. From six miles out and at 10,000 feet, both pilots launched a *Bat*. Both weapons traveled erratically and fell short of their intended targets. Due to the weight of the weapon system, the Privateers could not carry a conventional bomb load. Not wishing to try strafing attacks on the shipping, the Privateers headed back to Palawan.[44]

After the failed *Bat* attack, VPB-109 settled in for daily strikes against shipping and radio/radar installations throughout the Borneo and Malay coasts. After only a week at Palawan, it was obvious that no worthwhile shipping was located in the routine search areas to warrant *Bat* attacks. Having been sunk or driven into areas beyond the range of squadron aircraft, the only possible targets for

Palawan Island in the Philippines (pictured here) was the base of operations for VPB-106 and 109 Privateers, as well as VPB-111 Liberators beginning in April 1945. (Author's Collection)

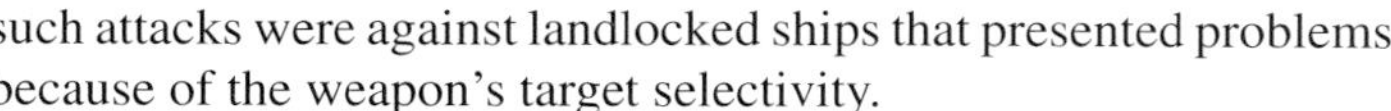

A coastal vessel burning off the Malay Coast after being set afire by strafing from a VPB-109 Privateer. Such vessels of wooden construction burned easily from .50-caliber incendiary rounds. (Courtesy: NARA)

VPB-109's Lieutenant (jg) Serbin's bow turret gunner shoots down a Japanese *Jake* floatplane on 2 May 1945 off Indo-China. The squadron was based at Palawan Island in the Philippines from April to May 1945. (Courtesy: NARA)

such attacks were against landlocked ships that presented problems because of the weapon's target selectivity.

Big Score for Lieutenant Vadnais

It soon became apparent to Commander Hicks and his men that the only shipping left were small, mostly wooden hulled coastal vessels (70 to 100 tons) that hugged the Malay and Borneo coasts. Borneo, which had supplied Japan's military with 40 percent of its oil, was rapidly being cut off by allied air and naval forces and, on 1 May, the invasion of Borneo began with landings by the Australian 7th and 9th Infantry Divisions at Tarakan Island on the northeastern coast.[45]

Lieutenant Robert Vadnais possibly conducted one of the most successful PB4Y-2 missions in the war when he extended his search along the western coast of Borneo on 3 May 1945. Following a marked ship channel from Pontianak Bay and leading up the Kapoeas-Kegil River, Vadnais sighted two wooden coastal vessels in a stream at anchor a half mile away on his starboard and a mile below the town. He immediately initiated a run on the ships at 50 feet altitude and dropped one AN-47-A2 depth bomb. The bomb missed but, after completing two more runs on the ships, one of them burned to the waterline, while strafing by the Privateer's gunners decimated personnel abandoning the ships. Circling to starboard upon completion of the run, and passing over a shipyard and lumberyard on the north bank of the river, he sighted more shipping upstream.

The Privateer headed upstream 20 feet off the water, strafing a two-masted 60-foot schooner and setting it ablaze. A few moments

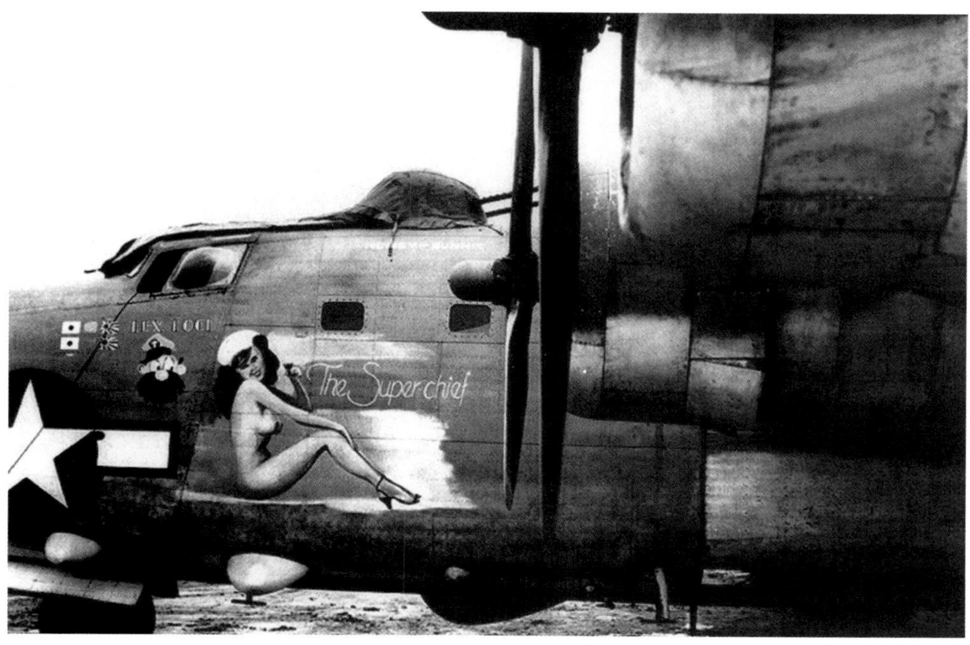

VPB-106's *Superchief* photographed on Palawan. Unfortunately, the Bureau Number remains a mystery at the time of this book's publication. (Author's Collection)

VPB-106's *Lucky-Leven* (Bureau Number 59397) later went on to serve with HEDRON 14 in the United States. It was destroyed in a crash near Miramar, California on 1 August 1946. (Author's Collection)

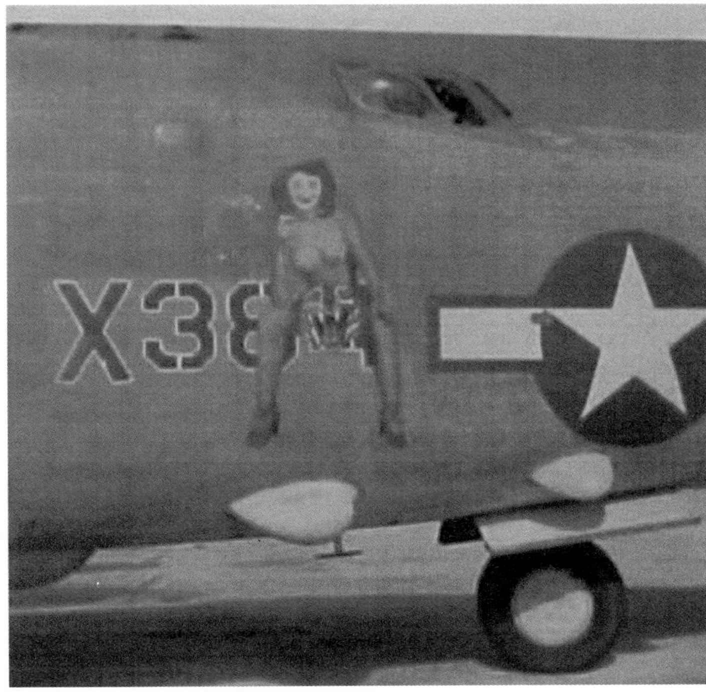

VPB-106's Bureau Number 59384 sported a rather unusual piece of nose art of a woman and a tiger's head. (Author's Collection)

later several shipyards were observed, along with a considerable amount of small shipping situated around an intersection of the river and a canal. Two coastal vessels at anchor near the intersection were attacked and left afire from heavy strafing. Continuing upstream, a shipyard just west of the intersection and containing four ways, each with a coastal vessel, was set afire by bombing and strafing and destroyed. Farther upstream, a large shipyard was heavily and repeatedly strafed during five runs, and an ensuing fire consumed a quarter of the yard before the Privateer left the area.

Lieutenant Vadnais then returned to the river and canal intersection to attack three coastal vessels anchored in the stream. During five strafing runs his gunners started fires that gutted and subsequently sank the vessels. Shortage of fuel and ammunition forced Lieutenant Vadnais to break off the attack, despite leaving an estimated 25 coastal vessels and two more shipyards untouched.[46]

VPB-109 Departs

There was real danger in flying a four-engined bomber on low altitude strikes, as William B. Edwards, an Aviation Machinist Mate, recalled when a fellow crewman and friend was killed during an anti-shipping strike on 5 May 1945. Edwards was operating the aft deck turret of Privateer Bureau Number 59529, piloted by Lieutenant Howard M. Turner, Jr., when a small ship was encountered at Parepare, in the Celebes, and the pilot began a bombing and strafing run:

"Joe Kasperlik was in the forward deck turret, and I didn't see anyone firing at us, nor did I see Joe get hit, but I noticed that my turret top was all covered with specks of blood. I turned my turret around and, seeing what had happened, called the pilot, 'Joe's been hit, someone get him out!'"

Bill Coffee went to get Kasperlik, while Lieutenant Turner, selecting to abort the bomb run, headed for Palawan, 950 miles away. The death of Joe Kasperlik was not the only loss suffered that day by VPB-109. Lieutenant Commander John F. Bundy, while heading for a strike against shipping at Pontianak, Borneo, was critically wounded by anti-aircraft fire over Papar. A day later, VPB-109 was transferred to the Central Pacific upon the arrival of the *Wolverators* of VPB-106.[47]

VPB-106 and VPB-111 continued to conduct strikes against the Japanese in the Far East by hitting shipping, transportation, and ground installations with patrols that extended 850 to 1000 miles covering Celebes, Borneo, Malaysia, and Indochina. However, reconnaissance proved to make up the majority of missions due to the upcoming invasion of Borneo scheduled for June and July 1945. During May VPB-106 claimed nearly 11,000 tons of shipping sunk or damaged; two enemy planes destroyed in the air, and two on the ground. Most of the ships attacked were small coastal vessels in the 75 to 250 ton range, but occasionally larger merchant shipping was encountered and dealt with by VPB-106 aircrews. Lieutenant (jg) W.B. Hoblin and his crew found an estimated 3,000-ton freighter while patrolling off Makassar, in the Western Celebes, and dropped a pair of 250-pound bombs; they left the vessel ablaze and listing 35 degrees. A careful search the following day revealed no evidence of the ship, and it was presumed sunk.

Lieutenant Commander Goodloe and his crew from VPB-106 pose next to their PB4Y-2. He and his crew were lost in action on 14 June 1945. One member of the crew on the far right has been identified as N.S. Smith. (Courtesy of Kathleen M. Smith)

Looking over Singapore

In late May VPB-106 and 111 were tagged with the mission of flying photographic reconnaissance missions to Singapore. Lieutenant Commander Goodloe flew the first such mission on the 23rd, flying a complete clockwise circle over Singapore and the surrounding area at 10,000 feet, taking photographs of shipping and installations without encountering any hostile fire. On retirement Goodloe's gunners worked over twin-engined aircraft parked on the runway and under trees at Changhi Point Airfield, leaving at least one Japanese aircraft destroyed. A week later, on the 30th, Patrol Plane Commander Lieutenant (jg) V.J. Smith scored the squadron's only two aerial kills. Ferreting the Malay coast, Smith and his crew spotted a Japanese cruiser and four merchant ships anchored at the mouth of the Pakang River; six miles south lay five picket boats at anchor in a semi-circle.

As Smith headed the PB4Y-2 towards the ships, an Aichi Jake floatplane fighter was spotted at a distance of four miles and closing towards the patrol bomber. The Japanese fighter open fire when the distance closed to within 1,000 feet, passing to starboard before making a 180-degree turn in an attempt to get on the Privateer's tail. Smith immediately followed the fighter's turn by making a 360-degree turn inside and came out on the Jake's tail and into range of the Privateer's gunners, and the gunners opened fire. Within a few seconds Smith closed the distance to within 50 feet and his

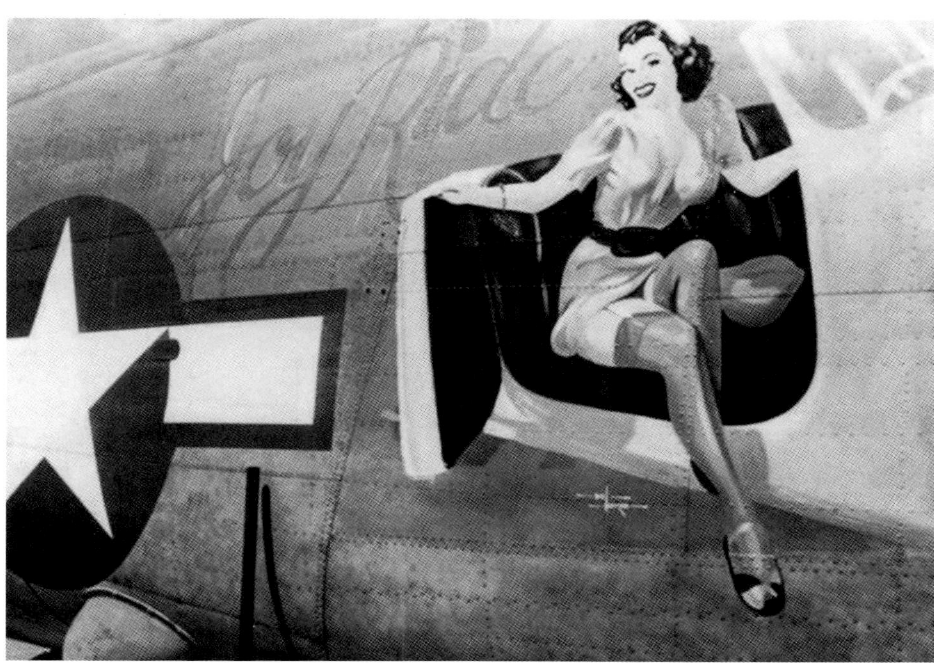

The art for VPB-106's *Joy Ride* (Bureau Number 59370) was applied on Tinian where the squadron was based until May 1945 and it went on to serve in the Philippines. (Courtesy: Earl Mann)

A view of Lieutenant "Pappy" Mears' Privateer Bureau Number 59563 on 1 June 1945 while on a joint reconnaissance mission to Singapore with a PB4Y-1 Liberator commanded by VPB-111's Lieutenant (jg) Roscoe Fred Heyler. (Courtesy: NARA)

gunners poured more than 800 rounds at the enemy aircraft, which crashed, sending up a huge volume of smoke and flame. The chase with the enemy fighter brought the Privateer to within a mile of the Japanese cruiser, which opened fire, and bursts of heavy anti-aircraft fire bracketed the aircraft but caused no damage. Smith changed course 150-degrees and almost immediately encountered a Nakajima Oscar fighter on a parallel course. The fighter made a flat 90-degree turn in an attempt to make a run on the Privateer's bow. Smith at first made the decision to turn away from the approaching fighter, but changed his mind and turned towards the advancing Oscar, which seemed to have confused the Japanese pilot, as the fighter flew past the Privateer without firing a shot. Smith's two top turret and port waist gunners opened fire as the Oscar crossed over the bow, scoring a number of hits in the engine area that knocked the cowling off. The starboard blister joined in and scored hits on the Oscar's tail section. The fighter's port wing dropped, and the fighter made a steep gliding turn to port before plunging vertically into the sea.

Through the remainder of May and into June 1945, VPB-106 conducted approximately 12 reconnaissance missions over the Singapore area, with most aircraft and their crews returning safely to Palawan. The first day of June brought a special coordinated snooper mission to Singapore involving 106 and 111. A VPB-111 Liberator piloted by Lieutenant (jg) Fred Heyler, carrying an Army photographic specialist, and a VPB-106 *Wolverator* Privateer piloted by Lieutenant Commander "Pappy" Mears arrived at the Malay coast after sunrise in a loose formation, with Commander Mears leading the way. Near Hong Kong, they encountered heavy anti-aircraft fire from shore batteries and ships, but it was ineffective, and the planes proceeded onward. Soon afterward they saw they had company—two Nakajima Oscar fighters were trailing them, but did not press in for an attack. Soon, another pair in front of the American patrol bombers joined the other two fighters.

As the two patrol planes neared Singapore a fighter peeled off and went for Mears and scored hits with 20-millimeter cannon fire on the Privateer's number three engine. The Oscar broke away, but came under fire from Heyler's gunners, and it went into the water. Mears' men tried to ward off the attack but were unsuccessful. The Privateer's engine caught fire, and the plane began to lose altitude. The Oscars came back and went after the damaged bomber, only to be beaten back by Mears' and Heyler's combined firepower.

Mears went on the radio and calmly told Heyler, "I'm afraid I'm going to have to ditch." The Liberator's pilot reduced speed to

Smoke streams from a damaged engine on Lieutenant "Pappy" Mears Privateer after being mortally damaged by Japanese fighters with VPB-111 on 1 June 1945. (Courtesy: Steve Hawley)

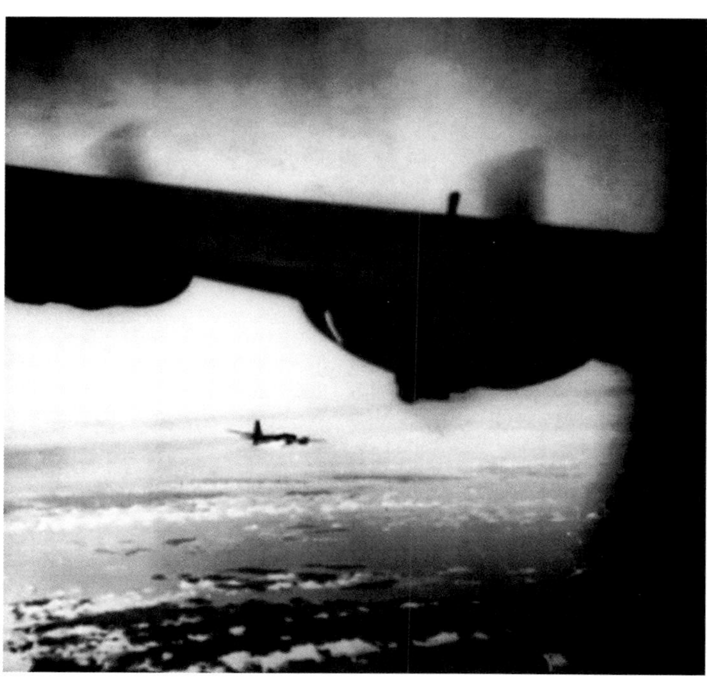

A photograph taken from the waist position of Lieutenant (jg) Heyler's PB4Y-1 Liberator shows flames streaming from Lieutenant Mears' Privateer moments before plummeting into the water off Malaya and killing the entire crew. (Courtesy: NARA)

stay with the crippled PB4Y-2 as Mears prepared for ditching. A few minutes later the flames appeared to go out, and Mears indicated he felt better about the situation. In fact, the fire was eating away the interior portion of the wing. The fire blossomed again, and he told his wingman, "I'm sorry, but I am going to ditch. Thank you for the way you stuck with me." It was his last transmission, as the number four engine went out 1,000 feet above the water. The Privateer banked sharply, and the starboard wing broke off between the engines 300 feet from the water; it flipped on its back and went into the water nose first, killing all on board.[48]

Seeing the Privateer go down, the Japanese fighter pilots tore into the lone Liberator and, for the next 20 minutes, the men aboard the aircraft counted 28 separate attacks. Heyler and his men fought bravely, turning back every attack without damage to the PB4Y-1. One Oscar was hit, then a second. One came within 50 feet and was hit hard by the bow, top, and starboard waist guns. The combined firepower blew pieces of the fighter away, smoke belched from the engine, and it was not seen again. Heyler and his crew fought on, with the Liberator dodging in and out of cloud cover to break free from the attackers. In all, 8 to 13 enemy fighters pursued the bomber before most became discouraged, ran out of ammunition, or ran low on fuel. After 14 hours in the air and after a running battle that lasted over an hour from altitudes ranging from 11,000 to 1,000 feet, the Liberator landed at Palawan without any damage to the plane and no injuries to the crew. Two weeks later, VPB-106 lost another plane and crew when Lieutenant Commander Green C. Goodloe and crew, the first in the squadron to reconnoiter Singapore, failed to return from a patrol on the 14th in Bureau Number 59412.

Crew M-28 photographed while serving with VPB-197 at Camp Kearney, California, before being assigned to VPB-117 in the Philippines. Front row from left to right: Aviation Machinist Mate 3rd Class (AMM3c) Edmund Sienkielewski, Seaman 1st Class (S1c) Ralph Allison, Aviation Ordnanceman 3rd Class (AOM3c) Lawrence Norton, Aviation Radioman 3rd Class (ARM3c) LeRoy Anderson, and Seaman 1st Class (S1c) Edwin Swanson. Back row from left to right: Seaman 1st Class (S1c) Paul Hartranft, Aviation Machinist Mate 1st Class (AMM1c) Max Trabert, Ensign W. Dale Whiteman, Lieutenant Orvis Fitts, Ensign Jack Braakman, Aviation Radioman 3rd Class (ARM3c) Billy E. Parrott, and Aviation Ordnanceman 3rd Class (AOM3c) Billy Hopson. (Courtesy: Orvis Fitts)

Crew M-28 of VPB-117 often flew this Privateer Bureau Number 59597 photographed at Mcguire Field, Mindoro, Philippine Islands. (Courtesy: Orvis Fitts)

Lieutenant Fitts and his crew in Bureau Number 59597 attacking a camouflaged ship in a channel at My Tho, MeKong River Delta, French Indo China on 7 July 1945. (Courtesy: Orvis Fitts)

The *Wolverators* and VPB-111 continued hunting for the small surface vessels that hugged the coastlines, with squadron planes claiming 55 vessels destroyed or damaged during June and July. Heavy rains in July briefly canceled operations from Palawan, and a detachment from 106 and 111 operated from Mindoro between the sixth and 19th; the squadron made only 17 strikes during the month. VPB-106 suffered their last combat loss when Privateer Bureau Number 59433, commanded by Lieutenant Joseph W. Swiencicki, failed to return from a patrol off mainland China on 30 July—it is presumed that he was shot down by enemy fighters.

Privateers to VPB-111

In May 1945 VPB-111 began receiving PB4Y-2s as replacements for their PB4Y-1 Liberators on Palawan, but the PB4Y-1 endured most squadron operations through the end of the war. One of the few combat patrols conducted by a VPB-111 Privateer was flown by Lieutenant Gordon K. Wilde. During an assigned search of the Celebes-Makassar area on 5 August 1945, Lieutenant Wilde and his crew participated in extracurricular activities by braving anti-aircraft fire from positions in Makassar. Inland from a dock area, he spotted three trucks and a motorcycle occupied by Japanese personnel about three miles on a major highway north of Makassar. Lieutenant Wilde immediately conducted a strafing attack that destroyed the vehicles and killed or wounded a dozen of their occupants. Meanwhile the motorcycle, with attached sidecar, ran off the road, climbed a ditch, and met head-on with a palm tree.

Swinging wide to the south of the city, Lieutenant Wilde came back into the harbor, avoiding the fire of at least three machine gun emplacements positioned along the embankment to the south of a commercial area. His gunners strafed a large lugger, damaging it slightly, and then saw ahead of his Privateer a large 110-foot tugboat tied up to a large wharf on which sat a three-story building. He leveled off at about 50 feet and dropped a pair of 100-pound general-purpose bombs, one of which went into the side of the ship and destroyed it, and the other skimmed over the ship and struck the building near the street level.

Continuing on patrol south of the Celebes, a large two-masted schooner was sighted. The sails were up, and the vessel was about 75 miles from land, so Lieutenant Wilde swung the Privateer around from 300 feet to look at the suspicious vessel. Probably seeing they were about to become the intended victims of the American patrol bomber, the vessel's occupants jumped overboard and climbed into a raft. A low pass was made over the vessel and attacked with incendiary cluster bombs, which missed, and with .50 caliber machine gun fire, which destroyed it.

VPB-106 remained in the Phillippines until October 1946, before returning to the U.S., where it was disestablished. VPB-111 returned to the United States between late October and November 1945, and continued as a PB4Y-2 patrol squadron for another five years. Between 1946 and 1950 the squadron went through three designations (VP-111 and VP-HL-11 in 1946, and finally VP-21 in 1948) while conducting ASW operations from bases at NAS New York, Atlantic City, and Patuxent River. In January 1949 VP-21 deployed to NAS Guantanamo Bay, Cuba, where one of its Privateers crashed, killing two crewmembers. In June 1950 the squadron began transitioning to the Martin P4M-1 Mercator.

Privateers on Mindoro

Privateers began to filter to the *Blue Raiders* of VPB-117 on Mindoro, Philippine Islands, in June 1945, where the squadron continued combat operations against the Japanese particularly in the Indochina area. One relief crew commanded by Lieutenant Orvis Fitts was one of the few in VPB-117 to fly combat missions in a PB4Y-2. On 7 August Lieutenant Fitts and his crew in Bureau Number 59597 hit shipping in the delta area of the Mekong River in French Indochina, and saw first-hand that the Japanese could still put up a fight:

"One of the crewmembers spotted a large river steamer that was moored against the north bank in one of the many delta river channels. It was well camouflaged with foliage. We were flying

A sailing junk suspected of being a Japanese picket vessel is strafed by Lieutenant Fitts and crew at Cape St. Jacques, French Indo China on 10 August 1945. (Courtesy: Orvis Fitts)

very low, but I had missed it. We turned back, and I gave the order to open fire. Several parallel runs back and forth were made so all gun turrets could bear on the target and fire. The ammunition (.50-caliber belts) had a tracer round, an armor piercing round, a standard round, and one I don't remember, in groups of four. When firing, it was easy to see the line of fire because of the tracer rounds. I did not want to drop bombs yet, as there could well be bigger targets in the delta area. The river steamer burst into flames, and heavy black smoke erupted skyward. It appeared there was a deck cargo of oil drums aboard. As we left the area, the river steamer was furiously burning, and I am certain it was destroyed.

We proceeded up the Mekong River delta, and not too far from the burning river steamer we spotted a ship in the river between an island and the town of My Tho. I maneuvered to make a low-level run from the ship's stern to the bow with the plane's bomb bay doors open. I ordered LeRoy (Aviation Radioman 3rd Class Leroy Anderson) in the forward top deck turret and Billy Hopson (Aviation Ordnanceman 3rd Class) in the bow turret to open fire when they were within range. I wanted to discourage any return fire. As we approached the stern, I pressed the bomb release button on the control wheel. Nothing happened—no bombs away. There was an electrical malfunction.

Just after we cleared the ship's bow there was a loud explosion, and I suddenly saw numerous holes appear in our bow area in front of me. Billy Hopson called on the intercom to say he was drenched in hydraulic fluid, that our hydraulic lines had been punctured, and there were holes all over the bow area, but he was okay and, for that, we were thankful. He also volunteered to go back to the open bomb bay, stand on the narrow catwalk between the port and starboard bomb bay compartments, and manually release the bombs in a second run on the ship. It was a courageous offer, but I vetoed it. First, I now realized we had been caught in a crossfire coming from the island and the waterfront of the town of My Tho. Second, another run would be suicidal. Third, it was too dangerous for Billy to stand on the narrow catwalk of the open bomb bay; any violent maneuver of the aircraft could throw him out.

While I did not think of it at the time, the war was in its final days, and the risk was simply not worth it. I have subsequently wondered if the ship was a deliberate decoy placed there to entice an attack and catch the attacking plane in a murderous crossfire. I do not remember any return fire from the ship, but LeRoy told me there was some return fire. I ordered an inspection to determine how much damage we had sustained. Our biggest problem was the loss of hydraulic fluid and pressure on landing. We jettisoned our bombs in the sea and set course for Maguire Field.

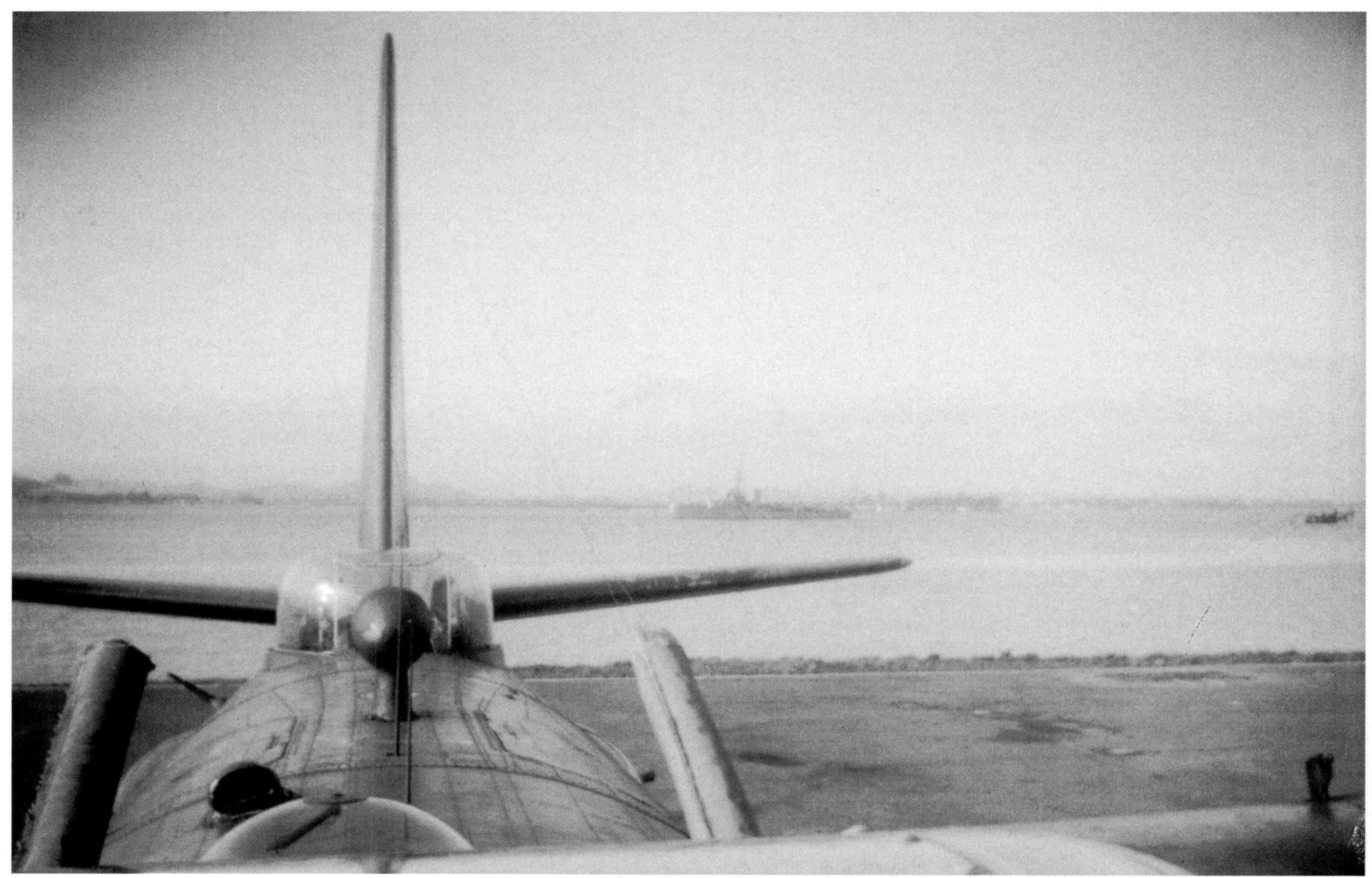

A PB4Y-2 Privateer sits on the tarmac at an unknown location in the Pacific circa 1945-46 with warships sailing in the distance. This photograph was shot just behind the forward top turret indicated by the covered machine gun barrels in the bottom center and left. (Author's Collection)

On approaching our home base I called and informed them of our situation. They told me emergency vehicles would be standing by. There were two hydraulic reservoirs for the brakes, one for each wheel. I knew I had pressure remaining in each one, but once I applied the brakes and released them there would be no remaining pressure. I tried to land as close to the near end of the runway as possible so I could let the plane roll to reduce speed before I applied the brakes. After I applied the brakes, I never fully released them until we were parked. After landing, we counted 15 holes in the bow. The loud explosion probably came from a 20-millimeter round striking the armor plate in the bow area directly in front of me. The armor plate was bowed in from the impact, and the nuts on the bolts holding the armor plate in place were gone. The bolts had been stripped, the nuts gone, and the armor plate could be moved back and forth. That piece of armor plate saved my life."[49]

Lieutenant Fitts' mission of 7 August 1945 was one of the few combat missions conducted by a PB4Y-2 Privateer assigned to VPB-117. Operations for the *Blue Raiders* of VPB-117 in the Philippines continued for another four days before the squadron was sent to Tinian. On 16 August it transferred to Tinian and provided weather reconnaissance flights. In September the squadron returned to the United States, where it was disestablished in December 1945.

8

Additional World War II Squadrons

PB4Y-2 combat squadrons of World War II provided an invaluable service in the defeat of Japan by providing a long-range platform to check enemy military movements, participating in aerial mine-laying operations, and conducting diversionary, harassing attacks against enemy bases, islands, and shipping. Between 1944 and 1945, Navy Liberators and Privateers flew 15,000 patrols and destroyed 504 of the 937 Japanese aircraft encountered in the air and on the ground, against a loss of only 18. Combat aircrews, operating under Fleet Air Wing One and Eighteen, are credited with destroying in the air 32 out of the 44 Japanese aircraft attributed to the PB4Y-2. In addition, FAW-1 Privateers served as the agent in the sinking or damaging of 353 Japanese ships with a combined weight of approximately 284, 000 tons.[50]

During the closing days of World War II PB4Y-2 squadrons served in the Aleutian Islands off Alaska, and a number of other units were in the process of transitioning to the PB4Y-2 when Japan surrendered, while a few more provided advanced flight training. Two squadrons, VPB-120 and 122, served in Alaska under the operational control of Fleet Air Wing Four (FAW-4) during the final days of the war with Japan. VPB-120 was originally commissioned as VP-12, a PBY-5A Catalina squadron, until October 1944, when it was redesignated as Patrol Bombing Squadron 120 and transitioned to the Privateer. On 19 July 1945 the squadron departed for Shemya Island, in the Aleutians, where it conducted photographic reconnaissance and anti-shipping missions to the Kurile Islands of Japan through September of that year. Afterward, it was deployed

In less than ideal flying conditions, VPB-122's Bureau Number 59775 prepares to taxi from a base in Alaska circa late 1945. According to Robert Feuilloy, an expert on the PB4Y-2 in French service, this particular aircraft later served with Flottilla 8F of the French Aéronavale in Vietnam. (Courtesy: Steve Hawley)

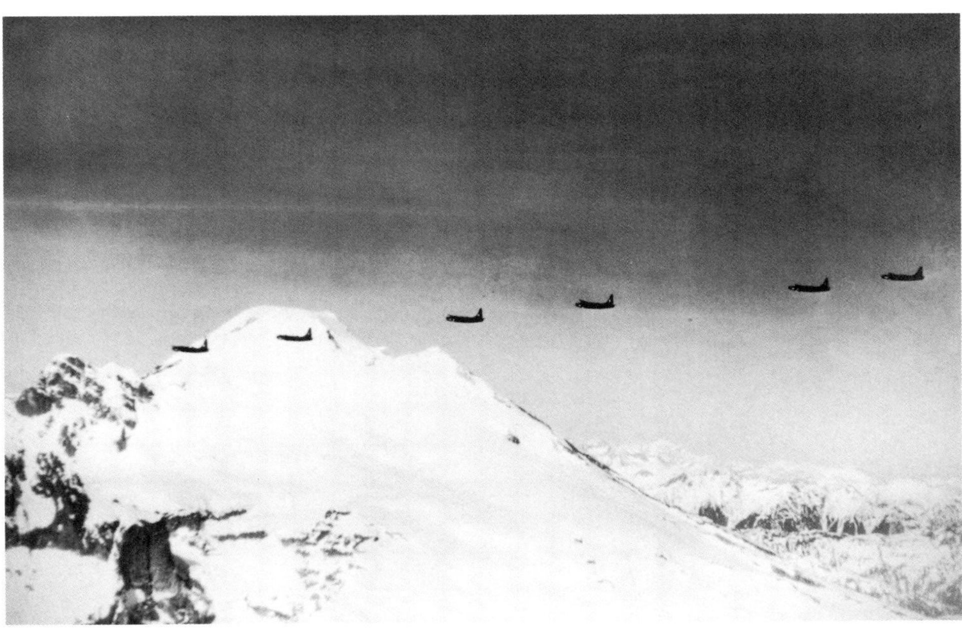

Two PB4Y-2 squadrons, VPB-120 and 122, served in the Alaskan Theater during the closing days of World War II. Here a formation VPB-122 Privateers cruise by snow-covered mountains of Alaska circa late 1945. (Courtesy: Eddie Harding, VPB-122 veteran)

to Attu and Kodiak until its disestablishment in March 1949, during which time it was redesignated as VP-HL-10 and finally VP-20.

VPB-122 became the second and last Privateer squadron to arrive at Shemya as the war with Japan ended. In August 1944 the squadron received its first PB4Y-2, but three months later six out of seven crews and every PB4Y-2 on hand was transferred to VPB-108. The squadron did not get back up to strength until March 1945, and even then, it had to train with the PB4Y-1 Liberator. The squadron received new Privateers in July 1945 and began advanced training at Whidbey Island, Washington. On 5 August VPB-122 began their movement to Shemya, with the last plane arriving on the very day the war ended. On 30 November 1945 one of the squadron's aircraft crashed, resulting in the largest single loss of life in the PB4Y-2's service history when Bureau Number 59777, on a flight to NAS Kodiak, Alaska, with a crew of eight and carrying 17 passengers went down, killing all aboard. Between 1946 and 1948, when the squadron was redesignated as VP-HL-12 and later VP-12, it was based at Kodiak, Alaska, where it conducted navigation training and ice patrols.

Veteran PB4Y-1 Liberator squadrons, upon ending tours of duty overseas in the Pacific or Great Britain, returned to the United States and were reorganized for training with the PB4Y-2, including VPB-101, VPB-103, 105, 107, and 115. VPB-101, a veteran Pacific Liberator squadron, upon completion of its second tour, reformed in May 1945 at NAAS Crows Landing and briefly trained with the

Shown here is Bureau Number 59777 of VPB-122 undergoing maintenance sometime in late 1945. This aircraft crashed during a transport flight on 30 November 1945, killing all aboard. (Courtesy: Steve Hawley)

Bureau Number 59646 of VPB-122 warming her engines up on a snow-covered tarmac at a base in Alaska circa 1945-46. (Courtesy: Steve Hawley)

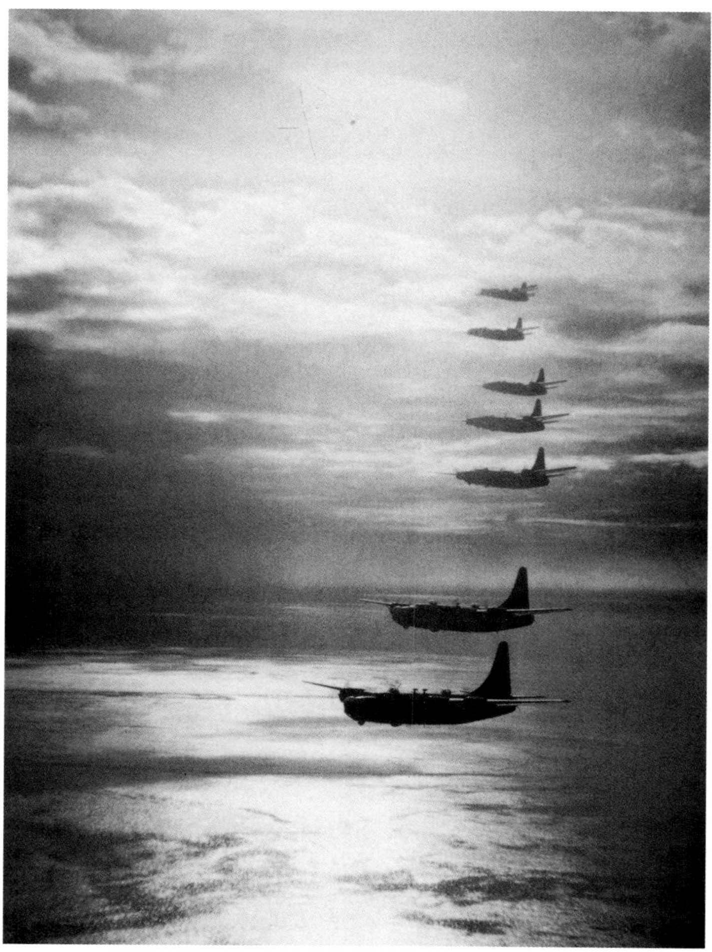

A flight of VPB-122 Privateers over the North Pacific circa 1945-46. (Courtesy: Eddie Harding, VPB-122 veteran)

PB4Y-2. The squadron reformed again at NAS Willow Grove, Pennsylvania, in July 1945, where it assigned the Navy version of the Boeing B-17 Flying Fortress, the PB-1W. Two veteran PB4Y-1 squadrons based at Dunkeswell, England, were VPB-103 and 105 which, upon returning to the United States in June 1945, began transitioning to the PB4Y-2. However, Japan's surrender hastened the disestablishment of both squadrons in September of that year. VPB-107 was another PB4Y-1 squadron, and during the war served in Brazil and later Upottery, England. In July 1945 the squadron reformed at Crows Landing as a PB4Y-2 squadron. Between November 1946 and January 1950 VB-107 Privateers flew out of Whidbey Island, Washington, and Kodiak, Alaska. Before being disestablished in January 1950 the squadron went through four different designations: VPB-107, VP-107, VP-HL-7, and finally VP-27.

Another veteran of World War II combat was VPB-115, which served in the South Pacific as a PB4Y-1 squadron from March to November 1944. The squadron reorganized, and upon transitioning to the PB4Y-2 at Crows Landing operated from Kaneohe between August 1945 and January 1950. In November 1946 it became one of only two squadrons selected to train and operate the ASM-N-2 *Bat* air-to-surface guided missile, the other being VP-24. During this period the squadron was redesignated as VP-HL-13, and then VP-25. Finally, VPB-143, a former PV-1 Ventura squadron, transitioned to the Privateer in June 1944 at Camp Kearney, California. In August 1945 the squadron transferred to Kaneohe, where it remained for nearly two years until its disestablishment in May 1947. In 1946 the squadron's moniker changed from VP-143 to VP-HL-5.

Bureau Number 59846 served with VPB-122, 197, and ATU-12. Here she is undergoing maintenance in Alaska circa 1946 when it served with VPB-122. (Courtesy: Steve Hawley)

A profile of Bureau Number 59846 shows it with the sea blue color scheme and with the five-digit serial number stenciled on the forward fuselage. (Courtesy: Steve Hawley)

VPB-143's Bureau Number 59824 in the foreground parked on the tarmac in NAS Kaneohe, Hawaii late 1945. The squadron deployed to Hawaii in August 1945 and began training but the end of hostilities ended its chance of combat in the Pacific. The squadron, redesignated VP-143 in May 1946 and VP-HL-5 in November 1946, remained at NAS Kaneohe until May 1947. (Courtesy: Norman Houle)

Three Privateers, Bureau Numbers 59634, 59493, and 59652 of training squadron VB-4 OTU flying in formation over Florida during the Second World War. The aircraft appear to have the tri-color camouflage.

Bureau Number 59587 in glossy sea blue coloring served with Operational Training Unit (OTU) VB-4, a training squadron based in the United States during the Second World War. Privateers of this squadron were typically identified by the last three digits of the serial number on the horizontal stabilizer and the letters X and B on the aft portion of the fuselage. (Author's Collection)

9

Cold War Service 1946-1956

Well after the end of World War II, the Privateer continued to serve with the United States Navy, and later the Coast Guard, in a variety of missions, consisting of maritime and weather reconnaissance, flare drop missions during the Korean Conflict, air-sea rescue, and intelligence gathering. In 1951 the designation of the Privateer as a patrol bomber changed, with the Navy reclassifying it as the P4Y-2; however, most veterans and aviation historians continue to refer to the aircraft by its original designation.

U.S. Navy Weather Squadrons

In the area of weather reconnaissance, the model PB4Y-2M took on the role of tracking hurricanes and typhoons, with squadrons VPB-114, VPW-1, 2, 3, VJ-1, and 2 serving in that capacity throughout the late 1940s and early 1950s. Specifically, Navy weather reconnaissance squadrons, operating from bases in the United States and the Pacific, provided in-flight weather observations and reports. Additionally, such squadrons based in the Pacific conducted sur-

This photograph showing a formation of Privateers in October 1945 was possibly taken over the Philippine Islands. (Author's Collection)

The same formation, consisting of over 30 Privateers, is shown approaching an unknown coastline in October 1945. (Author's Collection)

PB4Y-2M Number R57 with a B-24 style nose belonged to Navy Weather Squadron One (VPW-1). This aircraft is painted overall glossy sea blue with white lettering and is probably Bureau Number 59957 which crashed into a mountainside in the Philippines on 19 October 1946. (Courtesy: Ray Parsons)

veying missions of the American Trust Territories of Micronesia, air-sea rescue, and radiation monitoring during nuclear weapons testing.

In May 1945 VPB-114, a veteran PB4Y-1 Liberator squadron that conducted ASW patrols from the Azores during World War II, became the first naval unit officially assigned weather reconnaissance duty when a detachment of six aircraft and seven crews left the Azores for NAS Boca Chica, Key West, Florida. By November 1945 the detachment, now equipped with PB4Y-2s, rejoined the squadron, which had redeployed from the Azores to NAS Edenton, North Carolina. The squadron was re-designated VP-HL-6 in 1946 and VP-26 in 1948.

During the Second World War, patrol planes in the Pacific often flew weather reconnaissance missions tracking typhoons, which might endanger surface units operating in or near the storm's path. After the war, squadrons specially equipped with PB4Y-2Ms continued this mission, with Weather Squadron One (VPW-1) becoming the first such unit upon commissioning in November 1945. Conversion of the patrol bomber for weather flights consisted of removing all armament, including replacing the ERCO bow turret with a B-24D-style nose, the installation of observation windows in place of the side waist blisters, and waterproofing the electric and ignition wiring in the engine nacelles. To make the flights more comfortable for crews, PB4Y-2Ms of VPW-1 included an electric range and an icebox in the after station.

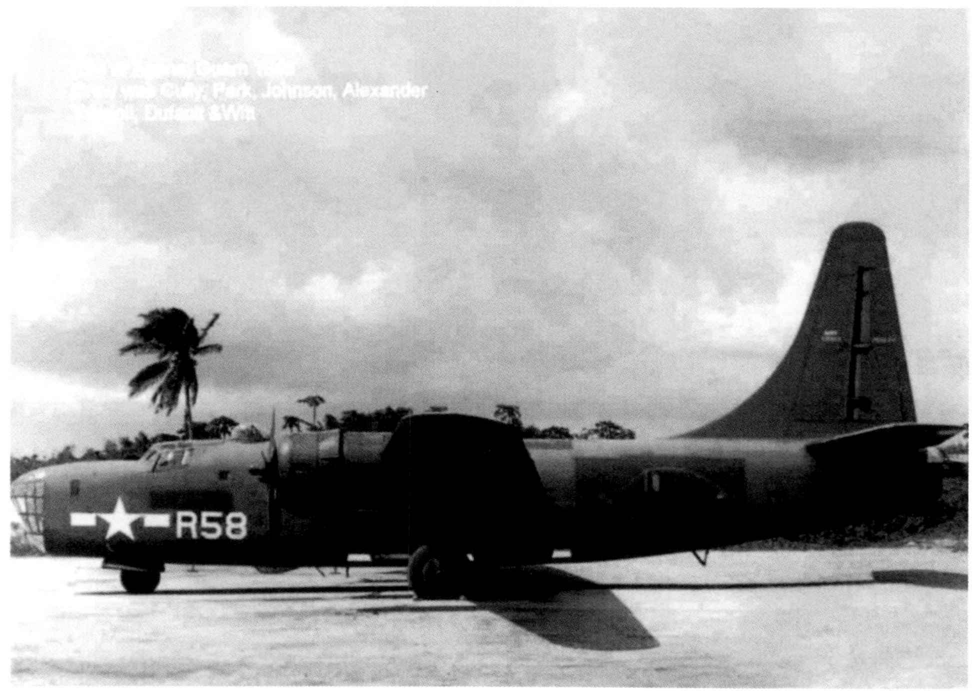

A side profile of VPW-1's R58 on Agana, Guam in 1946. The PB4Y-2M lacked weaponry and had the aft upper turret and side waist blisters removed. Note the color variation where the after upper turret and the waist blister have been deleted. (Courtesy: Ray Parsons)

Here is the squadron logo for Weather Reconnaissance Squadron Two (VPW-2) circa 1946-47. VPW-1 and 2 merged in 1946. (Courtesy: Ray Parsons)

This image shows a VPW-1 crew that was lost while flying a typhoon reconnaissance mission in PB4Y-2M Bureau Number 59957 on 19 October 1946. Back row from left to right: Lieutenant S.H. Castleton, Lieutenant J.L. Junkin, Lieutenant Nightingale (who was not on the flight), and Ensign D.E. Goerner. Front row left to right: Aviation Radioman 1st Class (ARM1c) Earl Vasso, Aviation Machinist Mate 1st Class (AMM1c) Robert W. Canada, Aviation Machinist Mate 2nd Class (AMM2c) Robert W. Cullen, and Aviation Radioman 3rd Class (ARM3c) James J. Walsh. (Courtesy: Ray Parsons)

VPW-1, with the nickname *Typhoon Chasers* and consisting of 14 PB4Y-2Ms, began weather reconnaissance and air-sea rescue flights from Guam in May 1946 under the operational control of Fleet Air Wing Eighteen. Between June and July of that year two detachments, three planes each, operated from Peleliu and Kwajalein, with the latter conducting weather reconnaissance flights for nuclear bomb testing off Bikini Atoll during Operation Crossroads, while the Peleliu detachment flew weather reconnaissance and air-sea rescue flights. A sister squadron, VPW-2, operated briefly from Guam before basing permanently at NAS Sangley Point, Philippines. Both VPW squadrons merged in November 1946 to form Meteorological Squadron One (VPM-1).

Flight crews on a PB4Y-2M normally consisted of eight men: four officers (patrol plane commander, co-pilot, navigator, and a weather expert with the title of aerologist), and four enlisted men (plane captain, second mechanic, first radioman, and second

A post-war view of an American airbase at an unknown location in the Pacific as viewed from the cockpit of a PB4Y-2. In the background is the tail of a Privateer with the "EL" letter code. The aircraft are painted overall glossy sea blue with insignia white tail lettering. (Author's Collection)

Crew 8 of VP-20 crew based at Kodiak, Alaska on 29 October 1948 six days before they were lost on a routine patrol in Privateer Bureau Number 59685. Back row from left to right: Chief Aviation Ordnanceman (AOC) Robert W. Eichorn, Aviation Ordnanceman 2nd Class (AO2) Lloyd O. Askildson, Aviation Electronics Mate (AL1) William L. Nevares, Seaman Apprentice (SA) James A. Wooley, Aviation Machinist Mate 3rd Class (AD3) Joseph D. Somers, Aviation Ordnanceman 2nd Class (AO2) Milton L. Russell, Aviation Machinist Mate 2nd Class (AD2) Norman M. Holland, and Chief Aviation Machinist Mate (ADC) Franklin E. Barden. Front row from left to right: Chief Aviation Machinist Mate (ADC) Robert W. Trenton, Ensign Harold R. Herndon, Lieutenant Paul R. Barker, and Midshipman William R. Musgrove. William L. Nevares and Milton L. Russell were not aboard the ill-fated flight but were replaced by ALC William G. Coleman and AO2 Bill Clark. (Courtesy: Jon Barker)

Bureau Number 59608 with the "MA" tail code shows that this aircraft was assigned to VP-23 sometime during the late 1940s. (Author's Collection)

Right: Bureau Number 59847 sporting a glossy red color scheme as a P4Y-2K target drone with Navy Utility Squadron Three (VU-3) at NAS North Island, California circa 1947. (Courtesy: Tailhook Association via Mahlon K. Miller)

Snow covered Privateers operated by an unknown squadron with the "EL" tail code circa late 1940s. (Author's Collection)

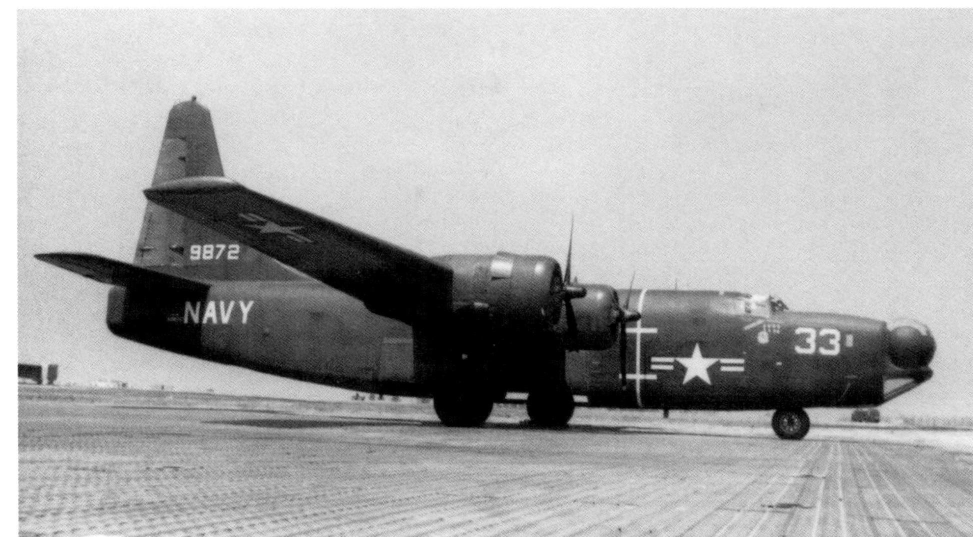

Bureau Number 59872 with the in-squadron number 33 is reported to have crashed at NAS Corpus Christi, Texas while assigned to VP (HL)-12 on 22 January 1948. (Author's Collection)

A VP-23 Privateer in flight possibly over the Atlantic Ocean circa late 1940s. (Courtesy: Naval Historical Center)

A VP-25 PB4Y-2B on the tarmac with a "Bat" guided missile. (Courtesy: NARA)

VP-26's Bureau Number 59645, with the in-squadron call sign HB-7, at Port Lyautey, French Morocco. Soviet fighters shot down this aircraft with the loss of all hands over the Baltic Sea on 8 April 1950. Missing and presumed killed were: Lieutenant J.H. Fetts, Lieutenant R.D. Reynolds, Lieutenant H.W. Seeschaf, Ensign T.L. Burgess, Aviation Electronics Technician 1st Class (AT1) F.L. Beckman, Aviation Machinist Mate 1st Class (AD1) J.H. Danens, Aviation Machinist Mate 1st Class (AD1) J.W. Thomas, (AL3) J.J. Bourasasa, Communications Technician 3rd Class (CT3) E.J. Purcell, and Aviation Electronics Technician 3rd Class (AT3) J.H. Rinnier. (Courtesy: U.S. Navy)

radioman-radar operator). During a typhoon reconnaissance flight, the aircraft would completely circle the typhoon at a minimum practicable radius, usually from a distance where surface wind velocity was approximately 60 knots. According to Ray Parsons, who was a member of VPW-1 and participated in a number of typhoon observations:

"We flew to the disturbance area and located the eye by radar. We flew in a clockwise direction, against the prevailing wind, around the outside of the eye at an altitude where we could monitor the sea to determine wind direction and speed. This altitude was generally in hundreds of feet, and always below the clouds, which were very low.

If turbulence was not too severe, the degrees of severity could only be defined by the crew's previous experiences with such storm systems.

We often could detect a weak spot in the eye and would enter the eye at that point. In the eye, we would gather the barometric pressure, sea conditions, and other information. Then we would ascend a couple of thousand feet and return to the base. During the circumnavigation of the eye we would send radio messages to the base at 15-minute intervals giving the information we gathered."[51]

VP-23 Hurricane Hunter Privateers over Miami, Florida circa late 1940s. (Courtesy: Tailhook Association via Mahlon K. Miller)

VP-24 PB4Y-2B at NAS Norfolk, Virginia in July 1951. (Courtesy: The Tailhook Association via Mahlon K. Miller)

Bureau Number 59852 parked at Barber's Point, Hawaii circa 1944-45 while assigned to VPB-200, which operated as a combat replacement unit. This particular aircraft was stricken from the Navy's inventory after crash landing at Port Lyautey, French Morocco in April 1951. (Author's Collection)

A spectacular view of a pair of Privateers Bureau Number 66261 (front) and 59868 (rear) from Weather Squadron Two (VJ-2) cruising over the Florida countryside in mid to late 1952. Note: the aft upper turrets of both aircraft have been removed. (Courtesy: Giorgio Salerno)

A number of Naval Reserve squadrons were equipped with the Privateer beginning in the late 1940s until replaced by the Lockheed P2V Neptune. Pictured here is Bureau Number 60008 at NAS South Weymouth, Massachusetts. (Author's Collection)

VPW-1 lost one aircraft and crew during its initial deployment to the Pacific when a PB4Y-2M flying a weather reconnaissance flight from Sangley Point, Philippines, crashed into Mount Banahoa, killing all hands onboard. Privateer Bureau Number 55957 and its crew of eight, commanded by Lieutenant Stanley H. Castleton, took off at 0508 hours on 19 October 1946, and afterward, the base received three routine messages from the aircraft but, on the third, transmission was abruptly interrupted, and no further contact was established. Planes of Fleet Air Wing Ten (FAW-10) commenced search operations, and the wreckage of Castleton's aircraft and the remains of the crew were subsequently found at the 3,100-foot level of Mount Banahoa. Apparently, reduced visibility from heavy clouds and precipitation were the primary factors that caused Lieutenant Castleton to fly into the side of the mountain.

While VPW-1 and 2 were conducting typhoon reconnaissance flights in the Pacific, VPW-3 flew hurricane-tracking missions from bases along the eastern seaboard of the United States. The third weather squadron operated PB4Y-2Ms from NAS Miami, Florida, with detachments at NAS Atlantic City, and Argentia, Newfoundland. Renamed VPM-3 in November 1946, VP-HL-3 a month later, and finally VP-23 in September 1948, the squadron was originally commissioned in May 1946 and manned by a number of personnel transferred from VPW-2. In addition to storm tracking, squadron planes and flight crews participated in filming a motion picture titled *Slattery's Hurricane*, starring Richard Widmark as a disgruntled Naval Reserve Officer who operates a smuggling operation while engaging in a tryst with the wife of a VP-23 patrol plane commander.

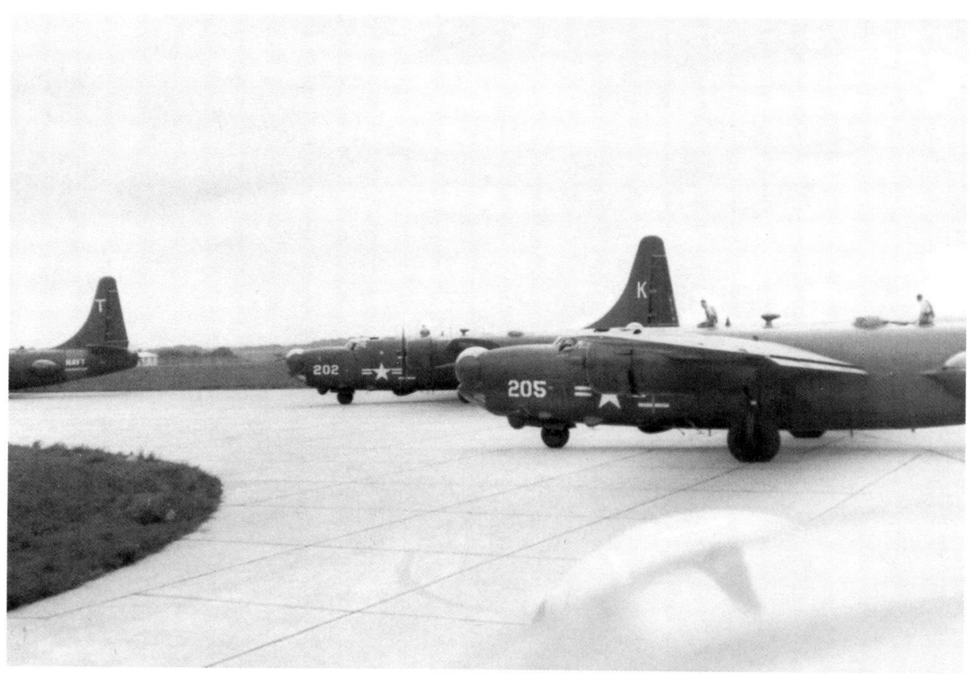

Three Naval Reserve Privateers prepare to depart for a two-week tour in Hawaii in 1954. The aircraft at the far left with the "T" tail code is a NAS Seattle, Washington based Privateer while the one in the back center with the "K" tail code identifies it as belonging to NAS Olathe, Kansas. (Marion C. Giorgini via David Giorgini)

This view shows USN Reserve Privateers preparing to depart from an unknown location circa 1954. (Marion C. Giorgini via David Giorgini)

During the 1949 Hurricane season squadron aircraft entered the eyes of 33 hurricanes. A year later, five of VP-23's Privateers sitting on the tarmac at NAS Miami were damaged by a hurricane that made landfall on 18 October 1950. In November 1949 VP-23 converted to the radar-equipped PB4Y-2S series and took on the additional role of ASW operations. Between December 1949 and October 1953, when VP-23 began transitioning to the Lockheed PV2-5 Neptune, detachments operated from Argentia, Newfoundland, Greenland, Brunswick, Maine, Reus Tarragona, Spain, and Port Lyautey, French Morocco.

In March 1952 a number of squadron personnel from VP-23 formed Weather Squadron Two (VJ-2), which operated six Privateers until those aircraft were replaced by the P2V3-W Neptune a year later. VJ-1 was another weather squadron established at Sand Point Naval Air Station, Seattle, Washington, in March 1952, and equipped with the P4Y-2S. The following year, the squadron was operating from NAS Agana, Guam, with detachments at NAS Sangley Point, Philippines, NAS Atsugi, Japan, and the United States Naval Embassy in Saigon, Vietnam. In September 1953 the squadron was redesignated as Airborne Early Warning Squadron Three

Shown here is VP-881's Number 206 commanded by Marion C. Giorgini in 1954. Closer inspection shows that a small observation blister has replaced the forward upper deck turret. The aircraft sported the typical glossy blue coloration of the period. (Marion C. Giorgini via David Giorgini)

Standing beside VP-881's Number 206 is the regular flight crew. Standing in the center is the patrol plane commander Marion C. Giorgini. The names of the others are unknown. (Marion C. Giorgini via David Giorgini)

A frontal view of a VP-881 P4Y-2 Privateer at an unknown location circa 1954. This aircraft retained the bow and side blisters along with the aft upper deck turret but an observation blister replaced the forward upper turret. (Marion C. Giorgini via David Giorgini)

This unidentified NAS Seattle, Washington, P4Y-2 apparently veered off the runway and became stuck in the mud. (Marion C. Giorgini via David Giorgini)

Mechanics work on the bow turret of a VP-881 Privateer at an undisclosed location circa 1954. (Marion C. Giorgini via David Giorgini)

(VW-3), and the P2V-5 Neptune began replacing the Privateers. While performing weather reconnaissance duties, the squadron lost a Privateer and its crew when Bureau Number 59176 crashed while on low-level penetration of Typhoon *Doris* on 16 December 1953. An intensive air and surface search failed to find any trace of the missing plane or crew. In June 1954 VW-3 was reported as being the last active duty squadron operating the Privateer.

Cold War Shootdown

During the late 1940s and early 1950s, especially between the years 1948 and 1953, the PB4Y-2/P4Y Privateer was used as a platform for electronics intelligence gathering (ELINT) against the Soviet Union. ELINT missions often entailed flying near Soviet-controlled territory, and during the course of such missions between 1950 and 1970, 40 U.S. aircraft were lost to hostile fire and over 200 U.S. service members perished. The first American aircraft lost while conducting an ELINT reconnaissance mission was a PB4Y-2 from VP-26. The squadron originally provided weather flights until 1949,

In this undated photograph is Bureau Number 66304 that is currently on display at the National Museum of Naval Aviation in Pensacola Florida. This P4Y-2G served with the U.S. Coast Guard between December 1952 and July 1958. Hawkins & Powers Aviation flew the plane for a number of years under the U.S. civilian registry N2870G before donating it to the museum in 1983. (Author's Collection)

Number 282 with the "T" tail code could be Bureau Number 66282 a Naval Reserve Privateer assigned to VP-881 at NAS Seattle, Washington. On 19 August 1954, it crashed at Chincoteague, Virginia. (Courtesy: Boche)

A PB4Y-2 of VP-23 on a Hurricane reconnaissance mission during September 1953, a month before the squadron transitioned to the P2V-5 Neptune. (Courtesy: U.S. Navy via Nevins Frankel)

when it took on the mission of electronic intelligence gathering of Soviet radar sites located in Eastern Europe; during one such mission a PB4Y-2 was intercepted and shot down by Soviet fighters. On 8 April 1950 four Soviet La-11s fighters belonging to the 30 GvIAP shot down PB4Y-2 Bureau Number 59645 with the in-squadron number HB-7, named the *Turbulent Turtle*, and carrying a crew of 10 commanded by Lieutenant John H. Fette.[52]

According to the American version, the incident happened over the Baltic Sea, while the Soviets claimed it happened over Latvia. Lieutenant Fette and his crew took off at 1031 hours from Wiesbaden, West Germany, and the subsequent loss of the aircraft and its crew occurred at 1739 hours. Four Soviet fighters piloted by Lieutenants Tezyaev, Gerasimov, Sataev, and Dokin were scrambled from an airbase at Liepaya and intercepted the Privateer some 70 kilometers off the Russian coast. Senior Lieutenant Boris Dokin, in

Four U.S. Coast Guard P4Y-2G Privateers with the Bureau Numbers 66306, 66304, 66302, and 66300 cruising above the coast of California in March 1958. At least three of the four aircraft Bureau Number 66300, 66302, and 66304 went on to serve as fire bombers with Hawkins & Powers Aviation. (Courtesy U.S. Coast Guard)

a memorandum dated soon after the incident, recounted the interception of Lieutenant Fette's plane:

"I received the order to take off. After the take off, I received the command to take altitude 4,000 meters and took course 360 degrees. I flew for 4 minutes on this course. At 1733 hours I received the command from the control point to take course 340 degrees. At 1737 hours I received the command to take course 360 degrees. At 1739 hours I made contact with a four-engined aircraft with American markings on a course of 135 degrees south of Lepaya, 8 kilometers from the settlement of Tsenkon. Having seen the aircraft, I approached it from the right and from behind and told the second pair, led by Senior Lieutenant Gerasimov, to force the violator to land. Gerasimov flew ahead and, sharply rocking his wings, turned to the left. The violator took a course of 270 degrees toward the sea and did not follow Senior Lieutenant Gerasimov. I then gave a 12 shot warning burst. The violator started to shoot at me. Seeing this, my wingman, Lieutenant Tezyaev, fired at the violator. The violator steeply descended and entered the clouds at an altitude of 500 meters, and supposedly, the aircraft crashed 5-10 kilometers from the shore."[53]

After the *Turbulent Turtle* failed to return, American, British, and Swedish vessels conducted a search, with debris from the aircraft being found consisting of life rafts, the nose wheel, seat cushions, radio logs, and other items. According to declassified documents, the Soviets conducted an extensive search of the area of the supposed sinking of the aircraft, a general area of 49 square miles (166 square kilometers), employing 45 different vessels and 160 divers, but nothing was found and the search was halted in June 1950.

P4Y-2G Bureau Number 66306, 66304, 66302, and 66300 from the U.S. Coast Guard Air Station at San Francisco, California on a morning patrol wing northward past the Golden Gate Bridge toward the hills of Marin County. (Courtesy U.S. Coast Guard)

This in-flight profile is that of Coast Guard P4Y-2G Bureau Number 66306 during the late 1950s. This aircraft apparently went on to serve as a fire bomber with the civilian registry N7974A until 22 July 1968 when it crashed at McGrath, Alaska while battling a forest fire. (Courtesy U.S. Coast Guard)

This aft view shows P4Y-2G Bureau Number 59688 at Coast Guard Station, San Francisco, California. The history of the plane shows that it was originally assigned to U.S. Navy Squadron VP-21 before the Coast Guard received it in January 1953, which then operated it until June 1957. (Courtesy U.S. Coast Guard)

A side view of a Coast Guard P4Y-2G with overall glossy sea blue color scheme at Barbers Point, Hawaii on 23 November 1948. (Courtesy U.S. Coast Guard)

The ultimate fate of the crew has yet to be determined and continues to be the subject of debate between the United States Government, Russian authorities, and the crew's families. Exacerbating the issue are reports from former German, Austrian, and Japanese POWs who, upon repatriation from the Soviet Union, claimed to have seen several members of Fette's crew alive and in Soviet work camps. However, the Soviets over the years issued statements denying the allegations. In 1951, the United States Government declared the crew dead; however, government agencies and private MIA/POW organizations are still pursuing all leads concerning the ultimate fate of Lieutenant Fette and his crew. Two months after the loss of the *Turbulent Turtle*, VP-26 transferred to NAS Patuxent River, Maryland, where it transitioned to the Lockheed P2V-4 Neptune.

On 8 April 2001, current members of VP-26 had the opportunity to return to Liepaja, Latvia, to pay their respects to fellow shipmates that were onboard the *Turbulent Turtle*. During the previous year the citizens of Liepaja, along with sailors of the Latvian Navy, unveiled a memorial plaque in honor of the 10 missing crewmen from Privateer HB-7. The bronze plaque, inscribed with the names of the lost crew, was placed on an existing Latvian monument for all sailors and fishermen lost at sea.[54]

Additional Privateer Squadrons of the United States Navy

Two additional active duty squadrons (VP-11 and VPW-1 (VP-51)) flew the P4Y-2 between 1949 and 1953. VP-11 was established in May 1952 and consisted of 12 P4Y-2S Privateers. Between January and June 1953, the squadron deployed to Argentia, Newfoundland. VP-11's use of the Privateer barely lasted a year, as it transitioned to the P2V-5 Neptune upon returning from Argentia. VPW-1, the second Privateer squadron to bear the designator, was established in April 1948 as the Navy's first Air Early Warning Squadron, and initially flew the Navy version of the Boeing B-17, the PB-1W Flying Fortress, until May 1949, when it began replacing the aircraft with the PB4Y-2S. In September 1948 the squadron was redesignated VP-51 due to the designation that was in use by another unit.

A considerable number of naval reserve squadrons and training units appeared to have flown the P4Y-2 until the mid-1950s. Some of them included Advance Training Units (ATU) 11 and 12, ATU-600, and Patrol Squadrons VP-21, VP-692, 722, 723, 791, 792, 801, 831, 832, 837, 881, 891, 893, 894, and 911, along with Fleet Aircraft Service Squadrons (FASRON). Although this is not a definitive list, it does show that the United States Navy, throughout the late 1940s and into the mid-1950s, equipped a considerable number of units with the Privateer.

United States Coast Guard Privateers

The United States Coast Guard (USCG) operated 13 P4Y-2G Privateers, primarily from San Francisco, California, and Barbers Point, Hawaii, for air-sea rescue work between 1946 and 1958. P4Y-2Gs were similar in appearance to the type operated by Navy weather reconnaissance units during the late 1940s and early 1950s, with a glass nose that closely resembled to that found on the B-24D Liberator, and observation windows in place of the waist blisters. Since the Coast Guard operated the aircraft until 1958, several of them were saved from being scrapped and went on to serve as slurry bombers with civilian companies.

10

Korean War

The rapid reduction of the armed forces after the end of the Second World War found the United States militarily unprepared to launch major combat operations when the Korean War began in August 1950. In Japan, short-manned, inexperienced, and ill-equipped American ground forces were rushed into the conflict, but advancing North Korean forces quickly pushed them back to the port of Pusan, at the tip of South Korea. Active duty and Reserve patrol squadrons in the United States, many manned by veterans of World War II, mobilized and went to Japan; among them were four United States Naval Privateer squadrons, VP-9, 28, 772, and 871. This new conflict saw the PB4Y-2's role change from that of shipping strikes conducted during the last months of World War II to that of searching for ship-borne Chinese infiltrators off the Korean coast, tracking merchant shipping destined for North Korean ports, and flying night illumination missions. During the Privateer's service in the Korean War not a single aircraft was lost to hostile fire, but operational accidents claimed 10 planes and many of their crews, with seven of them occurring during training flights within the United States.

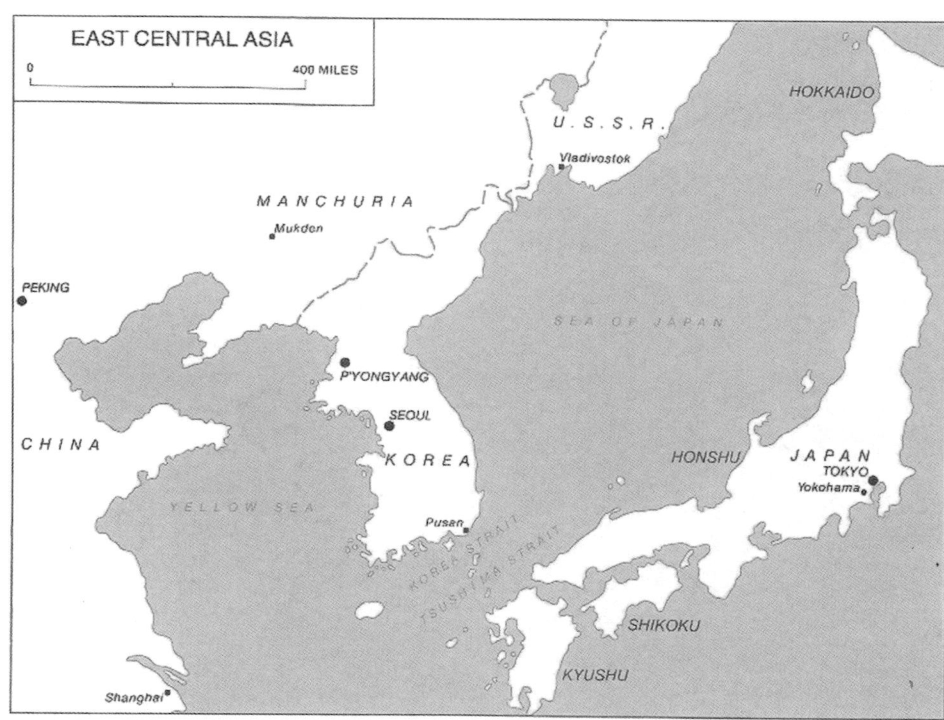

(Source: Billy C. Mossman, *Ebb and Flow: November 1950-July 1951*, Center of Military History)

A trio of VP-28 PB4Y-2S Privateers photographed somewhere over the Pacific Ocean in December 1951. (Courtesy: Mahlon K. Miller via Tailhook Association)

This VP-28 PB4Y-2S appears to be preparing for departure from an unknown location. The squadron operated from bases in Guam, Japan, Korea, and Okinawa during the Korean War. (Courtesy: Steve Hawley)

The Hawaiian Warriors of VP-28

The *Hawaiian Warriors* of VP-28 became the first Privateer squadron to support military operations in the Korean Theater. Established in July 1943 as VB-108 during World War II, the squadron served two tours of duty in the Pacific flying the PB4Y-1 Liberator and later, the PB4Y-2. Between December 1945 and April 1948 the squadron, designated as VP-108 in May 1946, VP-HL-8 in November 1946, and VP-28 in September 1948, operated from NAS Naha, Okinawa, conducting typhoon reconnaissance and air-sea rescue under Fleet Air Wing One (FAW-1). Based on Okinawa with a detachment at Guam between February and August 1950, the *Hawaiian Warriors* began flying patrols over the Formosa Straits, Foochow, and Shanghai, China, at the outbreak of hostilities in Korea. During one patrol on 26 July 1950, one of the squadron's planes encountered Chinese MIG-15s but safely returned to base without suffering damage. On 28 March 1951 the squadron's sec-

The officers and men of VP-772 stand on top and around a PB4Y-2 at NAS Sand Point, Seattle, Washington in 1952 prior to departing for Japan. (Courtesy: Jack Brown via Bob McLaughlin)

Chief Aviation Machinist Mate (ADC) Bert Degaetano instructs members of VP-772 on a PB4Y-2 engine at NAS Los Alamitos, California in October 1950. Students from left to right are: Aviation Machinist Mate 1st Class (AD1) Jacob Lowen, Aviation Machinist Mate 2nd Class (AD2) M.R. Balke, Aviation Machinist Mate 1st Class (AD1) Ralph F. Lower, Aviation Metal Smith/ Structural Mechanic 3rd Class (AM3) W.M. Davis, and Aviation Machinist Mate 3rd Class (AD3) James Godley. (Courtesy: NARA)

VP-772 Privateers, with BH-9 in the background, patrol over Korea during the squadron's first combat deployment. (Courtesy: Frank Tatu via Bob McLaughlin)

ond tour began with deployment to Itami Air Base, located in Southern Honshu, Japan. During its second tour, between April and October 1951, the squadron provided ship surveillance, anti-submarine patrols, weather reconnaissance missions along the Korean coast, and flare missions.

VP-28 had the distinction of having one of a handful of enlisted patrol plane commanders in the Navy. Robert G. Kirschner, Aviation Structural Mechanic First Class, flew 60 combat missions over Korea in the Privateer specializing in flare drop missions in support of Marine night fighters. As a patrol plane commander, he was over three commissioned officers and seven to eight enlisted men. However, commanding a patrol plane with an enlisted rating did prove troublesome on occasion when landing at airfields controlled by other armed forces. According to Kirschner, they would think he stole the plane and was just out on a joyride.[55]

In October 1951 VP-28's tour of duty in Japan ended, and it redeployed to NAS Barbers Point, Hawaii, leaving behind four Privateers and three crews assigned as "Detachment Able," which operated out of NAS Atsugi, Japan, which rotated one crew at a time out of Pusan, Korea. On 15 December Detachment Able, upon

A side profile of BH-9 of VP-772 in flight during the squadron's first deployment to Korea taken by Frank Tatu in the capacity as an official Navy photographer. (Courtesy: Frank Tatu via Bob McLaughlin)

AMS2 Jack Brown standing next to VP-772's Privateer Bureau Number 60006 possibly at NAS Iwakuni, Japan in 1953. Note the term P4Y-2 has replaced the PB4Y-2 designator under the horizontal stabilizer. (Courtesy: Jack Brown)

Three unidentified members of VP-772 pose for a photograph on their Privateer with two additional squadron aircraft in the background at Iwakuni, Japan in 1953. (Courtesy: Jack Brown via Bob McKlaughlin)

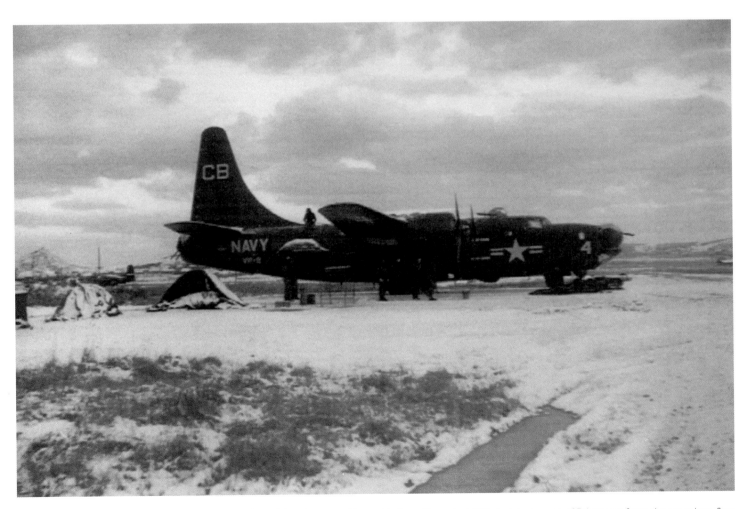

Personnel work on P4Y-2S Number 4 of VP-9 in the cold and snow at Pusan Air Base, Korea in 1952. A detachment of Privateers from the squadron flew flare-dropping missions from late June 1952 to January 1953. (Courtesy: A.G. Alexander)

Fighting the cold and snowy conditions in Atsugi, Japan on 21 December 1951, personnel from VP-871 prepare plane CH-6 for departure. The destination was Kimpo, South Korea and the mission was to resume flare-drop missions. (Courtesy: Stan Walker via Jeff Walker)

being relieved by VP-871, returned to Barbers Point and rejoined the rest of the squadron.

In June 1952 VP-28 deployed to Okinawa from Barbers Point and flew patrols along the coast of Communist China and the Straits of Formosa until December of that year. Nearly all patrols were completed without incident, but occasionally squadron aircraft did receive anti-aircraft fire from Chinese vessels, or were intercepted by Chinese or North Korean fighters. Jim Page was an enlisted member of a combat aircrew whose plane was attacked on 17 June 1952 by armed Chinese Landing Ships (LSM) during an early morning patrol that extended from Shanghai, China, southward to the island of Formosa:

"We had earlier test fired our guns and were just cruising along, flying along at about 1,000 to 2,000 feet, and the cloud cover may have been as much as about 500 feet above us. We had earlier transferred fuel from the auxiliary tanks, located in the forward bomb bay, to the wing tanks; this was a normal procedure to get the extra range. We came upon a group of junks that were clustered together; when we came in their range they separated, and there sat three LSMs converted to gunboats and armed with .50-caliber machine guns.

We were caught off guard. They unloaded on us, and we took numerous hits from tip to tail. We suffered a hit in the right landing

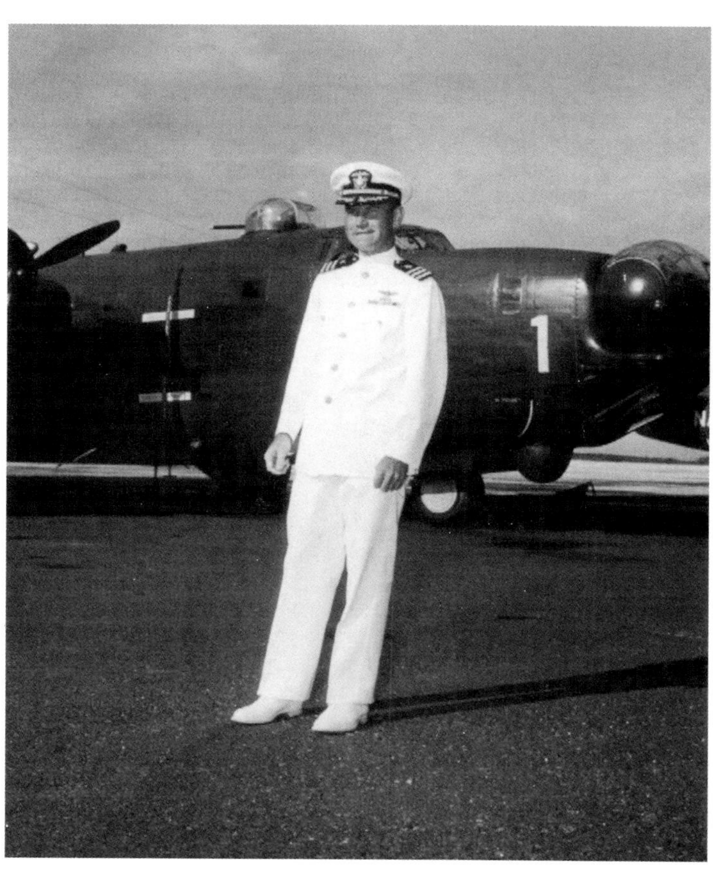

Commander Max P. Bailey, the first Commanding Officer of VP-9 stands proudly by one of the squadron's Privateers during his change of Command in April 1952. (Courtesy: A.G. Alexander)

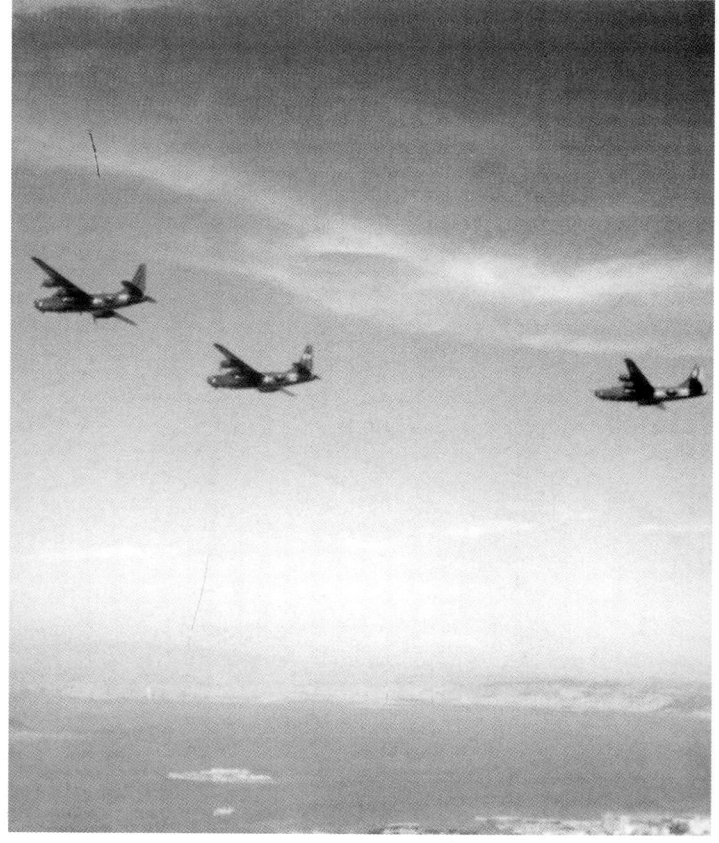

VP-871 Privateers seen here on the first leg of a TransPac in October 1951 fly over San Francisco Bay with Alcatraz Island in the bottom center. From Hawaii, the planes flew to Atsugi, Japan. (Courtesy: Maurice "Shep" Shapiro)

VP-871's Lieutenant Stan Walker braves the cold and snow next to CH-6 at Kimpo Airbase, South Korea in December 1951. (Courtesy: Stan Walker via Jeff Walker)

VP-871's CH-7 pictured here at Kimpo Airbase, South Korea in December 1951 was one of the squadron aircraft assigned flare-dropping missions. (Courtesy: Stan Walker via Jeff Walker)

gear well that opened a hole on the topside of the wing. The JFR antenna was severed and the wire trailed back, slapping the tail section. We had hits in the fuselage right over the radioman's head, and the self-ceiling auxiliary fuel tank was hit and smoking, which indicated a possible fire, so the pilot attempted to jettison the tank, but as it was released it lodged between the bomb bay door and the catwalk. I went into the bay with the doors open and proceeded to push and kick the tank free to where it would drop out. The catwalk was only about 18 inches wide, so it is hard to go through with a chute on, so I had no chute, which was somewhat scary. I succeeded in dislodging the fuel tank and went back to my station.

The pilot radioed back to Okinawa and got permission to secure the patrol. When we arrived back at Naha we were prepared to make a crash landing, I think every emergency vehicle on the base was awaiting us. When we touched down the fire trucks were right on our wingtips, just in case. Our pilot was a great guy and was due for rotation, and this was his last patrol with us. The landing he made was the best he ever made, strictly textbook."[56]

While conducting patrols off the Chinese mainland, VP-28 Privateers encountered Chinese fighters on two separate occasions, but were successfully driven off by the patrol aircraft's battery of .50 machine guns. Jim Page was one of the air gunners in a 12-man crew that participated in the two encounters with Chinese fighters. On 20 September 1952 Lieutenant Harvey R. Britt's P4Y-2S was attacked by two Chinese MIG-15s near Shanghai. The fighters made five attacks, exchanging fire with Britt's gunners:

"Our mission was to track shipping along the China Coast—whether it was goods or troops, the threat of invasion of Formosa was always present. The two MIG-15s came from above us and used the bright sun as their cover. They were on us rapidly, and fortunately, we were at battle stations and were ready for whatever came our way. We flew at around 1,000 to 2,000 feet, and the pilot's evasive action was to go as close to the water as possible and protect our belly, and he would fly directly at the MIG. In most cases, we could train at least 4-6 guns on target.

Once they were in range gunfire was exchanged; we carried 12 machine guns, while they had a 37-millimeter cannon and a 33-caliber gun in the nose. We were slow and could fly low, and they would have to throttle back to hold us in sight; at low altitude the MIG-15 was ineffective. The battle lasted about two minutes, but it seemed like an eternity. The MIGs broke off the fight and hi-tailed back to Shanghai; I think they suffered some damage, because they were smoking pretty good."

Before the squadron returned to the United States, one of its aircraft with Jim Page aboard was intercepted by a lone Chinese MIG-15. The interception occurred on 22 November 1952, only days before VP-28 went home:

"We were attacked by a single MIG-15. This attack was at about 500 feet at the start, and the plane came in from right to left and just under our tail. He was so close you could see the rivets on the plane, and I could see the pilot up close and personal. I called the pilot on the intercom and notified him, and he went into evasive action, and the fight was on. If you see one of those 37-millimeter tracers coming at you head-on, you get a scare. This fight was about the same length of time as the other; that's too long when you know the other guy wants to kill you."[57]

While preparing to rotate back to the United States, VP-28 transferred at least three P4Y-2S to the Republic of China Air Force on Formosa, and approximately one month later the squadron began transitioning to the P2V-5 Neptune.

The Golden Eagles of VP-9

VP-9 (the *Golden Eagles*) was established at NAS Seattle, Washington, in March 1951, and training of crews on the PB4Y-2 was conducted by FASRON 895. During the next several months the

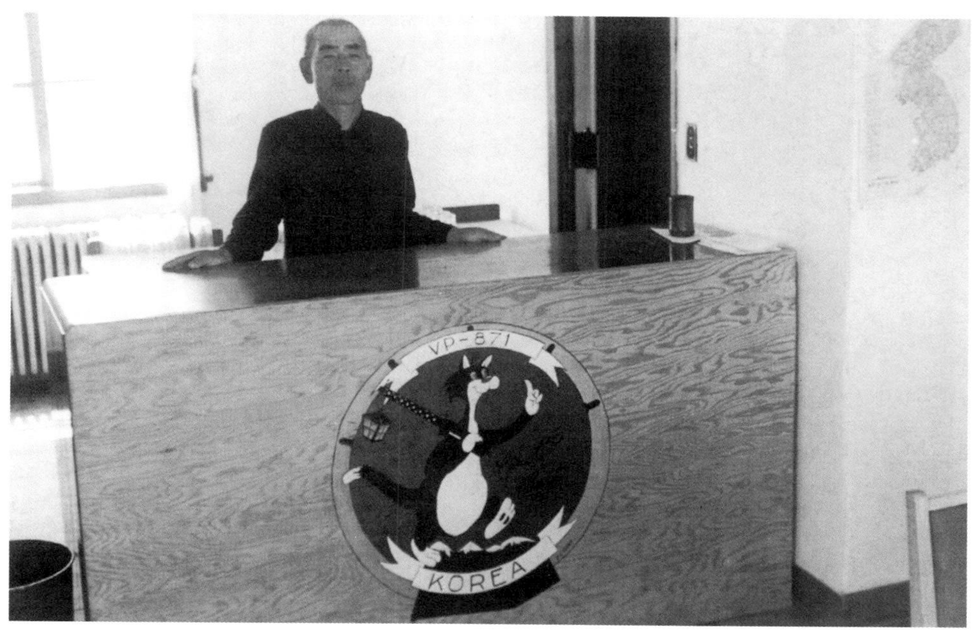

A bartender stands ready to take drink orders at The Sylvester Bar named after the cartoon character depicted on the VP-871 squadron logo. (Courtesy: Stan Walker via Jeff Walker)

squadron was plagued by a series of operational accidents. The first accident occurred on 21 June 1951 when Bureau Number 56263, piloted by Lieutenant Carl M. Hodge, crashed into Skagit Bay, approximately six miles from Seattle, Washington, during a low altitude bombing practice. When the plane hit the water, Lieutenant Hodge was thrown 50 feet through the windscreen into the water but survived; however, five crewmembers died and five more were injured.

In August 1951 the squadron suffered two more catastrophic accidents, resulting in the deaths of nearly two dozen men. The first occurred on the 12th when Bureau Number 66298 went missing some three hours after departing NAS Kodiak, Alaska. The wreckage and the remains of the 11-man crew commanded by Lieutenant Roy Edwin Park were found three days later at 900-foot level on Amak Island, approximately 20 miles northwest of Cold Bay, Alaska. The investigation board blamed the crash on pilot error. Less than three weeks later, on 31 August, VP-9 lost another Privateer and crew, but this time one of the crew survived the crash.

The accident occurred when Lieutenant Berdel A. Cook, piloting Bureau Number 66280, lost his bearings not long after departing NAS Adak, in the Aleutian Islands, and the aircraft crashed at the 800-foot level on Little Tanaga Island, some 16 miles from Adak. Miraculously Frank W. Mullick, the aircrew's third mechanic, survived after falling some 700 feet down a mountainside after the plane hit.

In February 1952 VP-9 transferred to NAS Alameda, California, and took on the role of the Navy's only Fleet Ready Mining Squadron. In June 1952 the squadron transferred to Iwakuni, Japan, with a detachment of aircraft operating from Pusan, Korea, between July 1952 and January 1953, in conjunction with Marine Corps night fighter F7F Tigercats and F4U Corsairs.

Flare-Drop Missions

As discussed earlier, Privateers were used in support of Marine Corps Grumman F7F Tigercat and F4U-5N Corsair night fighters conducting strikes against North Korean and Chinese supply movements during the Korean War. In the role of flare ships, bomb bay fuel tanks and electronic equipment were removed to enable the aircraft to carry between 150-250 high-intensity parachute flares, which were dropped to illuminate the target areas for the night fighters.

The reasoning behind the use of the Privateer in flare dropping missions during the Korean War stems from an idea formulated by the Commander in Chief Pacific Fleet, Admiral Arthur W. Radford. Before the introduction of the PB4Y-2 (redesignated the P4Y-2) in such missions, the Navy and Marine Corps flew Douglas R4D Skytrain transports to provide nighttime illumination of targets for attacking night fighters. Admiral Radford realized that the R4D, owing to its lack of speed and defensive firepower, was too vulnerable to enemy ground fire, and he therefore suggested that the heavily armed Privateer be utilized in such sorties.

The first evaluation flight was conducted by VP-772 on 12 June 1951, after Commander D.D. Nittinger and a full crew arrived at "K-1" Pusan Airbase in Bureau Number 59992 to support night attack operations of Marine Squadron VMF (N)-513. Three days later a second Privateer, Bureau Number 59742, belonging to the same patrol squadron, arrived to aid the flare-drop test. The evaluation was completed within a week, and both Privateers returned to Atsugi, Japan, between 17 and 20 June. Testing proved so successful that P4Y-2s from VP-9, 28, 772, and 871 were later allocated to fly what became known as Lamp Lighter or Firefly missions.

VP-9's experience with Lamp Lighter missions was chronicled in the article *Flares light the way for fighters*, published by Naval Aviation News during the Korean War, which typified the role of the Privateer in such missions:

"The pilot must first find his target in the blackest part of the night. Thoroughly taken up with the complicated job of handling a four-engine bomber and dodging the ever-present flak, the pilot would find his mission more tough if he did not have the assistance of a perfectly trained crew. It's nothing at all like handling a light plane on a Sunday afternoon.

Navigation must be perfect. To miss the target only slightly would be to waste flares and cause the fighter pilot to burn precious gasoline on a dry run. Wasted flares would give the enemy gun crews a good chance to take their time and search out the patrol plane with heavy AA fire, which to the patrol bomber ranks with the plague.

Under the guidance of the navigator riding in the nose of the plane, the man at the flare tube knows when to drop his flares. He may be any member of the crew who happens to be in the after station at that time. All hands turn to for the exhausting task of passing flares from the bomb bay to the tube. The high altitude makes the task hard and increases fatigue. At the end of a six-hour flight in which over 130 flares have been dropped, all hands are ready to 'hit the sack.'

Both members of the team, the patrol flare plane and the Marine fighter, are constantly on the lookout for signs of trucks on the roads below. Whenever a row of lights is seen, the word is exchanged and the flare plane navigator quickly fires instructions to the pilot and begins the run against the enemy.

'Easy port-more pore-easy starboard...Straighten her out a little...Steady, steady...After Station stand by to drop.
After Station standing by, sir.
Drop one, after station.
One away, sir.
Drop two.
Two away, sir.
Drop three and four away, sir. Flak bursting aft!
Hard port! Let's get the hell away from here. They're mad at us.'

The flares are set to ignite at whatever altitude the fighter pilot believes best. From high above in the flare plane, it's like looking directly into a photographer's flash. The country lights up brighter than day.

You wait to hear the report from the fighter below the flares. If the drop has been successful and there are targets on the road, the report runs something like this: 'Good drop! There's three of the (expletive) right under me. Watch for hits. I'm going in!'

Then silence. Then a few remarks by the flare plane crew questioning the family background of those below about to meet their ancestors. Then a flash down there, and the happy cry, 'We got 'em! Keep it lit up. I see three more!'

The flare plane encores the run, following the instructions of the fighter pilot and using the previous flares as markers. By this time, the enemy gun crews have you pretty well in their sights, and it makes the run a little more exciting. The performance is repeated until the fighter pilot is satisfied that there are no more targets, and then you pick another section of the road and start over again.

When the fighter runs out of ammunition and heads for home base, another is on its way to rendezvous for the second half of the operation that night. The evening flights are run in two shifts, keeping the Navy crews over the target areas anywhere from four to eight hours, longer than any other crews flying in the 'hot zones.'

After this continuous pasting in the middle of the night, the trucks have become a little leery, and there are times when targets are hard to find. This trick of attacking at night under flares has proved very effective, but the fact remains that in order for the enemy to continue the fight, he must have supplies. He must drive trucks down the only available roads at all times of the day and night. So, the Navy takes off every night with a load of flares, and the Marine fighter pilots do likewise a short time later.

The enemy does not take the dual attack lying down. He's mad as a hornet and just as active. The way he throws radar-controlled AA fire skyward, aided by our own flares, shows he means business. The fighter is vulnerable—he is flying low under the flares. The flareplane is vulnerable—he is flying slow and over the flares. It is a ticklish situation at either level, and all hands win gray hairs honestly in this type of night warfare.

The parachute flares used by the night marauders look a little like sono-buoys, being long and pencil-like. Two types are in use in Korea today: the Mk-5 flare, which turns out 730,000 candlepower, and the larger Mk-6, with a million candlepower. A new Mk-3 Mod-10 is just reaching the field. It burns for two minutes instead of three and turns out 1,230,000 candlepower.

The flares have static lines attached to the plane, which activate the fuse as the flare drops away from the aircraft. The delay in firing can be set so the flare will fall from 300 feet to 1,200 feet before igniting. A 13-foot parachute with asbestos shrouds keeps it from falling too fast, giving night fighters a chance to get plenty of 'look-see' time as it floats downward. A slow-burning magnesium compound pressed into cakes somewhat like a rocket motor furnishes the 'light' which turns the Korean countryside into day.

Because the light of the flare is so blinding to night-adapted eyes of pilots, the Navy experimented with putting an opaque parachute-like screen immediately above the flaming magnesium. This, however, did not operate too well, and tended to catch tire from the intense heat of the flare."[58]

VP-9's first deployment to the Korean Conflict ended on 3 January 1953, and the squadron returned to the United States, transitioning to the P2V-2 Neptune. However, soon after arriving back in the United States the squadron suffered the loss of one more Privateer and a crew when Bureau Number 59937 crashed on a flight to Whidbey Island, Washington, due to bad weather on 28

CH-6 of VP-871 on the ground at Atsugi, Japan in February 1952 getting ready for a maritime reconnaissance mission code named the ABLE Patrol. (Courtesy: Stan Walker via Jeff Walker)

January 1953, killing the 10 crewmen aboard. The wreck and the remains of the crew were found six months later.

VP-772

Two Naval Reserve Privateer squadrons were activated for duty during the Korean War, with VP-772, later nicknamed the *White Lightnings*, becoming the first such unit to serve in Korea, arriving in Japan in February 1951. Established as VP-916—a reserve squadron—in April 1946, its designation changed to Medium Patrol 66 (VP-ML-66) in November of that year, and to VP-772 in February 1950. Before called to active duty the squadron, based at NAS Los Alamitos, California, flew the Lockheed-Vega PV-2 Harpoon and the Consolidated PBY-5A Catalina. In September 1950 VP-772 began transitioning to the P4Y-2S at Sand Point and NAS Whidbey Island, Washington, by retrieving planes from Litchfield Park, Arizona, where they had been sitting since rolling off the assembly line in San Diego some five years before. As the Privateers were rescued from the baking heat of the Arizona desert one pilot remarked, "Our job was to rescue the aircraft from the desert, fly them back to civilization, and get them ready for the Korean War."[59]

The squadron arrived at NAS Atsugi, outside of Yokohama, Japan, on 2 February 1951 and began operations under Fleet Air Wing Six (FAW-6), while a detachment flew out of Iwakuni. Initial operations consisted of weather tracking and long-range reconnaissance, but flare dropping "Firefly" missions with the 1st Marine Air Wing soon followed, with two aircraft and crews operating from Pusan, Korea, between 12 June and 3 August 1951. The reconnaissance aspect included surveillance of Chinese, Soviet, and neutral shipping, the collection of electronic emissions from Chinese and Korean radar installations, and Combat Air Patrol (CAP) over American carrier forces. VP-772's patrol areas were called Fox and Able, and they covered the Yellow Sea between Shanghai, Tsingtao, and Port Arthur (Fox) to the Sea of Japan, east of Vladivostok and the Korean border (Able).[60]

The ship surveillance aspect of VP-772 missions entailed determining the type of cargo and what nations were supplying the North Koreans. A considerable number of the ships were Panamanian registered and, according to some accounts, manned by American crews, which created a considerable amount of anger and frustration among the flight crews of naval patrol squadrons. In a Time Magazine article from 1951, Lieutenant Bill McCord voiced his consternation of seeing a Panamanian-flagged ship laden with cargo destined for a North Korean port:

"They're not fooling anyone. They're American owned, American manned, and carrying American freight. I can't understand that. Not when we've lost 65,000 men in Korea already."[61]

The crews of naval patrol squadrons continued to report the movements of merchant shipping throughout the conflict, yet they were unable to stop the flow of war materials entering North Korean ports, as they lacked the authority to attack such shipping, since the vessels carried the flags of neutral countries. Some two years after Lieutenant Bill McCord voiced his consternation Wilmer L. Kerns, then a 20-year-old radioman with Crew 9 of VP-772, was on his second tour of duty with the squadron and remembered one particular ship surveillance mission off the Manchurian Coast on 22 January 1953:

"I located the ships by radar and directed the pilots to them. We circled the ships at a very low altitude, 50-100 feet, so that Lieutenant (jg) David E. Gates, the navigator, could take photographs that would provide clues regarding the nationality and type of cargo."[62]

VP-772's first tour in Japan ended in early August 1951 without the squadron losing one plane or crew to enemy action. After a brief period in the United States the squadron deployed to Barber's Point, Hawaii, in late January 1952, and served as the Pacific Fleet Mining Squadron, relieving VP-9, which had deployed to Japan. During its second deployment the squadron suffered one operational loss when Privateer Bureau Number 59992, which was the first to participate in flare drop missions with VMF (N)-531 a year before, crashed into Atada Shima Mountain while taking off from NAS Atsugi, killing the entire crew.

In July 1952 the squadron returned to Sand Point, Washington, where it suffered the loss of another plane and crew when Bureau Number 59923 crashed in the foothills of the Olympic Mountains on 12 November 1952, killing the crew of 10, as well as Captain G.R. Dyson, the Commander of Fleet Air Wing Four. In January 1953 the squadron re-deployed to Iwakuni, Japan, where it again took up weather tracking, long-range reconnaissance, and flare dropping missions. A month later VP-772 was augmented into the regular Navy as VP-17. During its second tour of duty in the Korean War the squadron flew 435 combat missions without a single loss of personnel or aircraft, and was the last squadron to fly the P4Y-2S in combat. In August 1953 the squadron returned to the United States and transitioned to the P2V-6 Neptune. It was the last active duty West Coast Squadron to fly the Privateer.

VP-871 The Big Red

The second reserve squadron to operate Privateers in the Korean War was VP-871, nicknamed *Big Red*, which operated out of Atsugi, Japan, between October 1951 and July 1952. The squadron was initially established as reserve squadron VP-907 in July 1946 and VP-ML-57 in November of the same year at NASS Livermore, California. In February 1950 it was redesignated as VP-871, called to active duty in March 1951, and transitioned to the P4Y-2S at NAS Alameda, California. The squadron suffered one operational loss while training in the United States when Bureau Number 59657 flew into the water near Smith Island, Washington, on 6 August 1951, killing the crew of nine.

In October the squadron deployed to Atsugi, Japan, and conducted ship surveillance over the Sea of Japan. Between 12 December 1951 and 7 July 1952 the squadron deployed a detachment to Kimpo, South Korea, and flew flare missions. It was during this period that it earned the nickname *Big Red*, in reference to the color of the flares dropped during interdiction missions. The detachment at Kimpo was composed of two aircraft and crews with the call signs Fatface 1 and Fatface 2. On night illumination missions an observer in the Privateer's bow turret would watch for signs of enemy vehicular activity, and when discovered, the patrol plane commander would call the night fighter in to destroy the enemy vehicles with a combination of napalm, bombs, rockets, and machine gun fire.

Living and working conditions at Kimpo were not ideal for the men of Fatface 1 and 2, especially during the winter months, according to Frank Durban, a member of VP-871's detachment at the time:

"The cold was terrible. We lived, flew, worked, and slept in our flight suits, so the smell was terrible when we got back to NAS Atsugi, Japan. We lived in big brown tents about 12 feet by 12 feet, with a big diesel oil stove, and when it would run out of diesel we would argue who had to go get more. We would often turn on all the showers as hot as we could stand it, and we would fall asleep on the shower floor. Then one by one we would get dressed and go on our precious four-day R&R. Then we would go back again."[63]

The squadron suffered only one operational loss while operating from Japan during the Korean War. Returning from patrol in poor visibility on 14 January 1952, Lieutenant Chester C. Johnson and his crew were killed when two engines failed on Bureau Number 59704 and the aircraft crashed. VP-871 left Japan in July 1952 and began transitioning to the P2V-2 and 3 Neptune and, in February 1953, the squadron was augmented into the regular Navy as VP-19.

11

French Aéronavale and RoCAF Privateer Operations

While Privateers of the U.S. Navy were conducting missions in support of the United Nations in Korea the aircraft began service with the French and Chinese. By the late 1940s, as the Cold War with the Soviet Union intensified, the United States Government began supplying allies with military equipment; two recipient nations of the PB4Y-2 were the French in Indochina (Vietnam) and the Nationalist Chinese on the island of Taiwan. Aéronavale, the air arm of the French Navy, operated PB4Y-2s for 10 years, at first in Indochina between 1950 and 1954, and later in Algeria from 1956 to 1960, while the Republic of China's Air Force (RoCAF) utilized the aircraft between 1952 and 1961. As with the United States Navy, as soon as more modern patrol aircraft became available the Privateers of the French Aéronavale and RoCAF were taken out of service and assigned to the scrap heap.

Flotilla 8F Privateers belonging to the French Aéronavale stand ready for operations at an airbase in Indochina in the early 1950s before the squadron was redesignated 28F. (Courtesy: Giorgio Salerno)

A Privateer of Flotilla 8F adorned with the squadron Wolf Head logo on the forward fuselage prepares for a mission against the Viet Minh in Indochina circa 1953. (Courtesy: Robert Feuilloy)

A close-up view of a Flotilla 8F Privateer circa 1953 shows the national insignia and the squadron Wolf insignia as the plane and its crew prepares for a mission against Viet Minh forces. (Courtesy: Robert Feuilloy)

Privateers of the French Aéronavale in Vietnam (1951-1954)

French colonial rule of Indochina began in the late 1800s, and its control of that country went uncontested until World War II. In September 1940 Japanese troops began occupying portions of Indochina under the pretext of a Franco-Japanese treaty that recognized Japan's pre-eminence in that country in return for a nominal recognition of French sovereignty. The French colonial government was allowed to maintain its own military and police forces; however, the Japanese maintained a considerable military presence and exercised nearly complete control of the colony's infrastructure. By March 1945, with the fall of the Vichy Government in France and the imminent collapse of the Hitler Regime in Germany, Japan ordered all French and Indochinese military forces to surrender.

In September 1945, soon after Japan's surrender, Ho Chi Minh and the Viet Minh, which exercised nearly complete control over much of the countryside, declared Vietnam's independence from France. However, the French were not about to relinquish its colonial rule and Viet Minh forces were ordered to disarm, which was answered by a series of attacks that culminated in the start of the French-Indochina War in December 1946.[64]

The decision by the United States to supply the French with military equipment, particularly aircraft, was largely based on the growing relationship between the Viet Minh and Communist China. Between 1950 and 1954 22 P4Y-2 Privateers were ferried to the French, with at least two United States Naval Patrol Squadrons, consisting of VP-772 and 801, being assigned the task of flying the aircraft to Saigon. VP-772 ferried the first seven aircraft to Saigon in November 1950 with VP-801, a reserve patrol squadron based in Miami, Florida, ferrying another 13 Privateers sometime afterward, but it is unclear which squadron delivered the remaining two Privateers.

The recipient unit of the Privateers was the French Aéronavale's Flotilla 8F, who initially used the aircraft extensively for surveillance work in locating Viet Minh forces. Nicknamed the *Wolf Head*

A side profile of French Privateer 28 F-8 on the ground at unknown location. The plane is overall glossy sea blue with insignia white lettering and has a flat black anti-glare panel. (Author's Collection)

Privateer Number 10 of Flotilla 28F possibly patrolling over Algeria in 1957. The aircraft's service with the Aéronavale ended a little more than three years after this photograph was taken. (Courtesy: Robert Feuilloy)

Squadron, Flotilla 8F began Privateer Operations in February 1951, and the number of sorties steadily increased throughout 1951, with over 170 operational missions being flown during the last quarter. The French lost only one Privateer in Vietnam during the first year of operations when number 8F2 crashed on landing at Tan Son Nhut on 20 December 1951, killing the pilot and injuring eight crewmen while returning from a reconnaissance mission.

A lack of spare parts in the latter part of 1951 reduced the squadron's number of operational aircraft to four, which coincided with a drastic decrease in the number of sorties flown from 170 in the last quarter of 1951 to 59 in the first quarter of 1952. However, the arrival of spare parts and additional Privateers, possibly ferried by VP-801, increased the capability of Flotilla 8F, and the number of sorties increased to nearly 200 by the end of the year.

The aircraft's ability to remain on station for a considerable amount of time, as well as its ordnance-carrying capability made the Privateer particularly useful as flareships, like the American counterparts then engaged in the Korean War, and in bombing missions. In July 1952 Aéronavale Privateers began bombing missions in support of French ground forces during the *Battle* of Na San between July 1952 and March 1953. During the battle, the aircraft were indispensable in preventing enemy forces from advancing on French positions by flying bombing missions at altitudes ranging between 8 and 10,000 feet. During the operation Capitaine de corvette Paul Audibert, Flotilla 8F's Commanding Officer, was killed, along three other passengers and eight crewmen aboard Privateer 8F7, former U.S. Navy Bureau Number 59839, when the aircraft crashed on take-off from Tan Son Nhut on 23 September 1951. Capitaine de corvette Gilbert Guyon assumed command of the squadron upon the death of Audibert.

In May 1953 Flotilla 8F was redesignated as 28F and was based at Tan Son Nhut, with a detachment of two planes at Cat Bi. Privateers of 28F were known by the call sign *Caesar* and participated in the vast airborne assault to reoccupy Dien Bien Phu, named *Opera-*

Four Republic of China Air Force (RoCAF) P4Y-2 Privateers fly in formation circa early 1950s. (Courtesy: Wings of China Publications, Wai Yip, Editor)

An aft view of a RoCAF Privateer as it prepares to depart from an airbase on Formosa. In the background are the tails of several more P4Y-2s. (Courtesy: Wings of China Publications, Wai Yip, Editor)

A flight line of RoCAF P4Y-2s prepare for patrol against a possible invasion from Communist-controlled Mainland China. (Courtesy: Wings of China Publications, Wai Yip, Editor)

An unidentified crew of RoCAF Privateer Number 37 standing next to their glossy sea blue aircraft with the Chinese National Insignia. (Courtesy: Wings of China Publications, Wai Yip, Editor)

tion Castor. This operation was viewed by General Henri Navarre, commander of French forces in Vietnam, as an essential step in halting a Viet Minh offensive in Laos. *Operation Castor* began on 20 November 1953 with French paratroopers occupying the town of Dien Bien Phu, who were then reinforced by units from the French military post at nearby Lai Chau.

Ho Chi Minh knew the French people had grown disillusioned with the war in Indochina and that the French Government was not prepared to commit additional military forces to the conflict. Therefore, he realized that a victory at Dien Bien Phu would provide the Viet Minh a considerable amount of leverage at peace talks scheduled for May 1954 in Geneva, Switzerland. By March 1954 the Viet Minh had concentrated nearly 50,000 regular troops, 55,000 support troops, and almost 100,000 transport workers near Dien Bien Phu.

U.S. Air Force General Benjamin Davis (right) and an unknown Chinese officer stand in front of a RoCAF P4Y-2. In 1951, Davis was the vice-commander of 13th Air Force and commander of Air Task Force 13 at Taipei, Taiwan whose primary responsibility was to build the RoCAF into a strong defensive force against Communist China. (Courtesy: Wings of China Publications, Wai Yip, Editor)

The Viet Minh launched their campaign to take Dien Bien Phu on 13 March 1954, during which time the French garrison numbered 15,000. In response, Flotilla 28F began around-the-clock bombing missions almost immediately, at which time the squadron had at its disposal seven to eight operational aircraft and six crews. During the month 164 sorties were flown, followed by another 176 in April against the steadily advancing Viet Minh. However, the Flotilla's bombing campaign was largely unsuccessful, since the Viet Minh had built an elaborate system of tunnels in the mountainsides that enabled them to protect its artillery pieces by continually moving them to prevent discovery.

Day missions were conducted between 10 to 15,000 feet, and the aircraft were often met with heavy anti-aircraft fire from Viet Minh positions, which accounted for the loss of two Privateers and their crews. Flotilla 28F's first combat loss occurred a little before noon on 12 April when Privateer 28F4, former U.S. Navy Bureau Number 59774, piloted by Ensign Alexis Manfanowsky, was shot down. After orbiting over the French base at 14,000 feet while another P4Y-2 conducted a bombing run against Viet Minh positions, Manfanowsky began a run by descending through a thick overcast. Immediately, enemy guns zeroed in on the aircraft and, within a few moments, it was hit. The Privateer banked to the left, bombs were jettisoned, and the aircraft spiraled into the ground, exploding on impact northwest of French positions, killing Manfanowsky and his crew.

Bombing missions continued, but failed to stem the concerted effort of the Viet Minh, and Dien Bien Phu finally fell on 7 May 1954; the siege had cost the lives of about 25,000 Vietnamese and more than 1,500 French troops. A day after the French surrender, Ensign Pierre Monguillon's Privateer 28F6, former U.S. Navy Bureau Number 59785, was shot down by anti-aircraft fire while fly-

RoCAF Privateers on patrol over Formosa during the 1950s. In 1961, all remaining P4Y-2s were stricken from the RoCAF inventory due to the arrival of more modern aircraft from the United States and from a lack of spare parts. (Courtesy: Wings of China Publications, Wai Yip, Editor)

Viewed from below, ten Privateers of the National Chinese Air Force display a show of force. Throughout the 1950s, RoCAF crews flying the Privateer conducted a variety of missions against Mainland China. (Courtesy: Wings of China Publications, Wai Yip, Editor)

ing near Dien Bien Phu, but two of the nine-man crew, Second Mates Kéromnés and Carpentier, survived to become prisoners of the Viet Minh.

The fall of Dien Bien Phu marked the end of French colonial rule in Vietnam; however, Aéronavale Privateer operations continued until 22 June 1954, when they were finally withdrawn to Saigon. It appears a detachment of Flotilla 28F Privateers remained in Vietnam until April 1956, when the squadron left for North Africa. It also appears that Flotilla 24F, the *Falcon Squadron*, briefly operated the aircraft in Indochina between May and September 1954 before turning the aircraft over to 28F.[65]

Privateers of the French Aéronavale in Africa (1956-1960)

Only months after the end of its colonial rule in Vietnam, France found itself embroiled in another war of independence in French North Africa. On 1 November 1954 Front de Libération Nationale (FLN) guerrillas launched a series of attacks in different parts of Algeria against military installations, police posts, warehouses, communications facilities, and public utilities. By 1956 a major source of supply for the FLN was Tunisia, and the French responded to the threat by installing an elaborate system of sensors, electrified fences, minefields, and forts along the length of Algeria's eastern border. By April 1956 *Aéronavale* Privateers were operating out of Algeria at Télergma, Lartigue, and Sénia in support of the French military by providing maritime surveillance missions (SURMAR).[66]

Privateers of Flotilla 28F, along with the Douglas A-26 Intruder, Lockheed P2V Neptune, and Avro Lancaster, were pressed into service to locate and suppress FLN operatives until the arrival of French-led ground forces. It was during one such mission on 21 May 1957 that Flotilla 28F lost an aircraft and its crew when Privateer 28F4, former U.S. Navy Bureau Number 59870, piloted by Ensign Claude Suret crashed in the Aures Mountains, located in the northeastern section of Algeria. Five of the crew survived the crash, and three were ultimately rescued by friendly forces, while two others may have been captured by the FLN. Support missions continued for another three years, but by the end of 1960, the harsh climate of North Africa, combined with the lack of spare parts and the arrival of the P2V Neptune in *Aéronavale's* inventory, signaled the end of PB4Y-2 operations by the French after 10 years of service.[67]

Privateers of the RoCAF (1952-1961)

The victory of Mao Tse-Tung's Communist forces and the establishment of the People's Republic of China in 1949 resulted in the retreat of the Nationalist president Chiang Kai-shek and his followers to Taiwan, formally called Formosa, from where the latter hoped to retake the mainland. Taiwan was placed under United States military protection soon after the start of the Korean War in June 1950, and the Nationalist Chinese military began receiving military equipment, including aircraft. Between 1952 and 1956 38 P4Y-2s were transferred to the Chinese; however, little information has

RoCAF personnel performing maintenance on the main landing gear of a P4Y-2. Note in the background that the propeller warning is written in English. (Courtesy: Wings of China Publications, Wai Yip, Editor)

RoCAF personnel performing maintenance on a Privateer's main landing wheel assembly. (Courtesy: Wings of China Publications, Wai Yip, Editor)

A supervisor looks on as RoCAF personnel perform engine maintenance. (Courtesy: Wings of China Publications, Wai Yip, Editor)

been forthcoming concerning the dates in which the transfer took place, the identity of all United States units involved in the ferrying missions, or which individual aircraft were actually sent. However, it has been established that in November 1952 VP-28 transferred three of their P4Y-2 Privateers to the Military Assistance Advisory Group (MAAG) in Taiwan. In March 1953 the United States Navy ferried another 12 Privateers to the Philippines, where personnel from the Republic of China Air Force (RoCAF) were waiting to take delivery. However, the aircraft were delivered in a somewhat derelict condition and required additional maintenance before they could be flown to Taiwan. Assigned to the 8th Air Group, they were used for bombing missions, coastal maritime patrol, and clandestine operations against the People's Republic of China, during which the RoCAF lost four of the aircraft. Chinese Privateers retained the standard dark blue United States Navy color scheme, but large one or two digit RoCAF serial numbers were added to the side of the fuselage ahead of the cockpit.

Between August 1954 and May 1955, nationalist and communist military forces fought in a series of engagements in the Taiwan Straits, which nearly prompted the United States to use nuclear weapons against mainland China. During the crisis, the RoCAF Privateers were used to bomb communist positions and gather electronic intelligence. On one such mission, RoCAF Privateer Number 12 was shot down by anti-aircraft artillery near Xiamen, China. In the summer of 1955, at the request of the United States military, the RoCAF began using a P4Y to gather intelligence over China. Special electronic equipment was installed in one of the aircraft, a crew was trained on the use of the equipment and, between 17 August 1955 and 12 April 1956, 14 nighttime missions, lasting between six to 10 hours, were conducted over the Chinese mainland to collect such intelligence data.

After the Communist victory in 1949 pro-Nationalist troops located in the Province of Wenan were forced to retreat to the jungles of Burma, where they established a stronghold for guerrilla warfare; RoCAF Privateers were used to supply this force. On 6 April 1958 a P4Y-2 with the RoCAF Serial Number 16 was involved in an airdrop, but was delayed by about an hour to identify the drop zone. Not having enough fuel to return to Taiwan, this P4Y-2 was forced to land in Hong Kong, where it was allowed to refuel and return to Taiwan two days later. Because of the spare parts problem, all surviving P4Y-2s were ordered to retire on 1 August 1958; however, it appears that some continued to fly re-supply missions for nearly another three years. RoCAF use of the Privateer concluded when Hawker Sea Fury fighters of the Burmese Airforce shot down P4Y-2 Number 423, possibly former USN Bureau Number 59423, on 15 February 1961 over Thailand while dropping supplies to the guerrillas.[68]

RoCAF P4Y-2 Privateer Losses

Date	Personnel Losses
12 September 1954	9 killed
15 February 1961	5 killed

12

Privateers Since 1961

Only a handful of the 736 PB4Y-2s that rolled off the assembly line in San Diego remain in existence. By the end of the 1950s, with both active duty and reserve squadrons equipped with the Lockheed P2V Neptune, a few remaining Privateers—four of them identified as Bureau Numbers 59779, 59935, 59758, and 59872—were sent to the missile testing center at Point Mugu, California. At Point Mugu, the aircraft were painted a bright orange-red and converted to remote control QP-4B drones, where they were ultimately destroyed during weapons testing.

The two last Privateers in the Navy inventory, Opposite 31 and Opposite 35, were destroyed in December 1963 and January 1964 over the Pacific Missile Test Range. Opposite 31, with the nickname *Lucky Pierre*, was brought down on 18 December 1963, and a month later, on 18 January 1964, Opposite 35—nicknamed *Clyde*—was destroyed by a Bullpup pilot-guided air-to-ground missile fired from an A-4 Skyhawk jet piloted by Bert Creighton of Navy Squadron VX-4. According to Creighton, when the Bullpup locked in and exploded over the Privateer, "It just blew the propellers off, and it flipped over on its back and spun in."[69]

With faded paint, a somewhat derelict Bureau Number 59713 awaits conversion to a P4Y-2K target drone. Barely visible behind the Privateer is a B-17 Flying Fortress probably waiting for a similar conversion. (Author's Collection)

Civilian Privateers

In the mid-1950s, approximately two dozen Privateers sitting in storage at Litchfield Park, outside of Phoenix, Arizona, were sold to private individuals and companies, who proceeded to remove all non-essential equipment in order to use the aircraft as crop dusters, transports, and in aerial fire fighting. The turrets and armor plating were removed, and the Pratt & Whitney R-1830-94 engines were replaced by the Wright Cyclone R-2600 to improve performance, which enabled the aircraft to hold up to 18,000 pounds or 3,000 gallons of fire-retardant chemical, which is also called *slurry mix*. Dubbed the Super Privateer, a few continue to perform aerial fire fighting duties with Hawkins & Powers Aviation, based out of Greybull, Wyoming. However, flying the World War II-era aircraft has resulted in the loss of several Privateers and their crews. Since 1968, four Privateers and their crews have been lost while flying slurry runs, while others have been destroyed or severely damaged in accidents.

Privateer Airtanker Fatalities (1968-2002)

Date	Serial Number	Location	Fatalities
22 July 1968	7974A	McGrath, Alaska	4
3 September 1969	1911H	Greybull, Wyoming	2
27 June 1974	7237C	Safford, Arizona	2
18 July 2002	7620C	Pinewoods, Colorado	2

Privateers in Latin America

During the late 1950s a few surplus Privateers found their way to Latin America, where they served as passenger or cargo planes with civilian companies or the military. Specific planes have been identified as operating out of Brazil, Honduras, and Mexico, while a few more may have been registered in Argentina, Chile, and Paraguay.

Bureau Number 59713 at the U.S. Navy's Point Mugu Missile Test Center after being converted to a P4Y-2K target drone in 1961. (Courtesy Giorgio Salerno)

Still in U.S. Navy markings, but with a newly applied civilian registration number N6814D, Number 205 with the Naval Reserve tail code letter "T" indicates that at one time it was assigned to NAS Seattle, Washington. (Author's Collection)

Her glossy blue coloring faded in the desert heat, Bureau Number 59614 a PB4Y-2S also waits the scrapper's torch at Litchfield Park, Arizona sometime in the early 1960s. (Author's Collection)

PB4Y-2S *Bouncing Betty* (Bureau Number 59741) waiting for her final fate in a storage area at Litchfield Park, Arizona sometime during the early 1960s. (Author's Collection)

Since the late 1950's two civilian Privateers have held the registration number N6884C. This is possibly the first, former Bureau Number 66284, which crashed on landing at Prescott, Arizona in June 1959 while serving as a fire bomber. (Author's Collection)

Converted to a fire bomber and operated by WenAirCo-according to the name stenciled below the co-pilot's station. N6816D was consumed by fire on the runway at Wenatchee, Washington on 27 July 1972. (Author's Collection)

Number 201 saw naval service at NAS Miami, Florida. Here it has the civilian registration N6816D shortly before the aircraft's conversion to a fire bomber. (Author's Collection)

N3191G Number 85 painted overall silver with orange tail and black anti-glare panel crashed at Diamond Lake, Oregon on 27 July 1970. (Author's Collection)

This photograph taken circa 1960s is of Hawkins & Powers N3739G. The former U.S. Navy Bureau Number 59819 was overall silver with both numbering and the anti-glare panel painted black. It is currently undergoing restoration at the Lone Star Flight Museum in Galveston, Texas. (Author's Collection)

Privateer Bureau Number 66293 was registered in Brazil as PT-BEO and served as a cargo plane with the civilian company Importadora e Exportadora of Rio de Janeiro beginning in February 1961. There is confusion whether a second Brazilian Privateer registered as PT-BEG actually existed, or if it was PT-BEO with a new serial number.

At least one, if not two Privateers operated in Mexico during the 1960s through the early 1970s. A substantial amount of information shows that former U.S. Navy Bureau Number 59946 operated in Mexico with the serial XB-DIT. During its service with the United States Navy, Privateer 59946 was assigned to training squadrons VB-4, ATU VP-HL-12, and NAMTC at Point Mugu, California, before being sold to Lysdale Flying Service and converted to a fire bomber with the U.S. civilian registry N6815D. This aircraft was sold to Mexico in 1959, painted an overall white, re-registered as XB-DIT, and began hauling fish along Baja, California. XB-DIT's ultimate fate is unknown. Some sources also suggest that a second Privateer with the former Bureau Number 59913 and U.S. civilian registry N6814 operated in Mexico as XB-DOD. [70]

Honduran Privateers served as transports. Parked next to several automobiles is FH-796. Both FH-792 and 796 went back to the United States in 1973. (Author's Collection)

Brazilian PT-BEO, former U.S. Navy Bureau Number 66293, served as a cargo plane in the early 1960s for a company named Importadora e Exportadora. (Author's Collection)

FH-792 was one of at least two Privateers the Honduran Air Force had in its inventory between 1956 and 1973. (Author's Collection)

Two Privateers with the former U.S. Navy Bureau Numbers 59742 and 59763 were purchased by the Honduran Air Force, Fuerza Aérea Hondurea (FAH), and served as transports with the FAH serial numbers 792 and 796. In addition, some information refers to an additional Honduran Privateer with the serial number FAH-794. According to military records, Bureau Number 59763 had a distinguished history, serving with VPB-106, 108, 111, 200; VP-23, VJ-2, and FASRON 103 before being sold as surplus in 1956. Positive identification of Honduran Privateers in terms of matching the FAH serials with either bureau numbers or U.S. civilian registration has yet to be completed. FAH-792 may have been Bureau Number 59742 with the U.S. civilian registry N7683C, and was briefly registered as HR-195-P. If this is correct, then FAH-796 was the former 59763, later registered as N7237C. Both aircraft operated from Honduras until 1973, when they were sold and converted to fire bombers in the United States with N7237C crashing during a slurry run on 27 June 1974, killing the two pilots.[71]

Museum Examples

The National Museum of Naval Aviation in Pensacola, Florida, acquired former Coast Guard P4Y-2G, Bureau Number 66304, for static display from Hawkins & Powers in 1983 after serving with the company as N2870G. The Lone Star Flight Museum in Galveston, Texas, is currently restoring to PB4Y-2 Bureau Number 59819, which served with Navy squadrons VPB-120 and VP-HL-10 before being sold to T&G Aviation of Chandler, Arizona, which converted it to a fire bomber with the civilian registry N3739G. On static display at the Yankee Air Museum in Belleville, Michigan, is Bureau Number 59876, which served with the Navy's VPB-197 and VPW-1 until the early 1950s, when the Coast Guard converted it to a P4Y-2G. In 1957 it entered the civilian market as N6813D and served as a fire bomber with Hawkins & Powers before being donated to the museum in 1986.

Color Gallery

Very few color photographs exist of World War II-era PB4Y-2 Privateers. Here is VPB-121's *Tail Chaser* (Bureau Number 59491) in faded tri-color camouflage at NAS Miramar, California upon its return from Iwo Jima in 1945. (Courtesy: Tailhook Association via Mahlon K. Miller)

One PB4Y-2 that did not make it back to Miramar was VPB-109's Bureau Number 59521 *Bachelor's Delight* shot down on 5 August 1945. In this photograph, taken in the Pacific, she sits company with two other USN land-based bombers, a PB4Y-1 Liberator in the back left and a PV-1 Ventura in the back right. (Author's Collection)

VPB-109's *Miss Lotta Tail* (Bureau Number 59522) with 59581 in the left background parked at NAS Miramar after returning from Okinawa. (Courtesy: Tailhook Association via Mahlon K. Miller)

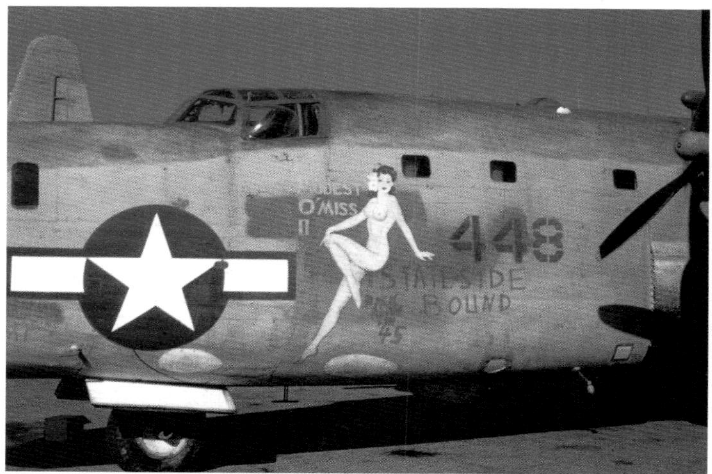

Modest O' Miss II (Bureau Number 59448) after arriving back in the United States in the fall of 1945 with an added phrase of "Back Alive in 45". (Courtesy: Tailhook Association via Mahlon K. Miller)

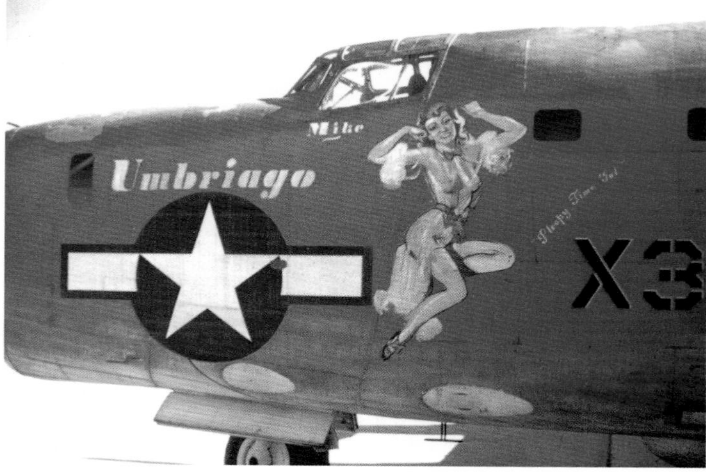

Shown here is VPB-106's *Umbriago* (Bureau Number 59390) at NAS Miramar in late 1945 after returning from Palawan Island, Philippines. (Courtesy: Tailhook Association via Mahlon K. Miller)

PB4Y-2 E-101 running her engines at NAS Miramar in 1945 may have served with either VPB-109 or 118 but its true squadron remains unclear. (Courtesy: Tailhook Association via Mahlon K. Miller)

Torchy Lena painted overall glossy sea blue and of unknown squadron lineage or bureau number, appears to have served rather well in the Pacific according to its 10 kill and 42 mission markings. (Courtesy: Tailhook Association via Mahlon K. Miller)

Chief Petty Officer (CPO) Coleman and Aviation Ordnanceman (AO2) John Smith of VP-871 at Atsugi, Japan in April 1952. (Courtesy: John Smith via Jeff Walker)

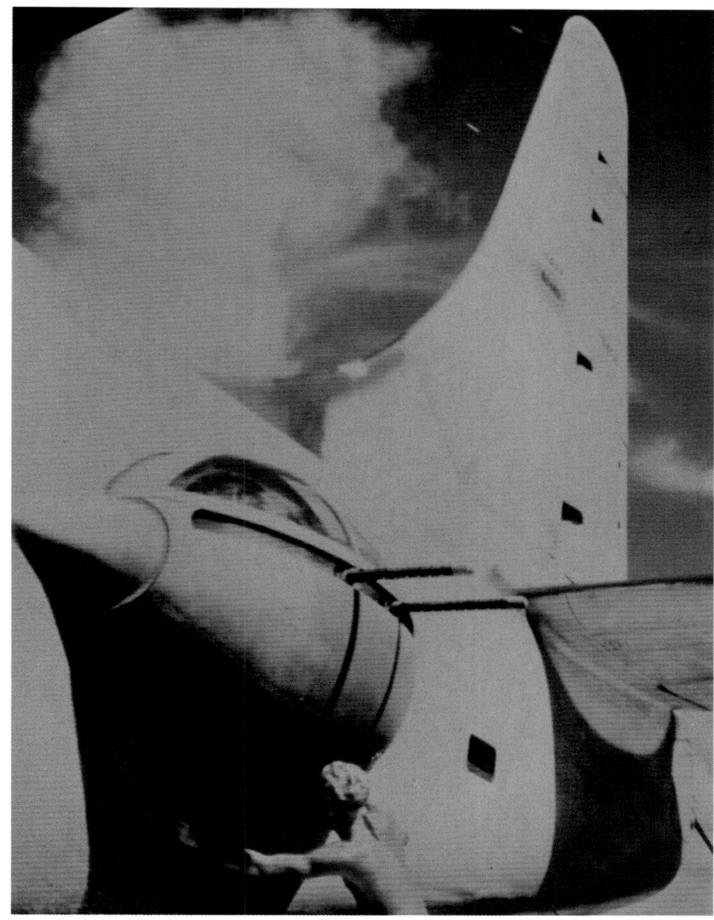

A member of an unidentified Privateer squadron inspects a waist turret somewhere in the Pacific during World War II. (Author's Collection)

Privateer CH-5 assigned to VP-871 on the ground at Atsugi, Japan, in April 1952. (Courtesy: John Smith via Jeff Walker)

Privateer CB-3 of VP-9 in flight circa 1951-52 when the squadron was serving in Japan during the Korean War. (Courtesy: A.G. Alexander)

E-141 leading a flight of Privateers with sea blue coloring possibly over California circa 1945. (Courtesy: Tailhook Association via Mahlon K. Miller)

A flight crew of VP-871 at Barbers Point, Hawaii on 5 December 1951 prepares for departure on the next leg of a TransPac to Johnson Island. The men identified in the back row from left to right: Bozzuto, Griffith, Gray, Millard, Waldrop, and John Smith. Front row from left to right: Reese, McArthur, Vic Westberg, Stan Walker, and Mearl Grisham. (Courtesy: John Smith via Jeff Walker)

This photograph shows the men that comprised VP-772's Crew 9 in 1952. Front row left to right: James A. Moen, plane captain, Lieutenant (jg) David E. Gates, navigator, Lieutenant William T. Vierregger, pilot, Lieutenant (jg) Harry G. Feldman, co-pilot, and Wilmer L. Kerns, radarman. Back row from left to right: Halton Q. Bittick II, 1st ordnanceman, R.L. Cosens, gunner, R.L. Miller, gunner, Philip G. Bernard, electronics technician and radioman, S.L. Shoemaker, 2nd radioman, and Shelby C. Andrus, 2nd mechanic. (Courtesy: Wilmer L. Kerns)

The Chief of Naval Operations in November 1944 approved VPB-106's official squadron insignia of a wolf riding a bomb. (Source: Naval Historical Center)

VPB-109's unofficial insignia of a Pirate riding a bomb, designed while the squadron was based on Okinawa, was apparently not submitted for approval to the Chief of Naval Operations. (Author's Collection)

VPB-118's unofficial squadron insignia of a penguin in a tuxedo carrying a bomb was probably not submitted for approval from the Chief of Naval Operations. The model for the insignia was Crows Landing Naval Air Station and a particular brand of bourbon. (Courtesy: Al Marks)

Squadron members between 1944 and 1946 apparently used VPB-119's unofficial insignia of a dragon devouring a Japanese flag, but there is no indication that it was submitted for approval from the Chief of Naval Operations. (Source: Naval Historical Center)

The Chief of Naval Operations in 1941 approved VPB-121's official squadron insignia of a Polar Bear. (Source: Naval Historical Center)

VPB-122's official insignia shows a Disney winged wolf character looking through a spyglass and was approved by the Chief of Naval Operations in late 1945. (Courtesy: Al Marks)

VPB-123's unofficial squadron insignia of a woodpecker mounted on a bomb and firing a machine gun commemorates the squadron's tour of duty on Okinawa in 1945. Donald Salmela, a member of the squadron, designed it. (Courtesy: VPB-123 Veterans Group)

The Chief of Naval Operations in March 1945 approved VPB-124's official insignia of a winged privateer sailing ship. (Author's Collection)

Privateer 59783 (71V) on a snow-covered runway in the Aleutian Islands circa 1945-1946. This aircraft, assigned to VPB-122, displays a variation in World War II camouflage consisting of a mottled appearance along the fuselage. (Courtesy: Giorgio Salerno)

Sunlight glistens off a flight of VP-24 Privateers circa late 1940s. (Courtesy: George Batho via Steve Hawley)

VP-871's CH-4 airborne out of Hawaii in December 1951 and heading for Japan to conduct maritime reconnaissance and flare dropping missions in support of combat operations in Korea. (Courtesy: John Smith via Jeff Walker)

This color photograph shows Flotilla's F28-7 of the French Aéronavale running its engines at an unknown location, possibly French Algeria circa 1957-60. (Courtesy: Giorgio Salerno)

Standing on the tarmac circa WB-223 provides a stunning example of the color scheme applied to late 1940s and early 1950s Privateers. (Courtesy: Giorgio Salerno)

Hawkins & Powers Number 123 with the registration number N7620C was a former U.S. Coast Guard P4Y-2G with the Bureau Number 66260. (Author's Collection)

Privateers of VP-9 parked on the tarmac at an unidentified location and time. (Courtesy: The Tailhook Association via Mahlon K. Miller)

A side profile of Hawkins & Powers Number 123 photographed in 1983. This aircraft crashed killing the two pilots aboard while conducting a slurry run on a wild fire near Pinewood, Colorado on 17 July 2003. (Courtesy: Giorgio Salerno)

Hawkins & Powers *Charlie 30* N3739G (USN Bureau Number 59819) shown here in June 1981 is now on display at the Yankee Air Museum at Ann Arbor, Michigan. (Courtesy: Giorgio Salerno)

At the time of this book's publication Hawkins & Powers Aviation, based at Greybull, Wyoming, continues to fly heavily modified and stripped down Privateers. Shown here is Super Privateer Number 126 (civilian registry N7962C) which formally held the USN Bureau Number 59882. (Courtesy: Hawkins and Powers Aviation, Inc)

Hawkins & Powers Number 126 releasing fire retardant possibly during a practice run. Records indicate this aircraft probably served with the U.S. Coast Guard during the 1950s. (Courtesy: Hawkins & Powers Aviation, Inc)

This photograph taken by VPB-118 veteran Elmor Jones shows Hawkins & Powers Number 121 in February 1991. Registered as N2871G, this aircraft is former USN and USCG Bureau Number 66302. (Courtesy: Elmor Jones via Earl Mann)

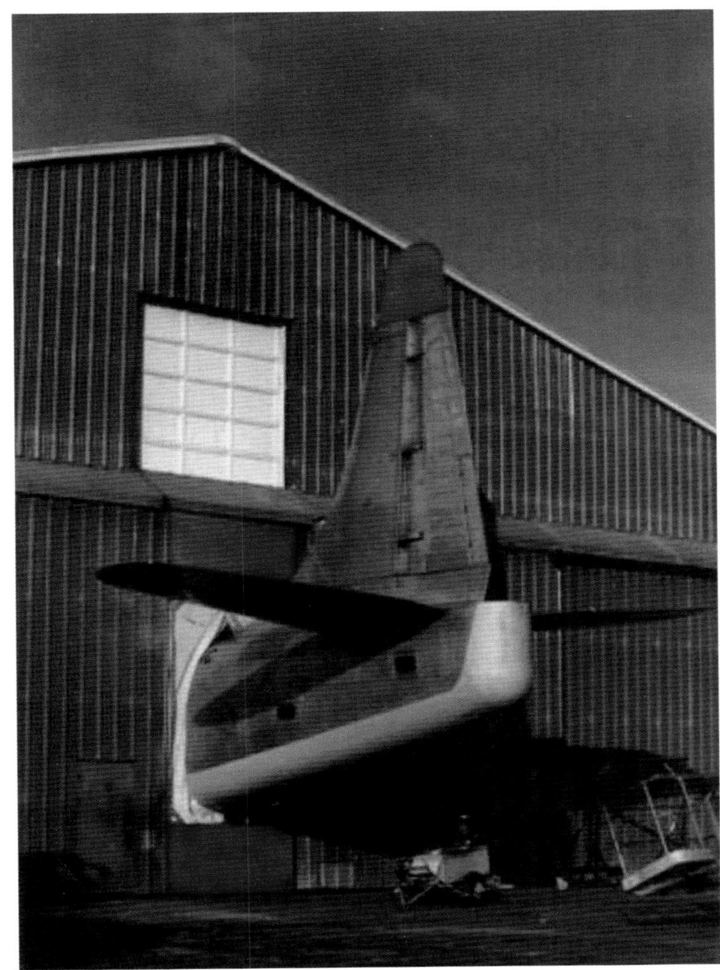

Another photograph taken by Elmor Jones shows the tail section of Hawkins & Powers Number 127 protruding out of a hanger at Greybull, Wyoming. (Courtesy: Elmor Jones via Earl Mann)

Wingless and broken, a derelict fuselage of a Privateer sits in a vacant lot somewhere in Florida circa 1980s. (Author's Collection)

The author photographed Privateer Bureau Number 66304 at the National Museum of Naval Aviation in Pensacola, Florida in October 2003 during a reunion held by veterans of VPB-109. It was the last squadron reunion attended by the author's father (Author's Collection)

VPB-118 veteran Elmor Jones took this photographing in December 1990 showing Hawkins & Powers Number 127 (former USN Bureau Number 59701) with the civilian registry N6884C. (Courtesy: Elmor Jones via Earl Mann)

Appendix A: WWII Aerial Kills by PB4Y-2 Patrol Plane Commanders

The following lists the dates, squadrons, patrol plan commanders (PPC), number, and types of Japanese aircraft destroyed in the air by PB4Y-2s during the Second World War (Original data compiled by James C. Sawruk). The author of this book takes responsibility for any errors that may have occurred during the editing process of Mr. Sawruk's data.

Date	Squadron	PPC	Type
05/30	106	Lt. (jg) Vernon J. Smith	Jake
			Oscar
			Total = 2
06/16	108	Lt. Charles T. Idle	Zeke
		Lt. Charles T. Idle	Zeke
		Lt. Charles R. Baumgartner	1/2 Oscar
06/20		Lt. William R. Hazlett	1/2 Oscar
			Total = 3
05/02	109	Lt. (jg) George Serbin	Dinah
			Jake
05/17		Lt. William A. Warren	George
			1/2 George
		Lt. George D. Fairbanks	1/2 George
05/24		Lt. Donald S. Chay	Rufe
		Lt. Floyd Hewitt	Tony
			Total = 6
03/11	118	Lt. Norman M. Keiser	Emily
04/27		Lt. Phillip E. Pettes	1/2 Val
		Lt. Leland P. McCutcheon	1/2 Val
05/05		Lt. August M. Lodato	Stella
		LCDR Arthur F. Farwell Jr.	Lorna
		Lt. August M. Lodato	1/2 Tess
		LCDR Arthur F. Farwell Jr.	1/2 Tess
05/07		LCDR Arthur F. Farwell Jr.	Val
05/16		LCDR Arthur F. Farwell Jr.	George
		Lt. Robert M. Finley	George
07/23		Lt. Robert M DeGolia	1/2 Topsy
		Lt. George H. Shortlidge	1/2 Topsy
			Total = 9
03/10	119	Lt. (jg) Virgil J. Evans	Oscar
03/12		Lt. (jg) Aubrey L. Althans	Jill
03/13		Lt. Frank D. Murphy	Oscar
03/18		Lt. William Lyle	Oscar
			Oscar
03/24		Lt. (jg) Aubrey L. Althans	Jake
04/01		Lt. (jg) Walter G. Vogelsang	Val
05/09		Lt. Frank F. Mattewson	Val
			Total = 8
07/31	121	Lt. Albert H. Magie Jr.	1/2 Zeke
		Lt. Richard V. Donahue	1/2 Zeke
08/03		LCDR Raymond J. Pflum	1/2 Pete
		Lt. Ralph E. Ettinger	1/2 Pete
		LCDR Raymond J. Pflum	1/2 Pete
		Lt. Ralph E. Ettinger	1/2 Pete
08/11		Lt. Thomas G. Allen	Zeke
			Total = 4
05/31	123	Lt. George W. McDonald	1/2 Frank
		Lt. Robert J. Monahan	1/2 Frank
06/03		Lt. George W. McDonald	1/2 Pete
		Lt. Robert J. Monahan	1/2 Pete
06/06		Lt. (jg) Erwin L. Klein	1/2 Tony
		Lt. (jg) Harold M. Sanderson	1/2 Tony
06/08		LCDR Samuel G. Shilling	Rex
		Lt. Alfred G. McCuaig	Tojo
07/03		Lt. Alfred G. McCuaig	Tojo
07/23		Lt. (jg) Richard L. Treat	Tojo
07/26		Lt. (jg) Terence P. Cassidy	Tojo
			Tojo
			Total = 9
07/06	124	Lt. John E. Ramsey	Val
07/07		Lt. (jg) Everett W. Osborn Jr.	Rex
07/24		John E. Ramsey	1/2 Oscar
		Lt. Gilbert E. Miller	1/2 Oscar
			Total = 3

Model and Types of Japanese Aircraft Engaged by PB4Y-2 Privateers

American Code Name	Model/Type
Dinah:	Mitsubishi Ki-46/2-engine Patrol
Emily:	H8K/two-engine flying boat
George:	Kawanishi N1K2 Shiden single-engine Fighter-Bomber
Frank:	Nakajima Ki-84 Hayate single-engine Fighter-Bomber
Kate:	Nakajima B5NS/single-engine Torpedo-bomber
Jake:	Aichi E13A1 floatplane fighter
Jill:	Nakajima B6N Tenzan single-engine Torpedo-bomber
Nick:	Kawasaki Ki-45/twin-engine fighter-bomber
Oscar:	Nakajima Ki-43 Hayabusa single-engine fighter
Pete:	Mitsubishi F1M2/single engine float-wing fighter
Rex:	Kawanishi N1K Kyofu single-engine floatplane fighter
Rufe:	Nakajima A6M2-N single-engine float-fighter
Sally:	Mitsubishi Ki-21/Bomber
Tess:	Two-engine transport
Tojo:	Ki-44 Shoki single-engine fighter
Tony:	Kawasaki Ki-61 Hien single-engine fighter
Topsy:	Mitsubishi Type 100 Ki-57 (L4M)/transport
Val:	Aichi D3A/single-engine dive-bomber
Zeke	Mitsubishi A6M Reisen single-engine fighter

Total Squadron Aerial Kills

Squadron	Aerial Kills	Squadron	Aerial Kills
118	9	121	4
123	9	108	3
119	8	124	3
109	6	106	2
		Total	44

Appendix B: WWII Squadron Combat Records

The following lists the combat records of World War II PB4Y-2 Squadrons found in individual squadron cruise books and combat diaries.

VPB-106
Ships Sunk: 30+
Ships Damaged: 78+
Aircraft Destroyed in Air: 2
Damaged in Air: 1
Destroyed on Ground: 2
Damaged on Ground: 2

VPB-108
Ships Sunk: 118
Ships Damaged: 159
Aircraft Destroyed in Air: 3
Probable: 1
Damaged in Air: 3

VPB-109 (The Reluctant Raiders)
Ships Sunk: 118
Ships Damaged: 87
Tonnage: 87,200
Aircraft Destroyed in Air: 6
Damaged in Air: 8
Damaged on Ground:1

VPB-118 (The Old Crows)
Ships Sunk: 100
Ships Damaged: 105
Aircraft Destroyed in Air: 9
Damaged in Air: 6
Destroyed on Ground: 5

VPB-119
Ships Sunk: 114
Ships Damaged: 124
Aircraft Destroyed in Air: 8
Damaged in Air: 3
Destroyed on Ground: 2
Damaged on Ground: 3

VPB-121
Ships Sunk: 8
Ships Damaged: 10
Tonnage: Less than 5,000
Aircraft Destroyed in Air: 4

VPB-123
Ships Sunk: 67
Ships Damaged: 38
Aircraft Destroyed in Air: 9

VPB-124
Ships Sunk: 16
Ships Damaged: 21
Tonnage: 27,136
Aircraft Destroyed in Air: 3
Damaged in Air: 1

Appendix C: WWII PB4Y-2 Combat and Operational Losses October 1944-August 1945

The following table lists the number of aircraft lost from all causes by PB4Y-2 combat squadrons during World War II. This list does not include losses incurred by training squadrons in the United States.

Squadron	Number
102	0
104	0
106	6
108	5
109	5
111	0
116	0
117	0
118	13
119	12
120	0
121	4
122	0
123	2
124	9
Total =	56

Appendix D: WWII PB4Y-2 Privateer Nose Art

The following is a partial list of aircraft with nose art, consisting of bureau numbers (if known), unit assignments during and after World War II (if known), the names of corresponding nose art, and a remarks section. Some information has been updated since the publication of *Above an Angry Sea*. Additional information was obtained from the following sources: Jim Augustus, David E. Bronson, Bill Duckett, Orvis N. Fitts, Steve Hawley, A.C. Jeanguenat, and Earl Mann.

BuNo	Unit(s)	Name	Remarks
32095		*Wart Hog*	XPB4Y-2 stricken 1946
59360	VPB-108/122	*Els Nocho*	
59378?	VPB-118		Possibly surveyed due to battle damage on 05/06/45.
59379	VPB-106/118	*Flying Tail?*	Surveyed due to battle damage on 05/26/45
59380	VPB-118	*Summer Storm*	Destroyed when a B-29 crashed into it on Tinian 04/22/45. Reported as belonging to VPB-119 in *Above an Angry Sea*.
59382	VPB-123	*La Cherrie*	
59383	VPB-118	*Navy's Torchy Tess*	Reported lost in action 05/06/45 in *Above an Angry Sea*.
59388	VPB-118	*Soaring Fin*	Ditched off Korea 05/07/45
59370	VPB-106	*Joy Ride*	
59390	VPB-106	*Umbriago*	
59392	VPB-118	*Miss Behavin*	Damaged while landing at Tinian 05/25/45
59396	VPB-106	*Blue Diamond*	Surveyed due to unidentified cause on 05/24/45
59397	VPB-106/Hedron 14-2	*Lucky-Levin*	Crashed near Miramar on 08/01/46
59398	VPB-106/197	*Baldy (Tortilla Flat)*	
59402	VPB-118	*Modest O Miss*	Crashed on landing at Iwo Jima 03/06/45
59404	VPB-118	*Pirate Queen*	Destroyed by enemy bombing on Okinawa 07/29/45
59405	VPB-118	*Miss Natch*	Caught fire and burned on the ground at Tinian 06/02/45.
59406	VPB-121	*Naval Body*	
59409	VPB-121	*Come N' Get It*	
59410	VPB-118	*Miss Lottatail*	
59413	VPB-119	*Holts Patches*	
59419	VPB-119	*Elizabeth Ann*	
59424	VPB-121	*Mr. Kip*	Surveyed due to unidentified cause on 05/29/45
59430	VPB-118	*Twitchy Bitch*	
59431	VPB-121	*Little Patrica*	
59432	VPB-106	*Tarfu*	
59438	VPB-123	*Lady of Leisure*	Crashed at Okinawa on 06/19/45
59441	VPB-108	*Accentuate the Positive*	Stricken due to landing accident 08/13/45
59446	VPB-108	*Lady Luck II*	Surveyed due to battle damage 06/11/45
59447	VPB-121	*Dangerous Dan*	
59449	VPB-118	*Vulnerable Virgin*	Lost in action on 05/06/45
59450	VPB-121	*Abroad for Action*	
59459	VPB-108	*Lady Luck III*	Identified as VPB-111 in *Above an Angry Sea*
59460	VPB-108	*Els-Notcho*	
59475	VPB-121	*Louisiana Lil*	
59476	VPB-123	*Pirate Princess*	
59478	VPB-121	*Buccaneer Bunny*	
59479	VPB-121	*After Hours*	Destroyed by fire on ground 05/28/45
59480	VPB-108	*Hippin Kitten II*	
59482	VPB-118	*Miss You*	
59484	VPB-121	*Lotta Tayle*	
59487	VPB-123	*Vagrant Verago*	
59489	VPB-108/121	*La Cherie*	
59491	VPB-121	*Tail Chaser/Red Wing*	
59492	VPB-121	*Pirate Princess*	
59498	VPB-108	*Super Slooper*	
59500	VPB-123	*Jackass Jenny*	Surveyed due to battle damage on 06/09/45
59501	VPB-109	*Punkie*	

59502	VPB-109	*Green Cherries*	
59504	VPB-124/123	*Pastime*	
59505	VPB-106/123/ VP-HL-12	*Red Wing/Indian Made*	
59506	VPB-123	*Little Skipper*	
59509	VPB-123	*Jacqueline*	
59510	VPB-123/VP(HL) ATU-12	*Jackson's Jail*	
59514	VPB-109	*Blind Bomber*	
59515	VPB-109	*Hogan's Goat*	
59520	VPB-123	*No Body Else's Butt*	
59519	VPB-124	*Gear Locked and Down*	Lost in action on 07/24/45
59521	VPB-109	*Bachelor's Delight*	Lost in action on 08/05/45
59522	VPB-109	*Miss Lotta Tail*	
59524	VPB-123	*Balls of Fire*	Crashed on landing at Camp Kearney, Californian on 01/28/46
59525	VPB-106/123	*Our Baby*	
59528	VPB-109	*Lambaster*	
59548	VPB-123	*Typhoon*	Surveyed after crashing on take off at Okinawa on 10/45
59564	VPB-121	*Ol' Blunderbuss*	
59566	VPB-121	*The Mad Frenchman*	
59582	VPB-116	*Miss Sea-ducer*	
59617	VPB-116/121/ VP(HL)-12	*Miss Milovin*	Crashed at NAS Corpus Christi, Texas on 09/12/47
59682	VPB-116	*Water Spy*	Crashed on landing at Tinian on 09/28/45
59745	VPB-120	*The Black Sheep*	
59755	VPB-122/116	*Peace Feeler*	
59760	VPB-116	*Cover Girl*	
Unknown	VPB-124	*Supreme Zu Zu*	
Unknown	VPB-124	*No Strain*	
Unknown	VPB-124	*Miss Pandemonium*	
Unknown		*Out of Bounds*	

Appendix E: PB4Y-2 Privateer Operational and Combat Losses 1944-1956

A considerable number of Privateers were lost through combat or operational accidents during its long service with the United States Navy. The following data consists of the individual bureau number, unit assignments, circumstances surrounding the loss, and date of loss for the Privateer from 1944 to 1956, in addition to those documented in the nose art section. This is not an exhaustive tabulation and, therefore, some omissions or errors possibly occurred while compiling this list. Source for this information was obtained from the Naval Aviation Safety Center Aircraft Accident Reports Roll 25 and World War II Squadron Combat Diaries.

BuNo	Unit(s)	Circumstance
59351	Unknown	Crashed on landing at Patuxent River, Maryland on 05/19/45
59356	VP(HL)-12	Surveyed due to unidentified cause on 03/28/48
59357	VPB-122	Crashed during training flight near La Conner, Washington on 08/13/45
59361	VPB-122	Surveyed after swerving off runway at Crows Landing, California on 04/01/45
59367	Unknown	Surveyed for unknown cause at Chincoteague, Virginia on 03/?/48
59369	VPB-121/124	Crashed on take off at Camp Kearney, California on 01/03/45
59377	VPB-118	Crashed while taxing at NAS Kaneohe, Hawaii on 12/25/45
59380	VPB-119	B-29 crashed into 59380 4/22/45 at west field, Tinian. Listed as belonging to VPB-119 in *Above an Angry Sea*
59381	VPB-118	Crashed while taking off from Midway on 12/17/44
59384	VPB-106	Surveyed on Palawan Island, Philippines on 06/?/45
59385	VPB-106	Surveyed due to unknown cause
59386	VPB-106	Struck coral boulder on runway at Tinian on 02/16/45
59387	VPB-118	Landing accident at NAS Kaneohe, Hawaii on 12/24/44
59389	VPB-106	Surveyed on Palawan Island, Philippines 06/?/45
59394	VPB-106	Ditched in Gulf of California on 10/24/44
59397	Hedron 14-2	Crashed near NAS Miramar, California on 08/01/46
59399	NAF Litchfield Park	Heavily damaged during engine run-up on 10/05/44
59401	VPB-118	Ditched two miles from Iwo Jima on 04/13/45
59407	VP-25	Crashed on landing at Agana, Guam on 12/29/48
59412	VPB-106	Lost in action 06/14/45
59414	VPB-119	Lost in action 04/11/45
59415	VPB-119	Lost on Typhoon flight from Clark Field, Philippines on 10/01/45
59422	VPB-119	Lost in action 05/19/45
59425	FAW-14	Ditched off Oahu, Hawaii on 05/29/45
59426	VPB-119	Lost in action 03/22/45
59427	VPB-119	Lost in action 06/17/45
59429	VPB-119	Collided with a PB4Y-1 at Clark Field, Philippines on 03/08/45
59433	VPB-106	Lost in action 07/01/45
59434	VB-4	Burned on ground at NAAS Whiting Field on 01/08/46
59436	VPB-121	Surveyed due to landing accident 02/15/45
59437	VB-4	Collided with PB4Y-2 BuNo 59721 over Munson, Florida on 05/10/46
59439	VPB-108	Unidentified loss on Iwo Jima on 05/11/45
59440	VPB-108	Possibly surveyed after raid on Marcus Island 05/09/45
59442	VPB-108	Ditched while on patrol on 04/08/45
59445	VPB-108	Surveyed due to battle damage in Marcus Island Raid 05/09/45
59448	VPB-118	Surveyed due to battle damage on 07/27/45
59452	VPB-119	Lost in action 04/01/45
59458	VPB-118	Lost in action on 07/22/45
59467	VPB-119	Surveyed after hard landing at Nichols Field, Philippines on 03/08/45
59473	VB ATU-1	Crashed on landing at NAS Hutchinson, Kansas on 07/12/46
59474	VPB-121	Lost in action 3/06/45
59477	VPB-121	Ditched while on flight to Kaneohe, Hawaii on 01/11/45
59495	VPB-121	Lost in action on 08/11/45
59497	VPB-106	Lost in action on 03/9/45
59513	VPB-124	Crashed due to fuel exhaustion on 06/06/45
59523	VPB-109	Destroyed on ground by enemy bombing on 05/24/45
59526	VPB-109	Destroyed in enemy bombing at Okinawa on 05/19/45
59529	VPB-109	Surveyed after being damaged on ground at Okinawa on 05/24/45
59530	VPB-109	Surveyed 06/06/45 after suffering battle damage on 05/30/45
59532	VPB-124	Lost in action on 06/26/45

59533	VPB-109	Possibly surveyed due to damage from enemy bombing on 05/24/45
59534	VPB-124	Surveyed due to battle damage on 07/02/45
59535	VPB-124	Lost in action on 06/27/45
59538	VPB-124	Lost in action on 07/07/45
59539	VB-4	Crashed during training flight near Sioux City, Iowa on 06/18/46
59543	VPB-119	Surveyed do to battle damage on 03/29/45
59544	Unknown	Crashed taking off from Lindberg Field, California on 11/22/44
59546	VPB-119	Unidentified loss at Clark Field, Philippine on 06/24/45
59549	VPB-124	Surveyed after landing accident at Tinian on 06/17/45
59550	VPB-118	Surveyed due to battle damage on 07/23/45
59553	VPB-119	Lost in action 06/24/45
59556	VPB-118	Possibly lost in action on 08/08/45
59557	VPB-124	Lost in action on 06/26/45
59558	VPB-119	Burned on ground at Clark Field, Philippines on 03/22/45
59559	VPB-119	Lost in action on 05/01/45
59563	VPB-106	Shotdown off Singapore on 06/01/45
59584	VPB-119	Crashed during on patrol near Homonhon Island, Philippines on 01/12/46
59588	VPB-102	Crashed on landing at NAS Agana, Guam on 08/23/46
59606	VPB-119	Engine exploded while taxing at Clark Field, Philippines on 07/24/46
59618	VB-4	Crashed near Master Field, Florida on 09/12/45
59620	VPB-119	Lost on air/sea rescue mission 09/28/46
59642	VB-4	Lost during navigation training from NAS Miami, Florida on 07/18/45
59644	FAW-4	Crashed on landing at NAS Kodiak, Alaska on 01/12/46
59645	VPB-122/VPB-107/VP-26	*Turbulent Turtle* Shotdown by Soviet fighters on 04/08/50
59646	Unknown	Unidentified cause on 06/11/52
59657	VP-871	Crashed near Smith Island, Washington on 08/06/51
59633	VPHL-8	Crashed on landing at NAS Kwajalein on 01/23/48
59685	VP-20	Went missing from NAS Kodiak, Alaska on 11/03/48
59695	VPB-143/VP-894	Crashed on take-off from NAS Sand Point on 08/26/56
59704	VP-871	Crashed near Atsugi, Japan after double engine failure on 01/14/52
59715	Unknown	Crashed on landing at Manteo, North Carolina on 08/22/45
59716	VP(HL)-12/VW-3	Lost during typhoon penetration on 12/16/53
59721	VB-4	Mid-air collision with BuNo 59437 near Munson, Florida on 05/10/46
59733	VPB-102	Crashed at Iwo Jima on 09/13/45
59734	VB-4 ATU-4	Crashed on landing at NAAS Whiting Field, Florida on 02/26/46
59747	VPB-124	Lost in action on 07/24/45
59750	VPB-104/119	Crashed off Mindoro, Philippines on 07/30/46[72]
59762	VP-21	Crashed while landing at Montgomery, Alabama on 11/16/48
59776	VP(HL)-13	Crashed into cliff in Marshall Islands on 08/12/48
59777	VPB-122	Crashed while on transport flight from Kodiak, Alaska on 11/30/45
59778	VPB-122	Surveyed after landing accident at Yonabaru, Okinawa on 10/16/45
59779	VPB-122	Crashed upon landing at Vancouver, British Columbia on 10/16/45
59799	VB-4	Crashed on flight from Little Rock, Arkansas on 6/18/46
59802	VPB-197	Crashed during training flight off Hawaii on 06/23/45
59811	VP-28	Surveyed after landing accident at Itamy, Japan on 07/11/51
59817	VP-29	Crashed during training flight near Mikallo, Oregon on 11/09/49
59821	VP-10/VP-HL-10	Crashed on landing approach Ault Field, Alaska on 07/22/47
59840	FASRON-895	Crashed during training flight near Coupeville, Washington on 09/19/50
59841	VPB-143	Crashed on landing at NAS Kaneohe, Hawaii on 08/31/45
59851	VP-HL-13	Crashed while landing at NAS Kaneohe, Hawaii on 11/18/46
59852	Unknown	Crashed on landing at Port Lyautey, French Morocco on 04/11/51
59853	VP-26	Crashed during taxi test at Port Lyautey, French Morocco on 10/14/48
59859	VP-25	Crashed upon landing at NAS Sangley Point Philippines
59860	VP(HL) ATU-12	Crashed while landing at NAS Corpus Christi, Texas on 04/25/48
59864	VPB-197	Crashed upon landing at NAAS Camp Kearney, California on 08/24/45
59872	VP(HL)-12	Surveyed at NAS Corpus Christi, Texas on 01/22/48
59881	VP-28	Crashed on landing at Itami, Japan on 07/11/51
59883	A&T Norfolk	Crashed on landing at NAS Norfolk, Virginia on 10/03/47
59884	Unknown	Crashed while on flight to Udine, Italy on 03/07/51
59885	VPB-197	Crashed during training flight on 08/22/45
59919	VP(HL)-4	Crashed during landing approach near Argentia, Newfoundland on 10/21/47
59923	VP-772	Crashed into South Mountain northwest of Shelton, Washington on 11/12/52
59937	VP-9	Crashed during a flight to Whidbey Island, Washington on 01/28/53
59953	VP(HL)-4	Crashed while landing at Goose Bay, Labrador on 10/02/47
59957	VPW-1	Crashed into Mount Bonphao, Philippines on 10/19/46
59959	VPM-1	Crashed on landing at NAS Agana, Guam on 07/04/47

59979	VP-26	Crashed near Port Lyautey, French Morocco on 03/23/49
59988	VP-24	Landing approach to NAS Argentia, Newfoundland on 10/06/52
59992	VP-772	Crashed on take-off Iwakuni, Japan on 07/27/51
60005	VP(HL)–10	Crashed while landing at NAS Whidbey Island, Washington on 06/26/48
66263	VP-9	Crashed into Skagit Bay, Washington on 21 June 1951
66267	VP-772	Crashed on landing at Atsugi, Japan on 02/14/51
66280	VP-9	Crashed into hill at Amak Island, Alaska on 08/12/51
66282	VP-881?	Crashed at Chincoteague, Virginia on 08/19/54
66298	VP-9	Crashed on take-off, Little Tanaga Island, Alaska 08/31/51
66320	VP-21	Crashed while on training flight near Patuxent River, Maryland River on 02/10/49

Appendix F: United States Coast Guard, Aéronavale, Civilian, and Latin American Privateer Data

P4Y-2G Coast Guard Privateers

BuNo	USCG Service Dates	Prior Naval Assignment
59598	07/01/46-01/20/48	
59628	Unknown	
59688	01/13/53-06/19/57	VP-21
59728	01/30/48-07/31/51	
59769	07/01/46-07/31/51	VPB-116
59848	01/20/48-?	
59876	02/05/53-02/19/54	
59967	03/23/48-10/07/48	
66260	10/19/52-02/18/54	
66300	12/11/52-07/19/58	
66302	12/11/52-07/09/58	
66304	12/11/52-07/01/58	
66306	01/14/53-09/05/58	

Privateers of Aéronavale

The following data lists 24 Privateers operated by the French Aéronavale between 1950 and 1960. (source: Robert Feuilloy)

USN BuNo	USN Service	Aéronavale	Date Received	Remarks
59659	VB-4 ATU 1	8F-1/28F-1	December 1951	Returned to US 2/55
59663	VP(HL)-8	8F-2/12	December 1951	
59665		28F-7	July 1953	Returned to US 2/55
59691		28F-10/28F-1	July 1953	
59753		8F-3/28F-3/13	December 1951	Returned to US 2/55
59771	VPB-118/124/108	24F-2	August 1950	Returned to US 2/55
59774	VPB-122	8F-4/28F-4/14	November 1951	Shotdown
59775	VPB-122	8F-5/28F-5/15	November 1951	Returned to US 1/55
59785		8F-6/28F-6/16	December 1951	Shotdown
59839		8F-7/24F-17	December 1951	Accident 09/23/52
59870		28F-4	May 1954	Loss 05/21/57
59891		8F-8/28F-19	December 1951	Retired 02/57
59898		8F-9/28F-18	November 1951	Returned to US 02/55
59899	VX-1	8F-10	December 1951	Accident 02/25/52
59783		24F-9/28F-9	July 1954	
59869		24F2/28F-12	May 1954	
59985		24F-7/28F-7	May 1954	
66004		24F-1	May 1954	Accident 06/08/54
66254		24F-3/28F-3	May 1954	
66259	VP-HL-10 VP-20	24F-8/28F-11	May 1954	
66270		24F-4/28F-10	May 1954	
66286		24F-5/28F-5	May 1954	
66294		24F-6/28F-2	May 1954	Accident 08/10/60
66318		24F-10/28F-6	March 1954	

Notes:
59691 (28F-10) changed to 28F-1
59663 (28F-2) changed to 28F-12
59753 (28F-3) changed to 28F-13
59774 (28F-4) changed to 28F-14
59775 (28F-5) changed to 28F-15
59783 (24F-9) became 28F-9
59785 (28F-6) changed to 28F-16
59839 (28F-7) changed to 28F-17
59869 (24F-2) became 28F-12
59870 designated 28F-4 after the loss of 59774
59898 (28F-9) changed to 28F-18
59891 (28F-8) changed to 28F-19
59985 (24F-7) became 28F-7
66254 (24F-3) became 28F-3
66270 (24F-4) became 28F-10 in 1955
66286 (24F-5) became 28F-5
66294 (24F-6) became 28F-2
66318 (24F-10) designated 28F-6 after loss of 59785

Civilian and Latin American Privateers

BuNo	Registry	Last Owner/Remarks
59763	N7237C	Honduras as FAH-792? Crashed at Safford, Arizona on 06/27/74. Section of aircraft currently owned by Ron Sathre
59701	N6884C	Hawkins & Powers
59742	N7683C	Honduras as FAH-796? Last owner Cameron Lazone
59819	N3739G	Lonestar Flight Museum
59876	N6813D	Yankee Air Museum
59882	N7962C	Hawkins & Powers as Tanker 126
59913	N6814D	Mexico as XB-DOD?
59946	N6815D	Mexico as XB-DIT
59991	N7621C	Ace Smelting Inc.
60001	N6814D?	Brazil PT-BEG?
66247	N7622C	Ace Smelting Inc.
66252	N9654C	World Aircraft Corporation
66260	N7620C	Crashed near Pinewoods, Colorado on 07/18/02
66284	N6884C	Crashed on landing at Prescott, Arizona 06/59
66293	Unknown	Brazil as PT-BEO
66300	N2872G	Hawkins & Powers as Tanker 124
66302	N2871G	Hawkins & Powers as Tanker 121
66304	N2870G	National Museum of Naval Aviation
66306	N7974A	Crashed at McGrath, Alaska on 07/22/68
Unknown	N6816D	Consumed by fire at Wenatchee, Washington on 07/27/70
Unknown	N3191G	Crashed at Diamond Lake, Oregon on 07/27/70
Unknown	N9681C	Crashed at Challis, Idaho on 07/17/64
Unknown	N1911H	Crashed at Greybull, Wyoming on 09/03/69

Appendix G: United States Navy PB4Y-2 Units 1944-1956

The following is a listing of individual units assigned PB4Y-2s, starting with the original unit designation, followed by subsequent designators and the approximate dates (if known) they were equipped with the aircraft. It is by no means exhaustive, and some errors or omissions may have occurred.

U.S. Navy	Dates
ATU-12/ATU-600	Unknown
VJ-1/VW-3	1946-?
VP-11	May 1952-June 1953
VP-51	May 1949-Jan 1950
VP-772/ VP-ML-66 /VP-17	1949-Aug 1953
VP-791	1952-?
VP-871	1950-1952
VP-981	Unknown
VB-4 O.T.U.	1944-?
VPB-100	Oct 1945
VPB-101	May-June 1945
VPB-102/VP-102/VP-HL-2/VP-22	July 1945-July 1950
VPB-103	June 1945-July 1945
VPB-104/VP-104/VP-HL-4/VP-24/VP-9	June 1945-June 1954
VPB-106/VP-106	Aug 1944-June 1946
VPB-107/VP-HL-7/VP-27	July 1945-Jan 1950
VPB-108/VP-HL-8/VP-28	Feb 1945-Dec 1952
VPB-109	Dec 1944-Oct 1945
VPB-111/VP-111/VP-HL-11/VP-21	May 1945-June 1950
VPB-114/VP-HL-6/VP-26	1945-March 1951
VPB-115/VP-115/VP-HL-13/VP-25	June 1945-Jan 1950
VPB-116/VP-116/VP-HL-1	June 1945-May 1947
VPB-117	June 1945-Dec 1945
VPB-118	Aug 1944-Dec 1945
VPB-119/VP-119/VP-HL-9/VP-ML-7	Aug 1944-Aug 1947
VPB-120/VP-120/VP-HL-10/VP-20	Aug 1944-March 1949
VPB-121	Oct 1944-June 1946
VPB-122/VP-122/VP-HL-12/VP-29	Sept 1944/March 1945-Jan 1950
VPB-123/VP-123	Dec 1944-Oct 1946
VPB-124/VP-124/VP-HL-3	Dec 1944-May 1947
VPB-143/VP-143/VP-HL-5	June 1945-May 1947
VPB-197	1945-46
VPB-200	Aug 1944-Oct 1945
VPM-1/VPW-1	Dec 1945-Nov 1946
VPW-2	Dec 1945-Nov 1946
VPW-3/VPM-3/VP-HL-3/VJ-2/VP-23/VW-4	May 1946-Oct 1953
VX-1	Unknown

Appendix H:
United States Navy Tail Codes
1946-1956

Squadron tail codes in use on regular and reserve USN Privateers from 1946 to 1956 are listed below. This data may not be complete.

1946

Squadron	**Code**
VP-HL-1 (ex VPB-116)	WC
VP-HL-2 (ex VPB-102)	WB
VP-HL-3 (ex VPB-124)	BC
VP-HL-4 (ex VPB-104)	HA
VP-HL-5 (ex VPB-143)	BD
VP-HL-6 (ex VPB-114)	HB
VP-HL-7 (ex VPB-107)	DC
VP-HL-8 (ex VPB-108)	AB
VP-HL-9 (ex VPB-119)	LB
VP-HL-10 (ex VPB-120)	DD
VP-HL-11 (ex VPB-111)	HC
VP-HL-12 (ex VPB-122)	DE
VP-HL-13 (ex VPB-115)	BB
VPM-3 (ex VPW-3)	ER
VX-1	XA

1948-1956

Squadron	**Code**
VJ-1	PM
VJ-2	PN
VP-7 (ex VP-HL-9/VP-ML-7)	HE (LB)*
VP-9	CB
VP-11	HB
VP-17 (ex VP-772)	BH (L)*
VP-19 (ex VP-871)	CH (PE)*
VP-20 (ex VP-HL-10)	DD
VP-21 (ex VP-HL-11)	HC
VP-22 (ex VP-HL-2)	AE/CE
VP-23 (ex VPM-3/VP-HL-3)	EH/MA
VP-24 (ex VP-HL-4)	HA
VP-25 (ex VP-HL-13)	BB
VP-26 (ex VP-HL-6)	HB/EB
VP-27 (ex VP-HL-7)	DC
VP-28 (ex VP-HL-8)	CF
VP-29 (ex VP-HL-12)	DE
VP-51 (ex VPW-1)	EW
VP-791	M
VP-881	T
VP-893	T
VP-894	T
VPW-1	(ex VPM-1) EW

*Prior Designation

Note: Privateers of an unidentified squadron appear in the book with a "EL" tailcode.

Appendix I: World War II PB4Y-2 Personnel Killed or Missing in Action 1944-1945

The following is a listing of personnel killed or missing in action while serving with World War II PB4Y-2 combat units. Some names may be misspelled based on the information contained in the after action reports. Information was obtained from *Naval Aviation Safety Center Aircraft Accident Reports*, individual squadron records obtained from the National Archives at College Park, Maryland, and the Navy Historical Center in Washington, D.C.

VPB-106
9 March 1945
E.W. Ashley, Lieutenant (jg)
R.M. Castiglia, Ensign
W.G. Bened Jr., Ensign
F.D. Blake Jr., AMMF2c
B. Brown, ARM3c
J.O. Campbell, AMMF1c
B.J. Grothe, AOM1c
O.L. Hackett, AOMB2c
W. Kish, ARM1c
F.O. McLaughlin Jr., AMMF1c
G. Mireles, S1c
J.W. Schroeder, AMMF1c

1 June 1945
H.F. Mears, Lieutenant Commander
R. Decker, Ensign
V. Carlson, Ensign
R.B. McCabe, AMM1c
J.J. Reiter, ARM1c
R.H. Blanton Jr, AFC1c
P. Davis Jr., ARM2c
A.J. George, AMM2c
E.L. Kitchen, AOM2c
H.E. Capen Jr., ARM3c
D.T. Morgan, AMM3c
B.R. O'Kane, S1c

14 June 1945
G.C. Goodloe, Lieutenant Commander
E.F. Conry, Ensign
N.S. Smith, Ensign
A.E. Krueger, AMM1c
R.B. O'Kon, AOM1c
Hernandez, ARM2c
D.J. Ashcroft, ARM2c
H.L Devasier, AMM2c
N.J. Kay Jr., AMM3c
G.G. Greenwood, AMM3c
G.F. Blakesley, ARM3c

30 July 1945
Joseph W. Swiencicki, Lieutenant
Jack Cranfill, Ensign
Robert K. Gunderson, Ensign
Leo E. Brown, AMM1c
William W. Ubl, AOM2c
Leo J.E. Babineau, AMM2c
James J. Sherman, ARM2c
Raymond R. Menendez, AOM3c
Fredrick A. Gidel, AMM2c
Robert D. Buscher, S1c
John K. Jones Jr., AMM3c

VPB-108
9 May 1945
John E. Muldrow, Lieutenant Commander
John C. O'Connell, Lieutenant (jg)
John J. Denton, AMM1c
James A. Brumley, ARM2c
Bill D. Martin, AOM3c
Daniel H. Webster, AFC3c
William P. Heaford, S1c (AOM)
Henry J. Struck, S1c (AOM)

VPB-109
5 May 1945
Joe W. Kasperlik, AMM2c

30 May 1945
Leo E. Kennedy, Lieutenant

5 August 1945
John D. Keeling, Lieutenant
Henry Baier Jr., Ensign
Keith W. Radcliffe, Ensign
William L. Willocks Jr., AMM1c
Frank R. Kramer, AOM1c
William J. Krier, ARM1c
Alexander J. Boyd, ARM1c
Melvin M. Rager, AMM2c
James R.T. Carswell, AFC2c
Peter G. Ilacqua, ARM2c
James E. Krieger, AMM3c
Lawrence R. Conroy, AOM3c

VPB-118
6 May 1945
J.A. Lasater, Lieutenant
M.L. Gibson, Ensign
C.J. Milner, Ensign
E.W. Smith, AMM2c
W.J. Hawkins, ARM2c
C.W. Jacobs, AMM3c
R.E. Miller, AOM2c
S.C. Bryant Jr., AMM2c
D. McAllister, ARM3c
H.F. Brockhorst, ARM3c
W.L. Thornton Jr., AOM3c
R.A. Carr, AMM3c

21 July 1945
L.P. McCutcheon, Lieutenant
F. Reeve, Lieutenant (jg)
W.E. Bucklwe, Ensign
O.A. Bunkers, AFC1c
A.D. Nelson, AMM2c
J.N. Welch, AMM3c

6 August 1945
D.C. Slator, AOM3c

8 August 1945
J.R. Park, Lieutenant (jg)
G. W. Lewton, Ensign
L.H. Lowe, Ensign
E.K. Hall Jr., ARM3c
M.E. Hedrick, S1c (ARM)
J.M. James, AMM3c
R.A. Koontz, AOM3c
C.A. McKinney, S1c (ARM)
M.M. Marich, ACOM
P. Preitz, S1c (ARM)
R.R. Reinhart, ARM3c
H.J. Wartzack, ARM3c

VPB-119
22 March 1945
Francis W. Greene, Ensign
Robert J. Jenson, AMMF2c
Andrew J. Wilson, AMMF2c
Nicholas J. Meo, AOM3c
James L. Doss, AOM2c
Calvin C. Gipson, S1c

1 April 1945
Raymond C. Bales, Lieutenant Commander
Roscoe M. Obert, Lieutenant
Robert L. Fox Jr., Lieutenant (jg)
Robert I Suhl, AMMF1c
Everett F. Fees, ACOM
William J. Wagner, ACRM
Joseph A. Howard, ACOM
Walter R. Gainer, AOM1c
Barney D. Guthrie Jr., AMMF2c
Edward L. Atkin Jr., ARM3c
John P. McKeon, AOM3c
Jack O. Ballard, S1c

11 April 1945
Aubrey L. Althans, Lieutenant (jg)
William C. Mathews, Lieutenant (jg)
Donald C. Kirby, Ensign
James W. Adams, AMMF1c
Casimer J. Bogacz, AMMF1c
George H. Stein, ARM1c
Francis J. Christiano. AMMF2c
Edward A. Jakubiak, AOMB2c
Charles A. Bagley, AOM3c
Wilson W. Harner, AOM2c
Harold H. Elfreich, S1c
Bearl A. Lawrence, ARM3c

1 May 1945
John W. Holt, Lieutenant
Firmin J. Urban, Ensign
Marshall C. Baker, Ensign
John F. Moe, ACMM
Milton F. Smith, ACRM
Adolph H. Busse, AOMB1c
Henry B. Babb, AOM2c
Livio J. Banda, AMMF3c
Jesse L. Middleton, ARM3c
Paul D. Wilson, ARM3c
Fred Kautz, AOM3c
Leno G. Benuzzi, S1c

7 May 1945
Lloyd Allen Whitten, S1c

19 May 1945
Walter G. Vogelsang, Lieutenant (jg)
Robert E. Graner, Lieutenant (jg)
Alvin R. Martin, Ensign
Edward W. Brooks, AMMF1c
Louis J. Oronoz, AMMF2c
Carl H. Swift, ARM1c
Donald C. Hulick, ARM2c
Jackie E. Rigsby, AOM3c
Walter T. Long, AOMB2c
Robert C. Molter, S1c
Leonal L. Smith, S1c

17 June 1945
Thomas J. Robinson, Lieutenant (jg)
Robert M. Cahow, Ensign
William R. Stuard Jr., AOM1c
Harold C. Everett, ARM2c
Ralph J. Henderson, AFC2c
Harold Snider, AOM3c
Edward M. Loeser Jr., AMMF2c

24 June 1945
Williard P. Comstock, Lieutenant
George Chadick, Lieutenant (jg)
Kenneth E. Shaffer Jr., Lieutenant (jg)
Marvin R. Denzig, Lieutenant (jg)
John Francis Geraghty, Lieutenant (passenger)
Oriel A. Roadifer, ACMM
Robert E. Morin, AMMF2c
Garr L. Rose, ARM1c
Henry E. Reed, ARM3c
Lyle W. Wagner, AMMF3c
Leonard Pukita, AMMF3c
Louis D. Meyer, AOM3c
Norman E. Baters, S1c

VPB-121
7 March 1945
William McElwee Jr., Lieutenant
R.L. Vannice, Lieutenant (jg)
R.E. Artz, Ensign
C.C. Gibbany, AMM2c
A.H. Hill, AMM3c
D.N. Gibbons Jr., ARM3c
W.E. Roarty, ARM3c
H.P. Garrison, AOM3c
L. Siscoe, Jr., AOMB2c
C.L. Weiss, S1c
F.E. Marstiller, S1c
J.T. Houser, AOMT1c

11 July 1945
J.M. Cumbach, AOM2c

11 August 1945
E.J. Heeb, Ensign
D.W. Mott, AMM1c
R.E. Guth, AMM2c
C.A. Bremer, S1c

VPB-123
7 August 1945
Joseph H. Farmer, AOM3c

VPB-124
6 June 1945
William C. Lawson, AOM2c

26 June 1945
Jack "R" Crist, Lieutenant (jg)
Grant W. Smith, Lieutenant (jg)
Ralph M. W. Frailey, Ensign
John E. Cain, AMM2c
Charles Wilson, ARM2c
Donald L. Bott, AOM2c
Theodore Noonan, AMM3c
John B. Kaighn Jr., ARM3c
Norman F. Surface, AOM2c
Bernard J. Moriarty, S1c
Earnest E. Pike, S1c
Norman I. Sayre, ART1c
Gerald W. Eves, Ensign
Jack "C" Camerson, ARM
Raymond J. Skulina, AOM1c
Thomas P. Metz, ARM2c

27 June 1945
Jack E. Vincent, Lieutenant (jg)
Arnold R. Hardman, Lieutenant (jg)
Adolph U. Johnson, Ensign
Cleo E. Grapes, AMM1c
James J. Carrico, ARM1c
Max C. Leir, AOM3c
Philip S. Anderson, AMM3c
Stephen W. O'Brien, Jr., ARM2c
Victor R. Davis, AOM3c
William V. Morgan, S1c
Eugene J. Stellern, S1c

7 July 1945
Ned B. Brown, Ensign
John V. Brennan, Jr, AOM3c
Robert J. Brower, Lieutenant
Stanley Sunshine, ARM3c
Earl K. Elias, AOM3c
Robert B. Watson, S1c
William H. Cates, AMM3c

21 July 1945
Gilbert E. Miller, Lieutenant
Ralph H. Hepworth, Lieutenant (jg)
Robert A. Littmann, Ensign
Orvill M. Osborn, AMM1c
Albert A. Comminiello, ARM1c
Joseph F. Cholasta, AOM3c
Francis A. Spencer, Jr., AMM2c
Madison R. Stacy, ARM3c
Raymond E. Davis, AOM3c
James B. Ivie, S1c
John M. Gay, AMM3c
Wilborn P. Raney, ARM2c
John B. Ramsey, Lieutenant
Robert P. Stengelin, Lieutenant (jg)
Merlin H. Williams, Ensign
Howard Hobbs, AMM1c
Robert S. Nicholls, ARM1c
William A. Yankow, AOM1c
John H. Anson, AMM2c
Hugh C. Wilson, ARM3c
Hoyt H. Hamlett, AOM3c
Allen E. Kallstrom, S1c
Russell L. Rummel, S1c
Robert T. Dumas, ARM2c

Appendix J: World War II-era Operational Facilities 1944-1945

The following is a listing of personnel killed or missing in the line of duty while serving aboard PB4Y-2 aircraft between 1944 and 1945. Information was obtained from *Naval Aviation Safety Center Aircraft Accident Reports*. Unfortunately, a few of the incidents are missing names, or only have the total number of personnel killed, because some reports are of poor quality and unreadable. Also, some names may be misspelled based on the information contained in the accident reports.

22 November 1944
C.C. Cappe, civilian
F.D. Sande, civilian
R.V. Skala, civilian
C. Bengston, civilian
R. Estis, civilian

29 March 1945
FAW-14
H.G. Morris, Ensign
Robert E. Clair, S1c

8 July 1945
Charles Henry Kliskey, AMM3c

VPB-197
18 July 1945
VB-4
C. M. Bailey, Lieutenant
R. H. Bower, Lieutenant (jg)
P. E. Mattingly, Ensign
F. W. Takkunrn, Ensign
M. J. Meola, AMM2c
C. C. Harran, ARM2c
C. S. McGowan, AMM2c
D. G. McLaughlin, ARM3c
F. M. Carroza, AOM2c
D. R. Strong, AOM3c
P. Kreple, ARM3c
D. Bradley, ARM1c
+3 unidentified

13 August 1945
FAW-6
L. F. West, Lieutenant Commander
R. H. Barden, Lieutenant
W. N. Konahan, ARM1c

22 August 1945
VPB-197
10 killed

12 September 1945
VB-4
J. G. William, Lieutenant
R. Bradburn, Ensign
L. L. Roof, Ensign,
N. D. Stockman, AMM3c
A. A. Cassiol, AMM3c
J. D. Robinson, ARM3c
R. E. Schlenker, AOM1c
F. Fleischer, AOM2c
C. E. Volk, AOM1c
R. V. Peterman, AOM3c
E. W. Chapman, AOM3c
J. E. McInytre, AOM3c
C. H. McClure, PHOM1c
T. H. Oswald, AOM1c

1 October 1945
VPB-119
Ralph F. Cook, Lieutenant (jg)
Oscar L. Smith, Lieutenant (jg)
Harold E. Raveche, Ensign
Kenneth D. Grifforce, AMM2c
Daryl B. Miller, ARM2c
James A. Dugan, AOM1c
Royce A. Lamb, S1c

11 October 1945
VPB-106
Robert C. Hoffman, ARM2c

30 November 1945
VPB-122
John E. McMilian, Lieutenant
John J. Ferguson, Lieutenant
Denorte Bondurant, Lieutenant
William F. Harper, Lieutenant (jg)
Joseph E. Osebold, Ensign
Charles W. Baker, ARM3c
Herman C. Bumpus, ARM2c
Benjamin Norman, AMM3c
John Plevelich, AOM1c
John G. Spenger, AMM1c
Haywood Waller, S1c
John G. Kativa, EM1c
Edward J. Bmolenski, SF3c
James E. Westfall, CCS
Dianiso A. Fajardo, ST1c
(?) Stringer, AOM3c
Harry B. Dawson, S1c
Francis J. Fries, AMM3c
Carl E. Behrens, AMM2c
Owen R. Tennat, AMM3c
Anthony W. Volk, AMM3c
Ludvek F. Medresek, AMM2c
+1 unidentified

Appendix K: Post World War II PB4Y-2 Operational Facilities 1946-1953

The following is a listing of personnel killed or missing in the line of duty while serving aboard PB4Y-2 aircraft between 1946 and 1953. Information was obtained from *Naval Aviation Safety Center Aircraft Accident Reports*. Unfortunately, a few of the incidents are missing names or only have the total number of personnel killed, because some reports are of poor quality and unreadable. Some names may be misspelled based on the information contained in the accident reports.

12 January 1946
VPB-119
William D. Regan, Lieutenant
Charles R. Embry, Ensign
Warren A. Bright, Ensign
James W. Croft, AMM2c
Ellis E. Scott, AMM3c
Doyle M. Lewis, ARM3c
Robert M. Silva, ARM3c
Richard H. Barton, ARM3c
John H. Provost Jr., ARM3c

10 May 1946
VB-4
23 Killed

30 July 1946
VPB-119
John F. Curran, Lieutenant Commander
E. V. Hall, AMM1c
J. F. Cox, AMM1c
R. C. Rifing, AMM2c
L. R. David, AMM2c
P. Pigapoulos, AOM2c
H. L. Woudard,ARM3c
D. E. McLellian, (rating/rank unidentified)
R. H. Meyer, (rating/rank unidentified)
T. E. Deaust, AOX1c

1 August 1946
Hedron 14-2
11 killed (names undetermined)

19 October 1946
VPW-1
S.H. Castleton, Lieutenant
J.L. Junkin, Lieutenant
D.E. Goerner, Ensign
Earl Vasso, ARM1c
Robert W. Canada, AMM1c
Robert W. Cullen, AMM2c
James J. Walsh, ARM3c

18 November 1946
VPHL-13
2 killed

22 July 1947
VPHL-10
W.H. Davis, Lieutenant
R.A. Kubber, Lieutenant
O.N. Jensen, ACMM
P. McAllister, ARM2c
(?) Hathaway, AOM3c

21 October 1947
John J. Perme, Lieutenant (jg)
Russell H. Scott, ACMM
Joseph J. Caworski, RM3c
Alton P. Herrington, ACM

25 April 1948
VPHL-12
O.W. Moll, Midshipman

12 August 1948
VPHL-13
Russell DeLany, Lieutenant Commander
T.C. O'Connor, Lieutenant
William Wise, Lieutenant (jg)
Walter Delaney, Midshipman
Charles D. Rudolph, AD1
Trafton B. Lee, ADC
John A. Beland, AD2
Carl H. Christiansen, AL2
Paul McDonald, AL3
F.A. Earle, unknown rating/rank
C. Pinkerton, AOC

3 November 1948
VP-20
Paul R. Barker, Lieutenant
Harold R. Herndon, Ensign
William R. Musgrove, Midshipman
Robert W. Eichorn, AOC
Lloyd O. Askildson, AO2
James A. Wooley, SA
Joseph D. Somers, AD3
Norman M. Holland, AD2
Franklin E. Barden, ADC
Robert W. Trenton, ADC
William G. Coleman, ALC
Bill Clark, AO2

10 February 1949
VP-21
Martin E. Kennedy, ADC
Edgar H. Perry, AN

9 November 1949
VP-29
Earhart H. Donovan, Midshipman

8 April 1950
VP-26
John H. Fetts, Lieutenant
Robert D. Reynolds, Lieutenant
Howard W. Seeschaf, Lieutenant
Tommy L. Burgess, Ensign
Frank L. Beckman, AT1
Joe H. Danens, AD1
Jack W. Thomas, AD1
Joseph J. Bourasasa, AL3
Edward J. Purcell, CT3
Joseph H. Rinnier, AT3

19 September 1950
FASRON-895
B.S. Bed, Lieutenant
L.W. Schmidt, Lieutenant (jg)
David G. Candler, ADE2
James D. Cook, ADE2
Edgar W. Monell, AL1
Vernon D. Alexander, ADC
+1 unidentified

7 March 1951
(unknown unit)
Elmer E. Jackson, Ensign
David R. Aiken, ET2
Andrew Andrews, ACC
Richard R. Radcliff, ADC
Donald E. Jones, AL3
Frank D'Acunto, ADAN
Ernest E. Craig, ADAN

21 June 1951
VP-9
Hilbert W. Hedquist, Lieutenant (jg)
Franklin P. Gaulburn, Jr., Lieutenant (jg)
Richard McDaniel, ALC
Anthony Bono, AL1
Donald W. Cunningham, AO3

27 July 1951
VP-772
James H. Marovish, Lieutenant
Walder L. McCord, Lieutenant
Allen Spund, Lieutenant
Eddie B. Cook, ADF1
Robert Gariel, ADE1
Coley G. Pridgen, AOU1
Willaim R. Still, AL1
Thomas J. Ricotta, AT2
Robert E. Overton, ALAN

VP-871
6 August 1951
E.W. Darrah, Lieutenant
R.A. Ward, Lieutenant
P.H. Lowe, ADEC
F.E. Thornton, AOU2
D.R. Gabbett, AT3

F.E. Partain, AL3
J.T. Andrew, AN
R.F. Bowen, ALAN
D. Lim, ADEAN

12 August 1951
VP-9
Roy E. Park, Lieutenant
Robert W. Conklin, Lieutenant
Henry H. Wood, Ensign
Leonard W. Sexton, AD1
Brooks A. Williams, AL1
Charles W. Elkins, AOM2
Edwen F. Busby, AT3
Ronald L. Hunt, AM3
Bobby Enloe, ALAN
Elnord E. Flinkfeld, ADAN
William S. Wagener, AOAN
Joseph D. Witherspoon, ATAN

31 August 1951
VP-9
Berdel A. Cook, Lieutenant
William H. Diana, Lieutenant
Frank H. Sudley, Ensign
James G. Mallard, ADC
George Y. Jenkins, AD1
Marvin P. Huber, ALCA
Don R. McNair, AN
Anthony C. Molina, ALAN
Wilford E. Tacie, ATAN

13 July 1952
VP-23
William G. Hearne, Lieutenant (jg)

14 January 1952
VP-871
Edmund C Hill, Lieutenant
Chester C. Johnson, Lieutenant
Lewis W. Seymour, Lieutenant
Leslie R. Humiston, AMC
John H. Jorgensen, ADE1
Joseph M. Wilkins, AT1
Robert M. Funk, ADE2
Oscar R. Anderson, AD3
Martin L. Cedeno, AL3
Leroy McMurray, AO3
Robert A. Rosa, AN
Ralph W Stacy, ALAN

12 March 1952
VPHL-12
W.E. Dozier, Lieutenant
B.M. Roeder, Lieutenant
D.E. Ruttledge, Lieutenant
R.G. Williams, Lieutenant
J.L. Daffenberg, AM3
R.C. Chase, ADAN
D.J. Givens, AA
R.H. Steinbaugh, AA
R.W. Augrain, CAD
R.B. Nye, CAD

6 October 1952
VP-24
D.A. Ellis, Lieutenant
F.B. Horton, Lieutenant
A.R. Kotko, Lieutenant
R. Meline, Lieutenant
M.E. Heintz, AD2
M. Demayo, ATAN

27 July 1952
VP-772

12 November 1952
G.R. Dyson, Captain
H.E. Francis, Lieutenant
L.S. Pyles, Lieutenant
S.C. Smith, Ensign
R.A. Carey, AT2
R.W. Elliott, AD2
A.D. Vandoren, AL3
S. Carter, ADAN
B.L. Isenschmidt, AOAN
G.E. Jones, AN
J.V. Simmons, AN

28 January 1953
VP-9
J.D. Greer, Captain
O.C. Everhart, Lieutenant
D.L. Jarvis, Lieutenant
L.R. Stegemerten, Lieutenant
C.C. Longacre, ADC
T.W. Huffman, AT1
J.A. Kerrigan, AO3
J.L. McDonnel, AO3
H.L. Ziemba, AO3
T.J. Whitehead, ADAN

15 December 1953
VW-3
9 killed

Appendix L:
Enlisted U.S. Navy Aviation Ratings

ACOM-Aviation Chief Ordnanceman
ACMM-Aviation Chief Machinist Mate
ACRM-Aviation Chief Radioman
AFC - Aviation Fire Control
AMM: Aviation Machinist's Mate
AMMC: Aviation Machinist's Mate C- Aviation Carburetor Mechanic.
AMMF: Aviation Machinist's Mate F- Aviation Flight Engineer.
AOM: Aviation Ordanceman
ARM: Aviation Radioman
AOMB: Aviation Ordnanceman-Bombsight Mechanic
AOMT Aviation Ordnanceman-Aviation Turret Mechanic

Post-World War II Enlisted U.S. Navy Aviation Ratings

AA: Airman Apprentice
AD: Aviation Machinist Mate
AD(AN) - Aviation Machinist's Mate (Airman)
ADE - Aviation Machinist's Mate (Engine Mechanic)
ADE (AN)- Aviation Machinist's Mate (Engine Mechanic) (Airman)
AE: Aviation Electrician's Mate
AEM: Aviation Electrician's Mate
AerM: Aerographer's Mate
AG: Aerographer's Mate
AL - Aviation Electronics Man
AL(AN) - Aviation Electronics Man (Airman)
AL(CA) - Aviation Electronics Man (Combat Aircrewman)
AM: Aviation Metalsmith/Aviation Structural Mechanic
AN: Airman
AO: Aviation Ordnanceman
AO(AN) - Aviation Ordnanceman (Airman)
AOU - Aviation Ordnanceman (Utility)
ART: Aviation Electronics Technician
AS: Apprentice Seaman
AT - Aviation Electronics Technician
AT(AN) - Aviation Electronics Technician (Airman)

Other U.S. Navy Enlisted Ratings

CT - Communications Technician
EM - Electrician's Mate
ET - Electronics Technician
PhoM: Photographer's Mate
RM – Radioman
S1c: Seaman First Class
ST - Sonar Technician (after 1948)

Appendix M: French Aéronavale PB4Y-2 Fatalities 1951-1957

The following is a listing of personnel killed or missing in the line of duty while serving with the French Aéronavale between 1951 and 1957. Information was obtained from Robert Feuilloy and Net Marine. *Histoire de la Flottille 28F*, http://www.netmarine.net/forces/aero/flo/28f/memoriam.htm.

20 December 1951
Edoward Perrault, Second Mátre, pilote

23 September 1952
Pierre LaSalle, Enseigne de vaisseau de premiére classe, commandant d'aéronef
André Dupont, Mátre mécanicien
André Rousse, Mátre radio
Pierre Coche, Second Mátre mécanicien
Michel Faget, Second Mátre radio
Robert Deberghes, Second Mátre navigateur
René Blin, Second Mátre armurier
Robert Depreux, Second Mátre armurier
Paul Audibert, Capitaine de corvette
Marc Venot, Capitaine de corvette
Francois Enault, Ingénieur Mécanicien
Henri Souret, Ingénieur Mécanicien de 1Ëre class

12 April 1954
Alexis Manafanowsky, Enseigne de vaisseau de premiére classe, commandant d'aéronef
Gay Gauthiez, Second Mátre pilote
Henré Ruello-Kermelin, Second Mátre navigateur
Pierre Puyjalinet, Second Mátre mécanicien
Charles Iltis, Second Mátre radio
Jackie Guiliano, Second Mátre radio
Marc Chaigne, Second Mátre radio
Serge Bourson, Second Mátre armurier
Jean Paumier, Second Mátre armurier

8 May 1954
Pierre Monguillon, Enseigne de Vaisseau de premiËre classe, commandant d'aéronef
André, Roissat Second Mátre pilote
Franck Bouyssou, Mátre mécanicien
Jean Hoog, Second Mátre
René Lacrosse, Second Mátre navigateur
Yves LeCoz, Second Mátre radio
Louis Stéphan, Second Mátre mécanicien

21 May 1957
Claude Suret, Enseigne de Vaisseau de premiére classe, commandant d'aéronef
Jacques Kervella, Enseigne de Vaisseau de 2e classe
Jean Cariou, Second Mátre mécanicien
Francois Gourmelon, Second Mátre navigateur
Jacques Granet, Second Mátre radio
René Josse, Second Mátre radariste
Michael Maton, Second Mátre macénicien
Gérard Roux de Vence, Second Mátre radio
René Delepine, Matelot armurier

French Aéronavale Commissioned Rank Structure and U.S. Navy Equivalent

Aéronavale	U.S. Navy
Capitaine de Corvette	Lieutenant-Commander
Enseigne de vaisseau de 1re classe	Lieutenant Junior Grade
Enseigne de vaisseau de 2e classe	Ensign

French Aéronavale Enlisted Rate Structure and U.S. Navy Equivalent

Mátre	Chief Petty Officer to Master Chief Petty Officer
Second mátre	Petty Officer 1st Class
Matelot	Seaman 1st Class

French Aéronavale Enlisted Occupational Specialty and Approximate U.S. Navy Equivalent

Aéronavale	U.S. Navy
Armurier	Ordnanceman
Commandant d'aéronef	Aircraft Commander
Ingénieur Mécanicien	Machinist Mate Engineer
Macénicien	Machinist Mate
Navigateur	Navigator
Pilote	Pilot
Radariste	Radarman
Radio	Radioman

Notes

[1] "It was a great aircraft to fly." Lieutenant Commander Orvis N. Fitts, USNR (Ret), *A Naval Aviator's Story World War II*, 83.
[2] The installation of ECM gear on the PB4Y-2 Privateer. Billy Woodward, *Patrol Bombing Squadron 104 (Third Tour): June 1945-November 1946*, 2.
[3] "We extended the fuselage seven additional feet forward of the wing." The extension also allowed the installation of bulky ECM gear which would not fit in the standard B-24 Liberator. *Reuben Fleet and the Story of Consolidated Aircraft*, 257.
[4] The deaths of Convair test pilots Marvin Weller and Conrad Cappe killed. An interesting note is that two of the Convair test pilots for the XPB4Y-2 project, Marvin Weller and Conrad Cappe were later killed in when a PB4Y-2 they were piloting crashed after losing a wing on take-off in November 1944. Email from Allan Blue to the author.
[5] Chief of Naval Operations, *U.S. Naval Aviation in the Pacific*, 6, 10.
[6] The sinking of a 1,200-ton freighter transport by VPB-118. James T. Pettit, *The History of Navy Bombing Squadron 118: The Old Crows*, 51.
[7] The loss of *Modest' O-Miss*. Pettit, 77-78.
[8] VPB-106's loss of Lieutenant Edward Ashley and his crew. Seaman 1st Class Raymond W. Gray Jr., and Seaman 1st Class Charles W. Reddon picked up by the Japanese. The entire crew was listed as killed in action in Alan C. Carey's *Above an Angry Sea: United States Navy B-24 Liberator and PB4Y-2 Privateer Operations in the Pacific (October 1944-August 1945)*, 79. Email from James C. Sawruk to the author.
[9] The destruction of an H8K Emily flying boat off Amami Shima by Lieutenant Mike Keiser and his crew. Pettit, 81-82 and Carey, *Above an Angry Sea*, 79.
[10] Ditching of Lieutenant Hazlett's Privateer. Carey, *Above an Angry Sea*, 81.
[11] VPB-118's *Modest' O-Miss II*'s rough day on 12 April. Pettit, 109-110.
[12] "My first command at sea, and I can't even get in the damn boat!" Pettit, 114-115. The quote also appears in a slightly modified manner in the October 1945 periodical of *All Hands*, 27. "Look, my first command at sea, and I'm not even aboard!"
[13] Installation of 20-millimeter cannons in VPB-108 and 121 Privateers. Carey, *Above an Angry Sea*, 80-81
[14] The ditching of Lieutenant Ebright's Privateer, Ibid.
[15] Lieutenant Mildahn took-off a few minutes after the first first six planes followed 40 minutes later by Lieutenants Stewert and Goodman. Lieutenant Commander Pressler, Lieutenants Barnes, Holohan, Stewert, Mildahn, and Goodman piloted VPB-102 aircraft.
[16] The raid on Marcus Island by VPB-102 and 108. Carey, *Above an Angry Sea*, 81-82.
[17] The analysis of Commander Pressler's desire to win recognition and thus advance his military career is from a source who wished to remain anonymous as it was an opinion formulated by those who participated in the attack soon after their return to Tinian. This opinion does not reflect official reports. This perspective is from an audiotape by an anonymous source to the author.
[18] Lieutenant Hazlett flying
Lady Luck II. Carey, *Above an Angry Sea*, 88-89.
[19] Deployment of VPB-121. Ibid, 75-77.
[20] VPB-121 and the rescue of Captain Mikes. *Pacific Privateers* and *Above an Angry Sea*.
[21] The downing of Lieutenants J.B. Rainey's plane. The pilot responsible for bring down the Privateer was Lieutenant (jg) Teizo Ota of the 302 Zu. Ibid, 93.
[22] Arnold G. Fisch,
Ryukyus. U.S. Army Campaigns of World War II.
[23] Deployment of VPB-118 to Okinawa. Ibid, 92.
[24] Ibid, 93.
[25] Strike on Kanoya Airfield by VPB-118. Petitt, 148-155 and Carey, *Above an Angry Sea*, 94.
[26] Anti-shipping strikes by VPB-118 on 5 May 1945. Carey, *Above an Angry Sea*, 95.
[27] Strikes by VPB-118 on 6 and 7 May 1945. Ibid, 96-98.
[28] The Japanese pilots involved in the battle were: Ens. Mitsuo Ishizuka, CPO Shigeru Aoyagi, CPO Tomio Yamamoto, PO1 Yasuo Matsumoto, CPO Toshio Tanaka, CPO Hideo Nakao(order to return and did not engage), CPO Hisamitsu Watanabe, PO2 Ei Hoshino, CPO Sanpei Shiono, CPO Shiro Hirotome, CPO Junichi Miyake, and PO2 Masayuki Tashiro. Email to the author from Sawruk.
[29] *Bat* attack by Hicks and Kennedy of VPB-109. Alan C. Carey, *The Reluctant Raiders: The Story of United States Navy Bombing Squadron VB/VPB-109 in World War II*, 145 and Carey, *Above an Angry Sea*, 106.
[30] The fighters possibly belonged to the 951 Ku based at Chinkai, Korea. Email to the author from Jim Sawruk.
[31] The interception of Chay and Hewitt of VPB-109 by Japanese fighters. Carey, *The Reluctant Raiders*, 143-44 and *Above an Angry Sea*, 105.
[32] For an in-depth discussion on the death of Lieutenant Jobe of VPB-109. Carey,
The Reluctant Raiders, 147-48 and *Above an Angry Sea*, 108-09.
[33] VPB-123's team of Lieutenant Al G. McCuaig and Lieutenant (jg) Kenneth F. Sanford. *Above an Angry Sea*, 122-38.
[34] Interception of VPB-124 Privateers by Japanese fighters. Ibid, 117-18.
[35] Loss of VPB-124's Commander Houston and his wingman, Lieutenant (jg) J.R. Crist. Ibid, 121-23.
[36] Various patrols conducted by VPB-124. Ibid, 123-24.
[37]The loss of Ramsey and Miller of VPB-124 remains a mystery. According to Japanese sources, it is known that JAAF fighters of the 25th Hiko Sentai intercepted two Privateers two kilometers north of Saishu-To Island. This is known as Cheju Do today, which is located off the southern coast of Korea. However, at the time, the squadron believed Ramsey and Miller were flying their sector on the Northwest coast of Korea, not the southern tip near Saishu-To Island. According to Japanese records, several of their Army fighters intercepted a pair of American bombers and one, flown by Sergeant Yamaguchi was shot down during the ensuing battle. The Japanese claimed to have downed both PB4Ys. But, if two American planes were shot down, did they belong to VPB-124? Information supplied by Jim Sawruk in an email to the author.
[38] VPB-109, 118, and 123 strike against rail transportation and railroad facilities in Northwestern Korea. Petitt, 284. Also see Carey,
The Reluctant Raiders 156-58, and *Above an Angry Sea*, 128-130.
[39] The loss of Lieutenant Keeling's crew on 5 August 1945 occurred exactly one year after the squadron lost another plane and crew to enemy action during its first tour in the Central Pacific.
The Reluctant Raiders, 159-60 and *Above an Angry Sea*, 130-131. The death of VPB-123's Joseph H. Farmer. *Above an Angry Sea*, 131.
[40] Loss of VPB-118's Lieutenant Park and crew of VPB-118. Petitt, 290-92 and *Above an Angry Sea*, 131.
[41] Lieutenant Holt's combat record.
Above an Angry Sea, 47.
[42] The reduction of Japanese merchant ships. *U.S. Naval Patrol Aviation*. 11.

[43] Missions by VPB-119. *Above an Angry Sea*, 52-55.
[44] The arrival of VPB-109 and the use of the SWOD Mk-9 *Bat*. *The Reluctant Raiders*, 117 and *Above an Angry Sea*, 57.
[45] Lack of large enemy shipping, Ibid, 58.
[46] Lieutenant Robert Vadnais attack on boatyards in Borneo. *The Reluctant Raiders*, 129-31. Also see *All Hands*, 25 and *Above an Angry Sea*, 59-60.
[47] "Joe's been hit, someone get him out!" *The Reluctant Raiders*, 131 and *Above an Angry Sea*, 60.
[48] The loss of VPB-106's Lieutenant Commander Green C. Goodloe and crew. *Above an Angry Sea*, 61-62, and Robert L. Wolpert, *The Story of One Eleven*, 77-84.
[49] "That piece of armor plate saved my life." Fitts, 107-111.
[50] Record for PB4Y-2 squadrons in World War II. *U.S. Naval Patrol Aviation*. 10, 43. Also see All Hands, 25.
[51] "...send radio messages to the base at 15 minute intervals giving the information we gathered," email from Ray Parsons to the author.
[52] Prior to being assigned to VP-26, the *Turbulent Turtle* served with VPB-107 and 122.
[53] "Supposedly the aircraft crashed 5-10 kilometers from the shore." U.S.-Russia Joint Commission on POW/MIAs, Task Force Russia, TFR Reports 27-5 and 27-7.
[54] Summation by AM1 (AW) Daniel Wagner, Team *Trident Remembers* and *The 53rd Anniversary of the First Cold War Shootdown VP-26's HB-7*.
[55]Enlisted patrol plane commander. *60-Mission Whitehat*, Naval Aviation News, May 1952.
[56] Letter from Jim Page to the author.
[57] "...that's too long when you know that other guy wants kill you." Letter from Jim Page to the author.
[58] "...catch tire from the intense heat of the flare." *Flares light the way for fighters* published by Naval Aviation News, date of publication unknown.
[59] "...and get them ready for the Korean War." Frank Tutu, *VP-772: A History-September 1950 through February 1953*.
[60] VP-772's patrol areas during the Korean War were called Fox and Able.
[61] "Not when we've lost 65,000 men in Korea already." Time Magazine 1951.
[62] "I located the ships by radar and directed the pilots to them," email from Wilmer L. Kerns to the author.
[63] Frank Durban email to the author.
[64] Ronald J. Cima, ed. *Vietnam: A Country Study*.
[65] Six of the French Privateers were returned to the United States between January and April 1955.
[66] Privateer operations in the Algerian War. Helen Chapan Metz, ed. *Algeria: A Country Study*.
[67] Privateers in service with the Aéronavale. Bail, René Bail. *Indochine 1953-1954: Les combats de L'impossible*.
[68] RoCaf Privateer shotdown on 15 February 1961, email to the author from Wai Yip.
[69] The two last Privateers in the Navy inventory, Opposite 31 and Opposite 35. Frederick A. Johnsen, *Privateer: The PB4Y-2 in Service*, 27 and Frederick A. Johnsen, *Bombers in Blue*, 22.
[70] XB-DIT's ultimate fate is unknown. Nicholas A. Veronico, *The Saga of Moby Dick: PB4Y-2 59946*, published in 2003 on the website The Latin American Aviation Historical Society at www.laahs.com.
[71] Both aircraft operated from Honduras for a number of years. The following sources were also consulted that contain information on the PB4Y-2 in Latin America: Davis, John. *The Convair Privateer in Latin America*, published in March 2002 on the website, The Latin American Aviation Historical Society at www.laahs.com. Also see, George Welsh's *Privateer: The PB4Y-1 and PB4Y-2 in Service (Privateer 50th Anniversary Issue)* and Frederick A. Johnson's *Bombers in Blue: PB4Y-2 Privateers and PB4Y-1 Liberators*.
[72] Both VPB-104 and 119 records show BuNo 59750 serving with both squadrons, however, I documented as belonging to VPB-119 in the book *Above an Angry Sea*. It could be possible that VPB-104 transferred the plane to VPB-119.
[73] There is a discrepancy concerning Aéronavale 28F-2, former U.S.N. Bureau Number 59663. According to information obtained from the Naval Aviation Safety Center Aircraft Accidents Reports Bureau Number 59663 was struck from U.S. Navy's inventory after crashing at NAS Kwajalein, Marshall Islands on 23 January 1948.

Bibliography

Government Sources

Appleman, Roy E., James M. Burns, Russell A. Gugeler, and John Stevens. *United States Army in World War II. The War in the Pacific. Okinawa: The Last Battle*. Center of Military History, United States Army. Washington D.C., 2000.

Cima, Ronald J., ed. *Vietnam: A Country Study*. Washington: GPO for the Library of Congress.

Coakley, Robert W. *World War II: The War Against Japan*. American Military History, Army Historical Series, Washington D.C.

Metz, Helen Chapan, ed. *Algeria: A Country Study*. Washington: GPO for the Library of Congress.

Naval Aviation Safety Center Aircraft Accident Reports.

Naval Aviation Combat Statistics: World War II. Air Branch, Office of Naval Intelligence, Office of the Chief of Naval Operations. Navy Department. OPNAV-P-23V No. A129. 17 June 1946.

U.S. Naval Aviation in the Pacific. Office of the Chief of Naval Operations. U.S. Navy, 1947.

Additional information was obtained from World War II Squadron After Action Reports and War Diaries that are available through the National Archives and Records Administration at College Park Maryland and Aircraft History Cards available through the Naval Historical Center.

Published Works

Bail, René. *Indochine 1953-1954: Les combats de L'impossible*. Charles-Lavauzelle. Paris-Limoges.

Carey, Alan C. *Above an Angry Sea: United States Navy B-24 Liberator and PB4Y-2 Privateer Operations in the Pacific (October 1944-August 1945)*. Atglen, PA. Schiffer Publishing Ltd. 2001.

Carey, Alan C. *The Reluctant Raiders: The Story of United States Navy Bombing Squadron VB/VPB-109 in World War II*. Atglen, PA. Schiffer Publishing Ltd. 1999.

Fitts, Orvis N. Lt. Commander, USNR (Ret). *A Naval Aviator's Story World War II*. Overland Park, KS. Fowler Printing & Publishing, 1998.

Johnson, Frederick A. *Bombers in Blue: PB4Y-2 Privateers and PB4Y-1 Liberators*. Bomber Books, Tacoma, WA, 1979.

Pettit, James T. *The History of Navy Bombing Squadron 118: "The Old Crows."* 1992.

Sanford, Kenneth F. *Crew Six*. Port Ludlow, WA, Sanford Publishing Group, 1996. Wagner, William.

Reuben Fleet and the story of Consolidated Aircraft. Fallbrook, CA, Aero Publishers, Inc. 1976.

Welsh, George, et al. *Privateer: The PB4Y-1 and PB4Y-2 in Service*. Skyword Press, San Diego, CA, 1993.

Wolf, Joseph. *Pacific Privateers*, 1976.

Wolpert, Robert L. *The Story of One Eleven: the Navy PB4Y squadron that served in England, North Africa and the Pacific during World War II*. Emerson Quality Press, Inc., Emerson, NJ. 1990.

Periodicals

Burgess, Rick. *Patrol Squadrons in the Korean War*. Naval Aviation News. July-August 2002.

Lewis F.H. "Bud." *Army vs. Navy at Atsugi*. Foundation Magazine. Spring 1994, 20-23.

Lucas, Jim. *False Flag*. Time Magazine. May 28, 1951, 15-16.

David Kesmodel, Kevin Vaughn, and Berny Morson,.

Two killed in crash: Slurry bomber falls out of sky at Big Elk fire. The Rocky Mountain News, July 19, 2002.

Lone Wolf Prowlers. All Hands Magazine. October 1945, 24-27.

Internet Sources

Augustus, Jim. "NAVAL LIBERATORS and PRIVATEERS Image Archive and Reference Center." http://www.navylib.com/index.html.

Baugher, Joseph F. "US Navy and US Marine Corps BuNos: Third Series (50360 to 60009)." http://home.att.net/~jbaugher/thirdseries6.html.

Baugher, Joseph F. "US Navy and US Marine Corps BuNos: Third Series (60010 to 70187)." http://home.att.net/~jbaugher/thirdseries7.html.

Carey, Alan C. "U.S. Navy Pacific-Based PB4Y Squadrons in World War II." http://alanc.carey.freeservers.com/

Davis, John. "The Convair Privateer in Latin America." Latin American Aviation Historical Society. http://www.laahs.com/art49.htm.

Marine Nationale. "Flottille 24F." http://www.defense.gouv.fr/marine/navires/unites/24f/index.htm.

Marine Nationale. "Flottille 28F." http://www.defense.gouv.fr/marine/navires/unites/28f/index.htm.

NetMarine: Histoire de la Flottille 28F: http://www.netmarine.net/forces/aero/flo/28f/histoire/index.htm.

Net Marine. "Histoire de la Flottille 28F. Les pertes de la flottille 28F depuis 1944." http://www.netmarine.net/forces/aero/flo/28f/memoriam.htm.

Veronico, Nicholas. "The Saga of Moby Dick: PB4Y-2 59946." Latin American Aviation Historical Society. http://www.laahs.com/art51.htm.

U.S.-Russia Joint Commission Documents. "TFR 27 Demarches on shootdowns and U.S. military personnel in Soviet prisons." http://lcweb2.loc.gov/frd/tfrussia/tfrhtml/tfr027-1.html.

Unpublished Works

Kerns, Wilmer L. *In Retrospect: Crew #9 of U.S. Naval Patrol Squadron VP-772 July 1952-July. 1953*.

Tatu, Frank. *VP-772: A History-September 1950 through February 1953*.

Wagner, Daniel, AM1 (AW). *Team Trident Remembers*, 2003.

Wagner, Daniel, AM1 (AW). *The 53rd Anniversary of the First Cold War Shootdown VP-26's HB-7*, 2003.

Woodward, Billy L. *Patrol Bombing Squadron 104 (Third Tour) June 1945-November 1946*.

Index

1
186th Regimental Combat Team 91
3
30 GvIAP 118
343Ku Air Group 67, 69
A
A-6 Tail Turret 10, 14, 32-33
Abroad for Action 57, 156
Accentuate the Positive 53, 156
Advance Training Unit 54, 103, 121
Aéronavale 7, 100, 133-137, 150, 161, 171
Aéronavale Commissioned Rank Structure and U.S. Navy Equivalent 170
Aéronavale Enlisted Occupational Specialty and Approximate U.S. Navy Equivalent 170
Aéronavale Enlisted Rate Structure and U.S. Navy Equivalent 170
Air Sea Rescue 49, 52-53
Airborne Fire Control Radar 22
Airborne Identification Radar 22
Airborne Multipurpose/Special Radar 22
Airborne Navigation Radar 21-23
Airborne Radar Auxiliary Assemblies 23
Airborne Radar Intercept Receivers 22
Airborne Radar Transmitters 23
Airborne Radio Intercept Receivers 23
Airborne Radio Navigation Equipment 22
Airborne Search & Detection Radar 21
Alexander, Alex G. 6
Algeria 135, 137, 150
Allen, H.D. 88
Allen, T. 55-58
Althans, A.L. 83, 85
Anderson, Leroy 96, 98
Antenna Systems 23
Ashley, Edward W. 39-41
Aspro 53-55
Audibert, Paul 135
Augustus, Jim 6, 156
B
B-24 Liberator Club 6
B-24D Liberator 24, 108, 121
Babe, Henry 87
Bachelor's Delight 64, 145, 157
Baldy (Tortilla Flat) 156
Bales, R.C. 82, 84
Balke, Roy 6, 64
Balls of Fire 157
Barlow, Jerry M. 45
Bat, SWOD Mk-9 15, 21, 34, 62, 67, 69, 73, 81, 90-91, 102, 111
Baumgartner, Charles 49-50
Berger, Donald 39, 66, 69
Big Red (see VP-871)
Binning, Edward G. 39, 66-67
Blind Bomber 67, 157
Blue Diamond 40, 156
Blue, Allan 6, 9, 25
Boeing B-17 Flying Fortress 47, 49, 102, 121, 139
Bonin Islands 37, 39-40, 44, 46, 54
Britt, Harvey R. 128
Bronson, David E. 6, 80, 156
Brower, Robert J. 72, 79
Brownlow, Curt 6
Buccaneer Bunny 56, 156
Bundy, John F. 93
C
Calwell, Benjamin F. 45
Camouflage and Markings 32-33
Castleton, Stanley H. 109, 114
Central Field, Iwo Jima 43-45
Central Pacific 37, 42, 45, 58, 80
Chay, Donald S. 69-70, 81
Clark Field 82-85, 87-88, 91
Clyde 139
Cold War Shootdown
Loss of a VP-26 Privateer 117-119, 121
ComAirPacSubComForward 46
Come N' Get It 58, 156
ComNavGroup China 89
Comstock, W.P. 87-88
Consolidated PBY-5A Catalina 49, 88, 100, 131
Convair 7, 9, 11-12, 24, 36
Cook, Berdel A. 129
Coronado, PB3Y-2 flying boat 79
Cover Girl 79, 157
Creighton, Bert 139
Crist, Jack R. 73
D
Dacier, George 79
David, Smith 6
Davis, Clifton B. 70
Davis, Dave 79
DeGolia, Robert M. 60
Detachment Able 124
Dien Bien Phu 135-137
Dodson, Thomas L. 60-61
Douglas A-26 Intruder 137
Douglas C-54 Skymaster 10
Douglas R4D 56
Duba, Harry V. 40, 60, 66
Duckett, Bill 6, 156
Durban, Frank 6, 132
Dyson, G.R. 131
E
Edwards, William B. 93
Electronics Gear 9, 21-23
PB4Y-2 21-23
ELINT 21, 117
Elizabeth Ann 156
Ellis, D.E. 75-76
Els-Notcho 43, 156
Eniwetok 37, 52, 58
ERCO 250SH-3 Bow Turret 10-11, 14, 28
ERCO 250-TH Waist Blisters 10, 14, 29-30
Ettinger, R.D. 53-55
Evans, H.W. 89
Evans, Virgil J. 83-84
F
Fairbanks, G.D. 67, 69
Farmer, Joseph H. 80
Farwell, Arthur F. 44, 59-61, 66
FASRON 121, 144
FASRON 895 128
Fette, John H. 87, 112, 118, 121
Feuilloy, Robert 6, 100, 161, 170
Finley, Robert M. 39, 60, 64, 65
Fitts, Orvis N. 6, 96-99, 156
Flare-Drop Missions 124, 129-131
Fleet Air Wing One (FAW-1) 37, 59, 79, 100, 123
Fleet Air Wing Four (FAW-4) 100, 131
Fleet Air Wing Six (FAW-6) 131
Fleet Air Wing Ten (FAW-10) 45, 114
Fleet Air Wing Eighteen (FAW-18) 37, 53, 72, 100, 109
Fleet, Reuben 9
Flotilla 24F 137
Flotilla 28F 133-137, 150
Flotilla 8F 133-134
Flying Tail? 42, 66, 156
Friel, R.G. 88
G
Gardner, Frank 79
Gates, David E. 131
Gear Locked and Down 76, 79, 157
Golden Eagles See VP-9
Goodloe, Green C. 94, 96
Gray Jr., Raymond W. 41
Green Cherries 157
Grumman F7F Tigercat 129
Guam 37-38, 81, 109
Guyon, Gilbert 135
H
Harding, Eddie 6
Harper, Kelly 38, 41
Hartgraves, Vern S. 48
Hartvig, Donald 45, 47-48, 50, 55
Hawaiian Warriors (see VP-28)
Hawkins & Powers 117-118, 139, 142, 144, 151-153
Hawley, Steve 6, 156
Henders, H.J. 49
Hewitt, Floyd 69-70, 79, 80
Heyler, Fred 95-96
Hicks, George L. 67, 69, 79-80, 91-92
Hippin Kitten II 156
Hoblin, Walter B. 41, 93
Hodge, Carl M. 129

Hogan's Goat 67, 69, 157
Holt, John W. 82, 85-88
Honduran Air Force 143-144
Hopson, Billy 96, 98
Houle, Norman 6
Houston, Charles E. 72-75
I
Indochina, Vietnam 133-137
Installation of the cannons
on the Privateer 44-45, 52, 56
Iwo Jima 37-42, 44-47, 50, 52, 54-55, 58, 81, 145
J
Jackass Jenny , 156
Jackson's Jail 73, 157
Jacqueline 157
Jallao 48-49
Jeanguenat, A.C. 6, 156
Jeffreys, Richard 6
Jobe, Joseph 69-70, 72, 75
Johnson, Chester C. 132
Johnston, Bob 75
Johnston, Robert D. 72
K
Kalmuk, Theodore 79
Kamada, Minoru 6
Kasperlik, Joe 93
Keeling, John D. 64, 80
Keiser, Michael 42-44, 61, 64, 66
Kennedy, Leo 69-70, 91
Kerns, Wilmer L. 131, 147
King, George L. 80
Kirschner, Robert G. 124
Klein, Erwin L. 71, 80
Krokoski, Chip 6
Kyogyoku Maru 60
L
La Cherie 156
La Cherrie 65, 156
Lady Luck II 50-51, 156
Lady Luck III 53, 156
Lady of Leisure 156
Lambaster 157
Lasater, Allan 59, 64
Lassiter, E.J. 49
Lefever, Robert C. 45, 50
Leik, Francis H. 39, 45
Lewis, Jack 79
Liberator C.IX 30
Little Skipper 157
Livesay, R.L. 49
Lloyd, William N. 78
Lockheed-Vega PV-2 Harpoon 131
Lodato, August M. 49, 60, 65, 78
Lone Star Flight Museum 142, 144
Lotta Tayle 52, 56, 156
Louisiana Lil 55, 156
Lucky Pierre 139
Lucky-Levin 93, 156
Lyle, William L. 83
Lysdale Flying Service 142
M
MAAG 138
Manfanowsky, Alexis 136
Mann, Earl 6, 10, 38-39, 156
Marcus Island 39, 46-49, 81
Marianna Islands 37, 40, 47
Marks, Al 6
Marshall Islands 37, 52
Marshall, Marion L. 78
Martin 250CE-16 and 250CE-17 Upper Deck
Turrets 10, 14, 31
Martin P4M-1 Mercator 97
Maxwell, W.E. 45
McAlister, Davis 6
McCord, Bill 131
McCuaig, Al G. 71
McCutcheon, Leland 59, 79
McDonald, George W. 71
McElwee Jr., William 52
Mears, Howard F. 45, 95, 96
Michaels, Walter C. 81
Mikes, E.H. 53-54
Miller, Gilbert 72, 75, 79
Miller, John M. 75
Miller, Mahlon 6
Mindoro 97
Miss Behavin 49, 156
Miss Lotta Tail 63, 157
Miss Lottatail 61, 156
Miss Milovin 54, 157
Miss Pandemonium 71, 157
Miss Sea-ducer 157
Miss You 67, 156
Modest' O-Miss 40-42, 44, 68, 146, 156
Monahan, Robert J. 71
Monguillon, Pierre 136
Montgomery, Mark V. 60-61, 68
Mr. Kip 156
Muldrow, John E. 44-45, 47-48
Mullick, Frank W. 129
Murphy, Frank 83, 86, 88
N
NAAS Crows Landing 101-102
NASS Livermore 131
NAS Adak 129
NAS Agana 81, 108, 115
NAS Alameda 129, 131
NAS Atlantic City 90, 97, 114
NAS Atsugi 81, 115, 124, 126, 130-132
NAS Barbers Point 81, 113, 124
NAS Boca Chica 108
NAS Edenton 90, 108
NAS Guantanamo 97
NAS Kaneohe 35, 104
NAS Kodiak 101-102, 129
NAS Los Alamitos 124
NAS Miami 114-115, 141
NAS Naha 123
NAS New York 97
NAS Patuxent River 10, 97, 121
NAS Sand Point 115, 123, 131
NAS Sangley Point 90, 115
NAS Seattle 114, 116-117, 128, 140
NAS Whidbey Island 101-102, 131
NAS Willow Grove 102
National Archives and Records
Administration 6
National Museum of Naval Aviation 144, 153
Naval Body 156
Navarre, Henri 136
Navy's Torchy Tess 38, 156
Nichirin Maru 82
Nittinger, D.D. 129
No Body Else's Butt 157
No Strain 72 157
O
Ofuna Prison Camp 75
Okinawa 38, 42, 55, 59-61, 65-68, 70-72, 74, 77, 81-82, 123, 145
Ol' Blunderbuss 55, 157
Old Crows See VPB-118
Operation Castor 135-136
Operation Iceberg 59
Osborn, Everett 72, 79
Osborn, O.M. 76
Our Baby , 157
Out of Bounds 77, 157
P
P2V-2 Neptune 89, 130, 132
P2V3-W Neptune 115
P2V-4 Neptune 81, 121
P2V-5 Neptune 115, 117-118, 121, 128
P2V-6 Neptune 131
P-4B 27
P4Y-2 27
P4Y-2B 27
P4Y-2G 27, 117-121, 144, 151
P4Y-2K 27, 139-140
P4Y-2S 27, 115, 125, 128, 131
Page, Jim 126, 128
Palawan 67, 91-92, 146
Palma, J. 49
Park, J.R. 80
Park, Roy Edwin 129
Parsons, Roy 6, 112
Pastime 56, 157
PB-1W 102, 121
PB4Y-2B 24, 67, 76, 111, 113
PB4Y-2K 24
PB4Y-2M 24, 106, 108, 109, 114
PB4Y-2S 24, 115, 121, 123, 140
Peace Feeler 157
Peleliu 44, 81, 109
Pflum, Raymond 52-55, 58
Pierce, Thomas 6
Pierce, Thomas F. 78
Pirate Princess 65, 156
Pirate Queen 41, 156
Post-World War II Enlisted U.S. Navy
Aviation Ratings 169
Price, John D. 59
Privateers in Latin America 7, 139, 142-144
Production PB4Y-2 24, 27, 30
PT-BEO Brazilian Privateer 142-143
Punkie 62, 156
PV-1 Ventura 35, 41, 102, 145
Q
QP-4B 139
Queenfish 15
R
Racenet, Joseph E. 6
Ragan, M.S. 85
Rainey, J.B. 55, 57-58
Ramsey, John E. 74, 78-79

Red Wing/Indian Made 65, 157
Reddon, Charles W. 41
Reluctant Raiders See VPB-109
Ripplinger, John F. 41
RoCAF 7, 133, 135-138
Rockcliffe Icewagon 30
Rowcliffe, Ted 6
RY-3 Privateer 30, 36
S
Sampson, William S. 39
Sanders, J.E. 72
Sanderson, Harold M. 71, 80
Sanford, Kenneth F. 71
Sawruk, James 6, 154
Sea Liberator 24
Serbin, George 69-70, 92
Serrill, Julian D. 60, 65
Shapiro, Maurice "Shep" 6
Shilling, Samuel G. 71
Ship Surveillance 122, 124, 128, 131
Shireman, Ted 6
Singapore reconnaissance missions 94-96
Slattery's Hurricane 114
Smith, V.J. 94
Soaring Fin 39, 156
Specifications, PB4Y-1 and -2 27
Super Privateer 139, 152
Super Slooper 53, 156
Supreme Zu Zu 74, 157
Suret, Claude 137
Swiencicki, Joseph W. 97
T
T&G Aviation 144
Tail Chaser/Red Wing 145, 156
Tailhook Association 6
Tarfu 156
Task Force 58 (TF-58) 40
The Black Sheep 157
The Mad Frenchman 157
Thompson, Harry J. 59-60, 64, 65
Thys, Bill 6
Tinian 37-40, 44-45, 47-49, 52, 59, 72, 81
Truk Atoll 37, 39, 81
Turbulent Turtle 119, 121
Turner, Howard M. 64, 75, 93
Twitchy Bitch 67, 156
Typhoon 77, 157
Typhoon Chasers 109
U
U.S. Navy Patrol Squadrons at www.vpnavy.com 6
Umbriago 41, 146, 156
United States Coast Guard Coloring and Markings 35
United States Coast Guard Privateers 7, 24, 27, 35, 117-121, 144, 152
United States Fifth Fleet 37, 39, 59
University of Washington 9
V
Vadnais, Robert 63, 92, 93
Vagrant Verago 61, 156
Van Thiel, W.A. 44
VB-4 OTU 104-105, 142
Vidal, Albert 63, 80
Vincent, Jack E. 72, 74-75
VJ-1 106, 115
VJ-2 106, 113, 115, 144
VMF (N)-531 129
Vodicka, E.F. 47
Vogelsang, Walter 82, 87-88
VP-9 6, 122, 125-126, 128-131, 147, 151
VP-11 121
VP-12 100-101
VP-17 131
VP-20 101, 110
VP-21 120-121
VP-22 81
VP-23 110-112, 114-115, 118, 144
VP-24 90, 97, 113, 150
VP-25 102, 111
VP-26 112, 117, 121
VP-27 102
VP-28 6, 51, 122-123, 128-129, 138
VP-772 6, 123-125, 129, 131, 134, 147
VP-801 134, 135
VP-871 6, 122, 127-132, 146-147, 150
VP-881 25, 116-117
VP-916 131
VPB-101 101
VPB-102 37, 44, 47, 53, 81
VPB-103 101, 103
VPB-104 6, 37, 87-88, 89, 90
VPB-106 37, 39-42, 44-45, 92-97, 144, 146, 148
VPB-107 101, 103
VPB-108 6, 37, 43-47, 49-56, 58, 144
VPB-109 6, 11, 15, 34, 37, 53, 62-64, 67, 69, 71-72, 74, 76-77, 79-81, 91-93, 145, 148, 153
VPB-111 37, 93-97, 144
VPB-114 106, 108
VPB-116 6, 37, 54, 79, 80-81
VPB-117 6, 7, 37, 51, 96-97, 99
VPB-118 6, 37-44, 50, 59-61, 66-69, 74, 77-81, 86, 145, 148, 152, 153
VPB-119 37, 82-91, 148
VPB-120 37, 100-101, 144
VPB-121 6, 37, 46, 52-56, 58, 72, 145, 149
VPB-122 6, 100-103, 149, 150
VPB-123 6, 15, 34, 37, 56, 61, 65, 71, 73, 74, 77-81, 149
VPB-124 6, 15, 34, 37, 51, 56, 71-73, 75-79, 81, 149
VPB-133 41
VPB-143 6, 102, 104
VPB-151 41
VPB-197 35, 96, 103, 144
VPB-200 35, 113, 144
VP-HL-1 81
VP-HL-2 81
VP-HL-3 81, 114
VP-HL-5 102
VP-HL-6 108
VP-HL-7 102
VP-HL-8 51, 123
VP-HL-10 101, 144
VP-HL-11 97
VP-HL-12 101, 111, 142
VP-HL-13 102
VPM-1 109
VPM-3 114
VP-ML-57 131
VP-ML-66 131
VPW-1 6, 106, 108-109, 112, 114, 121, 144
VPW-2 6, 106, 109, 114
Vulnerable Virgin 64, 156
VW-3 117
VX-4 139
W
Wallace, M.R. 48
Warren, William A. 67, 69
Wassner, William E. 70
Water Spy 157
Weather Squadrons 106-109, 112-115, 117
Weller, Nolan 65, 69
White Lightnings See VP-772
Wilde, Gordan K. 97
Wilson, R.W. 88
Wings of China Publications, Wai Yip, Editor 6
Wolf Head Squadron (*see* Flotilla 8F and 28F)
Wolverators (*see* VPB-106)
Woodward, Bill 6
World War II-Era Enlisted U.S. Navy Aviation Ratings 169
X
XB-DIT
Mexican Privateer 142
XPB4Y-2 9-10
Y
Yankee Air Museum 77, 88
Yontan Field 38, 59, 66, 67, 68, 72, 77, 81